MUSIC IN AMERICAN LIFE

D1484769

*A list of books in the series appears
at the end of this book.*

The Sound of the Dove

The
Sound of the Dove

Singing in Appalachian
Primitive Baptist Churches

Beverly Bush Patterson

UNIVERSITY OF ILLINOIS PRESS
URBANA AND CHICAGO

First paperback edition, 2001
© 1995 by the Board of Trustees of the University of Illinois
All rights reserved
Manufactured in the United States of America
1 2 3 4 5 C P 5 4 3 2 1

♾ This book is printed on acid-free paper.

Library of Congress Cataloging-in-Publication Data

Patterson, Beverly Bush, 1939–
    The sound of the dove : singing in Appalachian Primitive Baptist
churches / Beverly Bush Patterson.
        p.   cm. — (Music in American life)
    Includes bibliographical references and index.
    ISBN 0-252-02123-1 (cl.)
    ISBN 0-252-07003-8 (pbk.)
    1. Church music—Primitive Baptists. 2. Church music—Appalachian
Region. 3. Choral singing. 4. Music and society. I. Title.
II. Series.
ML3160.P28   1995
782.32'261'00974—dc20   94-1697
                                                                 CIP
                                                                 MN

Contents

Illustrations follow page 84

Preface

Much of the research for this study was carried out as part of a project called World and Identity in Ritual Action, an interdisciplinary study of American sectarian religion in the South. I was one of four outsiders from the academic community visiting Primitive Baptist churches in the central Blue Ridge Mountains and interviewing church members. I worked as a research assistant during the summers, primarily in 1982 and 1983, with the project directors, James L. Peacock (anthropology), who served as my dissertation adviser, Daniel W. Patterson (folklore), and Ruel W. Tyson, Jr. (religion). A partial report on this work was published by Professors Peacock and Tyson as *Pilgrims of Paradox* (Smithsonian Institution Press, 1989).

In addition to regular worship services, we attended association meetings, annual congregational meetings that included communion and foot washing, river baptizings, one wedding, and one funeral. The Primitive Baptists seemed to take as great an interest in their visitors as we took in them, and I was fortunate to be invited for visits of from one to five days in four homes during annual meetings, and to make other trips with members of one church community to attend meetings in another association.

Daniel Patterson and I supplemented the original fieldwork in North Carolina, Virginia, and West Virginia with additional field research in Primitive Baptist churches of eastern Kentucky during the summer of 1990. These churches, independent or members of various associations, are part of a larger informal network of congregations that are in general agreement on matters of doctrine and church polity.

Throughout the World and Identity project, we documented church meetings and interviews with sound recordings, field notes, photographs, and some videotape recordings. Materials from this project are in the Southern Folklife Collection of the Manuscripts Department in Wilson Library at the University of North Carolina in Chapel Hill. Recordings of eighty worship services and seventy-three interviews provided the primary research materials on which the present study is based. Quotations from these recordings and interviews are cited in this book using the form "WI-xxx"; a partial list of these recordings follows the notes at the back of the volume.

World and Identity in Ritual Action was funded by the National Endowment for the Humanities, the Wenner-Gren Foundation, and travel and research grants from the University of North Carolina. I gratefully acknowledge this support. I especially thank the project directors, Professors Peacock, Patterson, and Tyson, for the opportunity to further my long-standing interest in American sectarian religion and religious folksong. Their continuing interest and encouragement have been essential.

I am grateful also to Loyal Jones and the Appalachian Center at Berea College for a Mellon Fellowship that permitted additional library and field research in Kentucky. I owe particular thanks to William Tallmadge and to Shannon Wilson and the staff in Special Collections in Hutchins Library at Berea for making available materials from the Tallmadge Collection. I could not have asked for better cooperation. That research broadened my perspective and filled some gaps in my original study.

My deepest gratitude goes to all of the Primitive Baptists who have so generously and graciously responded to my interest and my questions. Among them are many knowledgeable elders and hospitable lay members to whom I remain greatly indebted. To Raymond and Nonnie Lee Nichols I owe debts I can never repay. Throughout this book I avoid using names of individuals or refer to most Primitive Baptists by pseudonyms, not only to comply with ethnographic methodology but also to respect Primitive Baptist practice of deferring to ordained elders as appropriate spokesmen for the church. I am especially grateful to Elders Billy Cook, Eddie Lyle, and the late Walter Evans and Dewey Roten, all of them eloquent and insightful interpreters of Primitive Baptist faith, doctrine, and practice.

1

Singing in Primitive Baptist Worship

Even a mockingbird cannot mock the sound of a dove.

—Primitive Baptist elder, Virginia, 1982

"I CAN REMEMBER WHEN I was real small, of passing the church out here and hearing them sing," responded a North Carolina woman when I asked her about the singing in her Primitive Baptist church. "I stopped there and stood behind a tree, listening to them. I thought it was really pretty, the singing was. I guess I must have been about eight or nine years old. I stood and listened, and it sounded like everybody in the church was singing, and the church was full. And, you know, it was in the summertime, they had the windows open, the doors was open, and you could hear them so plain" (WI-159).

Even now, as the wife of a deacon and the mother of a teen-age daughter, the woman communicated the irresistible attraction she had felt on first hearing Primitive Baptist singing. Those sounds were still vivid and fresh in her mind. She was not a musician herself and modestly insisted that she was not even a good singer. However, it did not surprise me that, even as a child, she was struck by the sound of Primitive Baptist singing.

It would not have sounded like the singing in the neighboring Missionary Baptist church where her mother, once a Primitive Baptist herself, took the children "because my daddy was a Missionary Baptist; she said she couldn't see her going one way and him going the other." The Missionary Baptists had a piano to accompany the singing, and a choir, and sometimes soloists and duos to sing "special music"; they used hymnbooks that had the music printed with the texts. By contrast, their Primitive Baptist neighbors always sang together as a whole congregation, unaccompanied, from a little pocket-sized book of hymn texts that had not changed since its first publication in 1887. Members relied on their memories to supply the old tunes for the hymns requested by the congregation and, after one good singer or another spontaneously started the tune, everyone joined the singing. When they sang it sounded different, especially to outsiders. Robert Palmer, a *New York Times* music critic, once described the sound of Primitive Baptist singing as having "an eerie luminosity that communicates the flavor of other-worldly religious experiences more vividly than any other sound [I have] heard on records" (1982).

The singing in these Primitive Baptist churches is so distinctive that it continues to set these churches apart. Readers who have sung many of these same hymns—even familiar texts and tunes such as "Guide Me, O Thou Great Jehovah" or "Amazing Grace"—may find the singing in Primitive Baptist churches to be absolutely and radically different from what they expect. It is a style of American religious folksong that has been centuries in the making.

Such singing is not simply a survival from older practice even though certain performances of lined-out hymns remind us of psalmody, one of the oldest forms of American religious song. It is a style with a history of controversy and one that continues to change. Since the late eighteenth century, well-meaning reformers have pronounced it backward and old fashioned. Clergy and musicians alike have denounced this old way of unaccompanied congregational hymn singing that was once common in many American churches. To a greater degree than most other denominations, Primitive Baptists resisted recommendations for musical change. Outsiders who find their singing distinctive may even imagine that these Old Baptists[1] have been impervious to such criticism and that they have stubbornly persisted in their old ways. But a closer look reveals that even the most remote Primitive Baptist churches have responded to pressures to modernize their practice of singing. Primitive Baptist singing is complex and all the more interesting because it continues to change while seeming to remain the same, holding on to some of the oldest features of its practice.

This congregational hymn singing is a powerful living tradition that is part of everyday life for a group of ordinary Americans. It is a tradition that continues to hold worlds of meaning—religious, social, and aesthetic—for the members and friends of Primitive Baptist churches. Field research and documentation suggest that Primitive Baptists actively use not only the words and melodies but even the musical sound and style of their singing to express and construct a complex religious identity, and this study will explore that hypothesis.[2]

The regular worship service provides the main context for this exploration. Typically, congregations meet one Sunday a month for a regular worship service, and they hold another service and business meeting on the preceding Saturday. Both services usually last an hour and a half. Some elements of the service are typical of Protestant services in general: congregational hymn singing, prayer, and preaching. The services, however, are set apart by the absence of mainstream Protestant features like printed programs, offertories, and special music interspersed throughout the service. They are also made distinctive by the inclusion of rituals like taking the hand of fellowship, or foot washing on Communion Sundays.

People arrive at a Primitive Baptist meeting well ahead of the hour announced for preaching, often forty-five minutes (or more) "early." They find ample parking on shady church lawns between the road and the meetinghouse, and there is usually plenty of seating inside. Most of these meetinghouses could accommodate two hundred people or more, but they are filled to capacity only on the special occasions that attract friends and members of their sister churches, such as association meetings. Attendance at regular meetings ranges from twenty to forty people, sometimes more, sometimes less. Spacing themselves comfortably in the open pews, most people sit toward the front of the church in the rows that directly face the pulpit. A few leading members customarily take places in pews that flank and face the pulpit on both sides. Separate congregational seating for men and women is no longer required in these churches, but a surprising number of couples continue to separate as they enter the church, women seating themselves on the right and men on the left.[3]

Church members come early to sing. They believe that the practice of singing is one of the church's original spiritual furnishings— that is, a practice authorized by Christ and his apostles in the New Testament. As one Primitive Baptist woman put it, "When the church was set up, it was thoroughly furnished and it doesn't need changing" (WI-110). Many members have their own copies of hymnbooks at home, and some bring these to church. The pastor or song leader (often the same person) quietly greets people as they come in, and he makes sure each person has a hymnbook before finally returning to his pew. He begins the singing by simply calling out the number of a hymn. From the moment he starts the first tune, almost everyone joins in singing, regardless of how few people are present and how strong or weak their voices are. Then, other members call out hymn numbers to make their song requests. Sometimes everyone sings in unison, sometimes a few singers add harmonies. Most of the texts they choose are eighteenth-century hymns by writers such as Isaac Watts and John Newton. Other favorite texts in the hymnbooks are those of gospel songs dating from the late nineteenth and early twentieth centuries. The congregation takes each request in turn, singing for half an hour or more before the preaching begins.

Finally, in a gesture that acknowledges the formal opening of the service, the congregation stands to sing one last hymn. If a visiting elder is present, the pastor often calls on him to "introduce" or open the service with prayer and any comments he feels led to make. Otherwise, the pastor will come forward to lead the prayer himself. He kneels on one knee near the pulpit and gives voice to a fervent extemporaneous prayer as members of the congregation sit quietly with heads bowed.

At the close of the prayer, the designated elder steps forward, leads a short preparatory hymn if he wishes, and "takes the stand" to preach. He uses no notes, only the King James version of the Bible, from which he reads his text. He typically begins his sermon with remarks about his own unworthiness and a disclaimer of having any ability to preach in and of himself. He expresses a hope that the Lord will deliver him in his subject and reminds the congregation of his dependency on God. If God does not give him anything to say, he promises, he will soon sit down. And if he says things that are not of God, he hopes they will soon be forgotten. Usually, he experiences liberty to preach and, as his subject unfolds, his voice gains strength and momentum. Some preachers shift into a musical chant as they feel empowered; others maintain a more conversational tone throughout. If several elders are present, they will all have an opportunity to speak. The style of delivery varies with each elder, but their messages are consistent. "I can tell you what *doesn't* change [in the Primitive Baptist church]," declared one deacon most emphatically, "and that's the preaching."

The sermons always reinforce the church's predestinarian doctrine of election and salvation by grace, a message the congregation never tires of hearing. Their doctrine of election distinguishes this branch of Primitive Baptists from a smaller group they call the "absoluters," an ultraconservative branch, often with churches in the same area but not in fellowship with these Primitive Baptists. The absoluters, they say, hold the erroneous and fatalistic doctrine that God predestinated *all* events and actions, both good and evil, whereas they themselves (the "conditionalists") believe that only salvation is predetermined.

They deny that God predestinated sin and evil. Before the foundation of the world, they say, God elected those whom he will save, and he gives them a hope of salvation in his own good time. They also distinguish themselves from an even smaller number of "progressive" Primitive Baptists who support Sunday schools and use musical instruments in their churches.

Their own singing is always unaccompanied by instruments, but it is accompanied by ritual at the end of each service. When the congregation stands to sing the closing hymn, the pastor announces that the doors of the church are open to receive new members. He and any visiting elders stand facing the congregation to participate in the ritual hand of fellowship during the singing. Members of the congregation offer their right hands to those standing nearest them, sometimes engaging simultaneously in handshake and embrace, left arms lightly encircling the shoulders of the others with right hands clasped between them. Then they walk single file, singing from hymnbooks held in their left hands, to shake hands with the preachers and with all others at the meeting. Anyone who wants to join the church will make that wish known to the pastor during this time, usually in a tearful request, often moved to this step by the power of the strong, slow-paced, soulful singing. The pastor then informs the congregation of this person's desire for a "home in the church," and invites the person to tell briefly of the "travels" or experiences that gave a hope of salvation. The church receives the new member by baptism or by letter (if coming from a sister church). Usually, however, no one requests membership and, after the hymn, the elders or deacons announce upcoming meetings at sister churches. The pastor closes the meeting with a short prayer.

Consistent with this simple, straightforward order of service are the plain meetinghouses that provide settings for these services. In the nine churches of the Mountain District Primitive Baptist Association,[4] where I most often visited, a rectangular brick or white-painted frame exterior still encloses a single meeting room with clear windows on either side. The plainness is deliberate, a silent testimony to Primitive Baptist belief that the church is a direct descendant of the original church described in the New Testament. A simple pulpit, or "bookboard," stands facing the congregation, centered on a platform that is elevated only a few inches. A small table in front of the pulpit may hold a modest arrangement of artificial flowers or a stack of hymnbooks, but its main purpose is to provide a place for the bread and wine served during the congregation's annual communion and foot-washing service.

Like regular services, this ritual retains a simplicity of form. Elders and deacons serve homemade unleavened bread and homemade wine to members of the congregation after reading appropriate Scriptures and briefly explaining the significance of each element. For the foot washing that follows, they distribute small basins of water and long homemade "towels" of plain cotton cloth that can be tied around the waist, leaving the hands free. Men are paired with men, women with women. Without speaking, they take turns washing each other's feet in a simple act that symbolizes humility and expresses bonds of Christian love.

The plain physical settings and uncomplicated order of service represent active resistance to any additions to the practice of religion that are not compatible with members' images of the church as already thoroughly furnished. The absence of education buildings, classrooms, church offices, telephones, choir rooms, and even musical instruments represents a rejection of what Primitive Baptists consider "human additions" or "innovations." Similarly absent are stained glass windows, crosses, steeples, dramatically elevated pulpits, enclosed pews, offering plates, candles and candelabra, vestments, and formal orders of worship. Although all of these churches practice baptism, none has a baptistry. Following New Testament examples, new members are baptized outdoors in nearby rivers, ponds, or creeks.[5]

This resistance to innovations and additions does not extend as far as some readers might imagine, however. Renovated interiors often include carpeting and pew cushions. Several congregations have built open sheds outdoors for serving "dinner on the ground" on communion Sundays, and a few churches have added fellowship halls for the purpose of serving these meals indoors. And indoor toilets have replaced most outdoor privies. Such changes are consistent with two of the guiding metaphors for the church: home and family. The interior walls of these churches are usually unadorned, but the exceptions continue to reflect these metaphors. One North Carolina church, for example, displayed a framed group photograph of former church elders on the wall behind the pulpit. Years ago another church had hung a photograph (approximately 8" x 10") of a soldier in World War I uniform, the son of long-deceased members. Below that was a familiar picture of Jesus. Those pictures had been there as long as church elders could remember.[6]

In its social organization, the Primitive Baptist church emphasizes the community, or congregation, rather than the individual. The congregation is not subdivided into separate groups that meet privately to focus on special projects, needs, or interests. Sunday School classes, youth groups, missionaries, and missionary societies do not exist in these churches, nor do opportunities for singing in choirs or serving as ushers and greeters. All worship and all church business are conducted publicly and openly, incorporating the whole congregation.

Churches like these have been part of the mountain culture and landscape in the central Blue Ridge Mountains for almost two hundred years, dating from the period of the earliest settlements in the region. Although the churches were not called Primitive Baptist in the 1790s, their spiritual descendants who now carry the name recognize the earlier Baptists by the predestinarian doctrine they held. By 1799, according to two Primitive Baptist historians, Sylvester Hassell and Elder Cushing Biggs Hassell (1886:906), the Mountain District Baptist Association had 1,193 members, 8 elders, and 20 churches. Since their split from the main body of Baptists in the early 1830s, however, when the dissenting conservatives began distinguishing themselves as "Primitive" or "Old School" Baptists, their numbers and influence have been eclipsed by the rapid growth of the more evangelical "missionary" Baptists. Even so, according to the religious census of 1890, Primitive Baptists still strongly outnumbered Methodists in Alleghany County, North Carolina, and Carroll County, Virginia, and they had significant strength in Grayson County, Virginia, where Methodists were in the majority.

Today, Primitive Baptists are less visible and less well known than their Methodist and Missionary Baptist neighbors in the central Blue Ridge region, even in counties where they were once dominant. Within their local communities, they are sometimes the victims of negative stereotyping as the "hardshell" Baptists. Outsiders, unfamiliar with the variety in sectarian religions, sometimes mistakenly confuse them with groups dramatically different from them, such as charismatic pentecostals, or even snake handlers. As one Primitive Baptist woman made clear, Primitive Baptists themselves distinguish their own churches from the neighboring Independent Baptists, Union Baptists, Free Will Baptists, Southern Baptists, Missionary Baptists, and Regular Baptists on the basis of adherence to the "hard" doctrine of particular election. I had asked her if there was any belief "that makes a difference to you between the Union [Baptists], and the Regular Baptists, and the Primitive Baptists." "Yes, there is," she said. "It's mostly on the way a sinner is saved. Now the other Baptists, they think that it's something you do on your own self. And [I believe] you're saved by the grace of God. He gives a new birth. There's nothing you can do to receive it, it has to come from him."

She, like other members of these churches, belongs to one church—

her "home" church—but she also attends several other sister churches that meet on the weekends that her home church does not hold
services. The churches that belong to the Mountain District Primitive
Baptist Association are all within an hour's drive of each other; some
are only a few minutes away. They are located on the outskirts of
towns and off rural mountain roads in a roughly triangular area defined by Sparta, North Carolina, (pop. 1,687) at its southern point;
Galax, Virginia, (pop. ca. 6,000) at its eastern point; and Independence,
Virginia, (pop. 1,112) at its western point. The churches cluster on both
sides of the North Carolina–Virginia state line—four in North Carolina, five in Virginia—and they are five to ten miles apart within these
clusters. "This country" is a phrase that members of these churches
use for the land that comprises their domain, more or less cotermi-
nous with the boundaries of their association. It is land that they, and
their families before them, have lived and worked on for most, or all,
of their lives (Peacock and Tyson 1989:6–12).

In their private lives, individual members remain somewhat separate socially from the larger local community. "The mountain environment, dispersed settlement pattern, and rather individualistic values
of most Mountain District Primitive Baptists encourage independence
and solitude." Their lives revolve around family, work, and church.
Although they will travel miles to attend meetings at sister churches,
they seldom engage in community activities beyond the church meetings, weddings, and funerals. Membership in civic, political, and vol-
untary activities is minimal (Peacock and Tyson 1989:26).[7] This community, then, is one that is bounded primarily by faith and practice and
only secondarily by geography, by kinship, or by economic or political ties.

Most Primitive Baptists maintain fellowship with their neighboring sister churches through an association of churches that agree on
matters of doctrine and practice. In *Pilgrims of Paradox*, James Peacock
and Ruel Tyson have observed that, in an association, "individualism is subsumed in deeply moving rituals of fellowship and communion, and practical jobs are grounded in carefully conceptualized theologies and cherished aesthetic forms." The association, they write,
"is a true cultural entity, but, in the view of the Primitive Baptists,
not just cultural. For them, the association and each church, though
fragilely human, are not merely human creations, but the Visible
Church—a manifestation on earth, despite all human limitations, of
the will of God and of His plan, as best the human intellect can dis-
cern it" (1989:27).

Peacock and Tyson have emphasized Primitive Baptist doctrine and polity by looking at sermons, tensions within the association, and the way the group negotiates conflict. Drawing on the same field research, my study complements that emphasis with a focus on singing and on those aspects of religious and regional culture that shape and influence this distinctive tradition of religious song. It offers insights on how Primitive Baptists experience their religion, and how they symbolize and express their ideals and aspirations. In addition, it explores apparent gender differences in the way men and women experience the church.

As important as Primitive Baptist singing has been to Primitive Baptists themselves, and as striking as it has been to a few observers, that singing has received little scholarly attention until recently. R. Paul Drummond, a Primitive Baptist himself and a student of choral music, wrote a doctoral dissertation in 1986 covering the publication history of Primitive Baptist hymnbooks, analyzing their contents, and tracing the flow of this denominational tradition of folk hymnody into the larger stream of American choral music. Brett Sutton had earlier pioneered an anthropological approach in substantial notes for his record album *Primitive Baptist Hymns of the Blue Ridge* (1982). In this essay, he documented the singing of African-American and Anglo-American Primitive Baptists and compared the singing of these two cultural traditions.

My focus is different from either of these studies in its attempt to explore the relationship of religious song and performance to social and cultural patterns—one of the most difficult and problematic of analytical tasks. The academic disciplines in which I work—anthropology, folklore, and ethnomusicology—do not yet offer very serviceable theories to explain that relationship, so I attack the question by combining methodologies from these and several other disciplines. My primary research method has been participant-observation in worship services, supplemented with interviews. But I have also made tune transcriptions and analyzed musical form and variation in the singing, studied song texts, and researched the historical background of this song tradition in documents related to late-seventeenth-century English Baptists.

As part of this interdisciplinary approach, I have also tried to learn more about the singing by considering women's historical and current relationship to it. Historical records from the early English churches, for example, include men's arguments about whether women should be allowed to participate in congregational singing. This is not an issue in these churches now, but it does provide background for a paradox inherent in present Primitive Baptist belief. Members assign unequal roles to men and women in the church, and, at the same time, defend a predestinarian doctrine that is strongly egalitarian. Singing, and hymn texts in particular, offers a window on how this group resolves this seeming contradiction. I will speculate that these older texts suggest that Primitive Baptists have held a richer conception of womanhood than has prevailed in less conservative Protestant groups since the rise of evangelical religion. Although such issues are somewhat incidental to my musical concerns, I will give them some attention because of their possible interest to those in the field of contemporary feminist studies.

In the chapters that follow, I show how these various strands—musical, textual, historical, religious, and social—interweave and link members of this community in constructions of meaning and identity. But the most illuminating insights come from the self-descriptions offered by Primitive Baptists in interviews. It is they who unfold what they mean when they characterize their singing as the sound of the dove.

2

Roots of Old
Baptist Song Practices

We believe we go with the Book, or else we've been awful
deceived, awful deceived.

—Primitive Baptist deacon, Virginia, 1982

THE FEATURE OF Primitive Baptist singing that outsiders notice
first—that they most often ask church members about—is the absence
of musical instruments for accompanying congregational song. In
mock seriousness, one church elder explained to us that Primitive
Baptists did not allow anything in the church that had not been baptized. And baptizing a piano, he said, would ruin it. In actual practice, however, the exclusion of musical instruments is a matter that
congregations continue to consider carefully. During the period of our
research, for example, one congregation somewhat reluctantly decided
that it could not grant permission to the daughter of its preacher when
she asked if she could have a piano brought into the church just for
her wedding (Peacock and Tyson 1989:24–26).

For regular meetings, the absence of instruments means that not
only is there no accompanied singing, but also there are no preludes,
offertories, postludes, or any other forms of incidental instrumental
music common in many other churches. In maintaining this practice,
Primitive Baptists in the Mountain Association are in agreement with
almost all other Primitive Baptists. Their position was once shared
by many other American churches—not only other Baptists, but Presbyterians, Methodists, Campbellites, Shakers, the Amish, and the
Mennonites, to name but a few. Now, however, they are out of step
with mainstream American churchgoers, for whom church music is
hardly conceivable without choirs and musical instruments, especially
an organ or piano.

Primitive Baptists are not indifferent to the charms of instrumental music, for there are a number of skilled musicians among them; and the question of using organs in the church arises from time to time among those who wish to be more progressive. By and large, though, most Primitive Baptists still agree that the voice is the only instrument appropriate for public worship. Their response to a question about their position on instrumental music in the church is usually a brief explanation that there is no evidence in the New Testament that musical instruments were included in the establishment of the church, and that Primitive Baptists do not believe they are necessary now.

Other features that contribute to the unique pattern of musical practice in these churches are seldom, if ever, debated within church circles. Only an outsider would be likely to ask, for example, why the church meets to sing for half an hour or more before preaching begins, why the members select songs only by verbal request at the time of meeting, or why they allow no singing except by the congregation as a whole. Church members often respond to such questions by vaguely referring to preference and custom and often couch their explanations in phrases such as "we like it that way," or, "we've always done it that way." These responses suggest that most features of the pattern are so habitual—so often repeated and so well accepted—that they arouse little or no curiosity or desire for change within the church.

The repertory of hymn texts and tunes, the deliberately slow tempos, the sometimes irregular rhythms of unison singing, the sometimes unconventional touches of harmony, and the self-effacing but important role of song leader all contribute to a distinctive style that can seem quite foreign to a listener who is from outside the church community. Some outsiders might fail to appreciate this sound because they hear in the solemn singing of untrained voices a sound that is outdated, raw, and unsophisticated, or even unpleasant. Others might think that the singing is merely peripheral and is less important than preaching and prayer. Singing is no less significant for being on the periphery, however. In fact, singing frames the service, opening and ending it, and setting its tone.

Nevertheless, the deeper meanings and the aesthetic values that singing holds for Primitive Baptists remain almost inaccessible to outsiders. Even for church members, it is preaching and not singing that formally provides the central focus of the worship service, and it is the preaching and church doctrine rather than the practice of singing that they most readily talk about. How, then, may an outsider gain some understanding of this singing?

One way to illuminate Primitive Baptists' attitudes is to place their practice of singing in historical perspective. This approach, which is essentially an exploration of the relation of singing to church doctrine, will be the focus of this chapter. Primitive Baptists defend their practice of unaccompanied singing, as Old Baptists have always done, by claiming scriptural authority. Published explanations of the Scriptures have circulated within the church during periods of controversy, and these explanations offer a glimpse of that religious world in which Primitive Baptists are deeply rooted. According to Paul Drummond (1989:28), the majority of the published articles that deal with music in Old Baptist worship were written in opposition to attempts around 1897 by a few of the churches in Georgia to introduce instrumental accompaniments (i.e., organs) as aids to congregational singing. He found that, between 1890 and 1930, numerous articles appeared in Primitive Baptist periodicals to clarify the rationale for opposing musical instruments (1989:135–44; see also Haynes 1959:228).

A representative statement, written by a Primitive Baptist elder in 1909, offers essentially the same reasoning that Primitive Baptists use today. Characteristically, his argument makes distinctions between the temple or ceremonial worship described in the Old Testament and the worship in the early Christian church described in the New Testament:

> Under ceremonial law we . . . find many forms and customs, many types and shadows, many priests with priestly robes, many sacrifices, festivals, tithings . . . and finding them there let us wisely leave them there. Had they been needed in the church Christ would have brought them over. . . . And this applies as strongly to instrumental music as to other temple services and legal ceremonies. . . . Christ established His church and thoroughly furnished her with all good works and useful things and the only safe rule by which to measure the service of God's House, to glorify Him and benefit His people is that the things needful for the church of Christ were placed in the church by Christ and His Apostles and the absence of a thing is its divine disapproval and everlasting condemnation. (Pittman 1909:382)

With the exception of two passages in the book of Revelation that Primitive Baptists would consider irrelevant to the establishment of practice in the early church, there is indeed no mention in the New Testament of musical instruments accompanying singing. There the only verses that mention singing appear in the King James version as follows:

And when they had sung an hymn, they went out into the mount of Olives. (Matt. 26:30 and Mark 14:26)

And at midnight Paul and Silas prayed, and sang praises to God: and the prisoners heard them. (Acts 16:25)

. . . I will sing with the spirit, and I will sing with the understanding also. (I Cor. 14:15b)

How is it brethren? When ye come together, every one of you hath a psalm, hath a doctrine, hath a tongue, hath a revelation, hath an interpretation. Let all things be done unto edifying. (I Cor. 14:26)

. . . [B]ut be filled with the spirit; Speaking to yourselves in psalms and hymns and spiritual songs, singing and making melody in your heart to the Lord. (Eph. 5:18b–19)

Let the word of Christ dwell in you richly in all wisdom; teaching and admonishing one another in psalms and hymns and spiritual songs, singing with grace in your hearts to the Lord. (Col. 3:16)

Is any among you afflicted? Let him pray. Is any merry? Let him sing psalms. (James 5:13)

Saying, I will declare thy name unto my brethren, in the midst of the church will I sing praise unto thee. (Heb. 2:12)

Clearly, these verses give no explicit instruction to the New Testament church concerning musical instruments or whether singing should be performed either with or without instrumental accompaniment. Primitive Baptists argue, however, that there is great significance in what is not said; and their interpretation rests on combining the absence of an explicit, New Testament statement authorizing the use of musical instruments with the claim that religious practice in a New Testament–based church is necessarily different from the worship described in the Old Testament.[1] For these Baptists, the only proper interpretation of the practice of singing mentioned in the New Testament is that it was unaccompanied, because that is the interpretation that best harmonizes the three factors that have to be taken into account: the absence of specific New Testament instructions about singing; the absence of instruments in New Testament descriptions of worship; and the belief that Old Testament and New Testament patterns of worship are different.

These twentieth-century Primitive Baptist arguments for exclud-

ing musical instruments from public worship have historical parallels in arguments about the place of music in Christian worship made
in sixteenth-century Europe during the Protestant Reformation. The
theologian with the greatest influence on dissenters in the British Isles,
John Calvin, had preached that musical instruments were tolerated
in the time of Law because the people were in their infancy with respect to their spiritual growth. The worship described in the Old Testament, he said, was figurative and terminated with the Gospel, where
he found no support for the use of musical instruments (Reyburn
1914:83–86; Scholes 1934:336; Stevenson 1953:14).

Even though the Primitive Baptists of the Mountain District Association and churches in fellowship with them do not formally
identify themselves as Calvinists,[2] they jokingly acknowledge ties
to Calvinism when they refer to Presbyterians as "uptown Primitive Baptists." Musically, Primitive Baptists, like most contemporary
Presbyterians, would reject any attempts to limit the texts of their
religious songs to metrical versions of the Psalms, a reform in church
singing that Calvin supported. On other points, however, there is a
remarkable similarity between ideas about music that Primitive Baptists hold today and those that Calvin supported.[3] Although Calvin
was not a musician, he eventually concluded that congregational
singing was a necessary part of public worship. Congregational singing, he thought, was closely linked to prayer. Prayer, the preaching
of the Word, and the administration of the sacraments were the
"three things which our Lord has commanded us to observe in our
spiritual assemblies," and prayer, as Calvin described it, could be
either spoken or sung. In his argument, Calvin appealed to New
Testament Scripture as an account of church history and claimed that
the introduction of congregational singing in sixteenth-century Europe was a restoration of early church practice and not an innovation as others argued.

> It is evident that the practice of singing in church . . . is not only
> a very ancient one but also was in use among the apostles. This
> we may infer from Paul's words: "I will sing with the spirit and
> I will sing with the mind" [I Cor. 14:15]. Likewise, Paul speaks
> to the Colossians: "Teaching and admonishing one another . . . in
> hymns, psalms, and spiritual songs, singing with thankfulness
> in your hearts to the Lord" [Col. 3:16]. For in the first passage
> he teaches that we should sing with voice and heart; in the sec-
> ond he commends spiritual songs, by which the godly may
> mutually edify one another. (Calvin 1960, 2:895)

Calvin recommended that all participants in worship—men, women, and children—sing. He saw no need for choirs or soloists in the church. He thought songs must be sung by the whole congregation with intelligence and understanding, exercising the mind in thinking of God. The words, he wrote, should be "in the language of the people which can be generally understood by the whole assemble [*sic*]. For this ought to be done for the edification of the whole church, which receives no benefit whatsoever from a sound not understood" (Calvin 1960, 2:896). He also stressed singing from the "deep feeling of the heart" and he argued that songs sung from the tip of the lips and from the throat rather than from the heart constituted an abuse.

Calvin believed that music had moral as well as emotional power. He argued that a melody could deliver a text with more intensity than words alone. In the following excerpt, translated from his *Epistle to the Reader* (1542, 1543), Calvin reasoned that a song text had to be chosen with great care to assure that singing it would be beneficial rather than harmful: "It is true that every evil word (as St. Paul says) perverts good morals, but when the melody is with it, it pierces the heart that much more strongly and enters into it; just as through a funnel wine is poured into a container, so also venom and corruption are distilled to the depth of the heart by the melody" (Garside 1979:33).

To engage the mind appropriately and to lend dignity and grace to spiritual assemblies, Calvin advocated the creation of a musical style that represented a complete break with the familiar. It was to be characterized by new tunes that would be "neither light nor frivolous, but have gravity and majesty" (Garside 1979:32). Such songs would be a means to spiritual joy and would distinguish the truly sacred from mere entertainment.

Although the general musical direction that Calvin established for the church—unaccompanied, solemn, and heartfelt congregational singing of carefully chosen texts—remains evident in Primitive Baptist practice, we discover no simple or direct process of transmission. We find, instead, that the practice of singing favored by Primitive Baptists reflects a much broader and more complex historical background. Other Reformation theologies of music, particularly those of Huldreich Zwingli and Martin Luther, have undoubtedly had their effects. Zwingli's position, however, is reflected more in arguments about singing among early Baptists than in any current practice.

Garside (1966, 1967) argues that although Zwingli was the best musician of the major reformers, he had concluded that music had no place in worship because it had no theological dimension. Music was for Zwingli, writes Garside, an exclusively secular medium that could neither communicate the Word of God nor function as an agent for the operation of the Spirit. Therefore, Zwingli interpreted New Testament references to "making melody in your heart" (Eph. 5:19) and to "singing with grace in your hearts" (Col. 3:16) as literal instructions to sing silently "in the heart," not with the voice. Musical sound of any sort in public worship was, he thought, contrary both to Scripture and to the practice of the early church. At Zwingli's urging, Scripture reading was substituted for singing, and all music, vocal and instrumental, was eliminated from the liturgy of Zurich in 1525.

While Zwingli and Calvin led the most radical reforms of musical practice in public worship, Martin Luther advocated relatively moderate reforms (Garside 1967). Unlike Zwingli or Calvin, Luther never included music in his list of offending practices of the Roman church. His primary musical aim was to add congregational singing in the vernacular to the existing musical practices of the church. Unlike Calvin, he did not limit song texts to metrical versions of the Scriptures, nor did he find objections to putting familiar tunes from a variety of sources in the service of newly composed vernacular hymn texts for public worship. A singer, lute player, and composer himself, he not only insisted on congregational singing, he also supported elaborate polyphonic music that only trained choirs could perform, and he encouraged financial support of church musicians. He kept organs and other instruments in the churches, and though they were not immediately used to accompany congregational singing there was nothing in Luther's concept of church music to oppose the eventual acceptance of accompanied congregational singing.

Luther published his first hymnal in 1524, setting the texts to melodies, or adopting melodic styles, that were already familiar to the congregation through Gregorian chant, processional hymns, Latin spiritual songs, or secular tunes. Although the congregation sang in unison, the melodies were harmonized in the hymnals, suggesting the possibility of part-singing eventually. In practice, the congregation sometimes sang a unison melody in alternating parts, the choir or instruments giving variety to the sound from one verse to the next.

The most common musical pattern found in American Protestant churches today, even in mainstream Baptist churches, follows generally in the direction advocated by Luther. This larger pattern, which was not at all evident in the practice of early English Baptists and still stands in contrast to that of contemporary Primitive Baptists, is characterized by worship services that include instrumental music, accompanied congregational singing, and rehearsed choirs or soloists performing music composed for the church. While Primitive Baptists clearly reject all of these practices, they do continue to adapt folk and ballad tunes to their hymn texts. Even so, their singing style remains consistent with their Calvinistic emphasis on the doctrine of election because neither their song texts nor their way of singing deliberately encourages the conversion of sinners. To further frame this relationship between doctrine and song style, we have to look closely at musical developments among the early English Baptists, for this is the direct historical source for the congregational song of modern Primitive Baptists.

Several members of the Mountain District Association I interviewed reported feeling a close spiritual kinship with the Strict and Particular Baptists in England. Some remembered hearing Elder Charles Alexander, from Liverpool, preach in North Carolina, and one woman had subscribed for years to a Strict and Particular Baptist periodical that featured his columns. She showed me the stack of papers she had saved because she was impressed by his finding "spiritual applications to things that most people read over as literal" (WI-109).

The doctrines and applications that link these Baptists in America and England and separate them from other Baptists are longstanding. In seventeenth-century England, several divisions occurred among Baptists, but one of the earliest—and one that Primitive Baptists find most important—developed between the Particular Baptists and the General Baptists. Thomas Crosby, an early Baptist historian, wrote that "there have been two *parties* of the *English Baptists* in *England* ever since the beginning of the reformation; those that have followed the *Calvinistical* scheme of doctrines, and from the principal point therein, *personal election,* have been termed *Particular Baptists*: And those that have professed the *Arminian* or remonstrant tenets; and have also from the chief of those doctrines, *universal redemption,* been called *General Baptists*" (Crosby 1738–40, 1:173).   ˙

Musical differences between Baptists also developed early—differences linked to these two doctrinal positions.[4] Reestablishing singing in the church in a form consistent with New Testament Scriptures was a concern of all English Baptists throughout the seventeenth century. And, like other dissenting groups, they were not agreed among themselves on how to achieve such a restoration (Allen 1691; Claridge 1697; Collins 1680). By the end of the seventeenth century, the Particular Baptists and the General Baptists had not only adopted distinctly different doctrines regarding salvation, but they had also developed distinctly different ideas about singing.

The chief exponent of the General Baptist position on singing was one of its ministers, Thomas Grantham. In principle, Grantham favored singing in public worship and even argued that singing psalms, hymns, and spiritual songs was an ordinance of the Christian church. In a published opinion (1678), he noted briefly his agreement with the belief, widely held in England, particularly among Calvinists, that the use of musical instruments was a borrowing from Jewish practice and should not be admitted in Christian worship. His primary concern, however, was not the use of musical instruments; instead, it was that he saw no clear scriptural basis for congregational singing, a practice accepted among many Protestants by that time. Grantham argued that there were only two modes of performance of spiritual songs: one was "by Art, as those do who only speak what another puts into their mouths"; the other was "by the gift of Gods Grace and Spirit." The first he dismissed as "counterfeit Psalmody," an empty sound of words without Spirit that had no place in public worship (Grantham 1678:99). Grantham advocated the second mode, singing with the Spirit or with "Affections raised to Godward by his Grace."

Those who performed the service of singing in public worship, Grantham insisted, should be gifted for it by the Spirit of God just as surely as those who would preach, teach, pray, or prophesy in public. This gift to sing in public worship was uncommon and required not only skill but also a certainty on the part of the singer that there was grace in his own heart so that his song might benefit himself as well as exhilarate, edify, or comfort the church. In addition, the words had to be spontaneous, inspired, and in accord with the Scriptures. The "matter" or text of a spiritual song, as Grantham saw it, must be the Word of God as it is "seated in the soul of the Christians, and not as it may be read to them out of a Book only and then repeated by them." David's Psalms were to be considered examples and precedents, but they were not to be simply repeated or translated into meter and sung, as Calvin had advocated. Grantham called singing such translations a "bare recital." Anyone could read a Psalm, he reasoned, and so the scriptural reference to "having a Psalm" surely meant "something further than to be able to read or sing them out of a Book, or as set forth by another" (Grantham 1678:100). As for other composed texts, Grantham dismissed them in the following manner:

> . . . Alas, what a groundless Practice have we here? [T]he Holy Scripture is a stranger to it, none of the Apostles used to do thus, that we read of: Nor is there any reason that any man's Verses should be introduced in the Church as a part of the Service of God, or that all should be tyed to one Man's Words, Measures,

and Tones in so great an Ordinance. . . . Surely this new Device of Singing what is put into mens Mouths by a Reader makes a fair way for Forms of Prayer to be introduced together with it . . . Have we not seen both the Spirit of Prayer and Praises greatly taken away where these formalities have prevailed? (1678:105)

Grantham believed that the manner of singing he advocated was the practice of the Primitive or New Testament church and was "lawful, very profitable, and fully warranted by I Corinthians 14," whereas, for a whole congregation to sing together would be to make "all the Body a Mouth and wholly to take away the use of the Ear," a practice not warranted by any Scripture (1678:101–2). Given these conditions, he concluded that only

> such persons as God hath gifted . . . and upon whose hearts God hath put a lively sense of present Mercies, should have their liberty and convenient opportunity, to celebrate the high Praises of God, one by one, in the Churches of God, . . . And that all this be done with a pleasant or chearful [*sic*] voice that may serve to express the Joys conceived in the Heart of him that singeth, the better to affect the Hearts of all the Congregation. . . . And thus he that hath a Psalm, becomes a useful Minister in the House of God. (1678:112–13)

In a variation on the theology of music formulated earlier by Zwingli, Grantham thought that every Christian hearing such a song "ought to apply or bring the matter of the Psalm to his own heart, and there to make melody to the Lord" (1678:101). All Christians could sing, of course, but just as they were to pray in private, they also ought to sing in private. In practice, this position seems to have eliminated congregational singing in public worship among the General Baptists until well after it was common practice among Particular Baptists.

But Particular Baptists themselves did not arrive at a general acceptance of congregational singing without a period of controversy. Although their arguments are comfortably remote in time, space, and even content, their opposing points of view—one rigidly literal and narrow and the other more metaphoric and typological—will be familiar to many Primitive Baptists today.

We see evidence of these mind sets in the records and reports of the London ministry of Benjamin Keach, one of the most influential ministers among the Particular Baptists in late-seventeenth-century England.[5] In 1668, at the age of twenty-eight, Keach was chosen as an elder by a Particular Baptist congregation in London. Keach had been baptized at the age of fifteen and was preaching among the General Baptists when he was eighteen, but he eventually joined the Particular Baptists after a move to London brought him in contact with them and some reflection brought about a change in his views.[6] He served his congregation in London until his death in 1704, meeting in a private house until the building of a meetinghouse at Horsleydown. Convinced that "singing the praises of God" was a holy ordinance of Jesus Christ, Keach labored with his congregation "earnestly and with a great deal of prudence and caution" to introduce "singing the praises of God in the assembly for public worship." For this purpose, he composed over three hundred hymns for the members to sing (*Spiritual Melody* [1691]). Keach first introduced congregational singing in 1673 after the Lord's Supper and labored patiently about fourteen years before he obtained agreement from the church "to sing the praises of God on every Lord's day" (Crosby 1738–40, 4:298–99). The agreement was not unanimous, however, and adopting the practice resulted in a split in the church.

Keach's primary opponent in the controversy was Isaac Marlow, a member of Keach's own congregation. Marlow was an outspoken critic of congregational singing, and he circulated his argument in several publications. Keach, who was no stranger to controversy, responded in print. From these documents we can see the reasoning behind the practice that finally prevailed among the Particular Baptists in England and Wales and was carried by them to America. In their argument about what kind of musical expression was appropriate in public worship, Keach and Marlow seem to have agreed only that there was New Testament authorization for singing by the church. They found nothing in common in their ideas for establishing that practice.

Marlow's argument was similar to that of the General Baptists, but it was more strident in its tone and more extreme in its position. Marlow rejected the use of precomposed or "humane Forms" as texts for singing on grounds that reliance on human compositions in verse form denied the power and rejected the gifts of the Holy Spirit (1690:20–21). He also argued that these forms—"rhime and metre"—were not natural:

For our Natural Light teacheth us that we should praise God, when in vocal worship, after the best, most apt and freest way that we are naturally capable to express our Hearts to God in, which is to praise him in Prose, with a plain voice, otherwise

for any to justifie the mode of singing their praises in Rhime and
Metre to be their natural duty, they must first make it manifest
that they can naturally express their Praises most aptest, and freest that way, which I believe but few, if any can, pretend unto;
because Rhime and Metre are more properly the fruit of Art than
the simple Gift of Nature, the which [*sic*] we have no Command
nor Example so to improve by Art for Gospel-worship. (1696:26)

Marlow objected to congregational singing on numerous other
grounds also. He found "not . . . one Text of Scripture . . . to shew that
ever, the Ministers and People sung with conjoined Voices in the Instituted Worship of God under the Law." Singing, for him, was a "cir-
cumstantial, accidental, and occasional Duty to the great Ordinance
of Thanksgiving and Praising of God" and it was never established
as a "constant continual Ordinance for Gospel worship" (1690:22).

Marlow did not stop with these fairly conventional arguments but
went to the unusual extreme of objecting to congregational singing
because it would include women.

The Womens vocal singing in the Church, a practice in common
use, is chargeable with breaking the positive and express Laws
of Christ, which are so plainly, clearly and fully worded, that I
know not how such Women can satisfie their Consciences in that
practice, unless it be through ignorance of the Scriptures wherein
it is forbidden; nor how any Gospel-Ministers can open their
Mouths for it, seeing Women are commanded not to teach, nor
to speak in the Church, but to learn in silence, and to be in silence; for the Apostle's Words imply, that for Women not to learn
in silence in the Church, but to break their silence there, by teaching or speaking in proper Church-worship, is a usurpation of
Authority, and Disobedience to the Law [I Cor. 14.34. I Tim.
2.11,12]. It's true, Women may speak to give their Evidence, or
an account of their Faith, or in an orderly way to give their As-
sent or Dissent in matters of Church-Discipline, for in such cases the Scriptures do allow their speaking; but in more proper
Acts of Divine Worship, as Prayer, Praising and Teaching, those
Scriptures do forbid them, or else they have no Sence nor Meaning at all in them: But such is the plain and common sence of
them, that you must first perswade me contrary to natural Sence
and Reason, that Womens vocal, audible singing of matter of
Praise and Doctrine, which thing the Scripture calls teaching,
and speaking [Col. 3.16. Eph. 5.19.] is neither of them, but is a
keeping Silence, learning in Silence, and is being in Silence, be-

fore I can believe that Women are permitted vocally to sing in the Worship of God in his Church. (1696:13–14)

Marlow made explicit in one of his early publications the reasoning underlying his argument. In insisting on women's silence in the church, he wrote the following: "But some will object and say, That these Scriptures that forbid Womens teaching and speaking in the Church, and that command them to learn in silence, do intend only that they should not be the Mouth of the Church as in Prayer and Doctrine, to speak to God for them, or from God unto them; . . . This Objection . . . cannot possibly be the Mind of Christ in them, because it is contrary to the Letter of those Texts . . ." (1692:96–97).

Keach may have prompted Marlow's statement with an even earlier attack. In 1691, he published his objections to Marlow's position, disagreeing not only with Marlow's ideas, but with his literal way of interpreting scriptural texts. "To take the bare letter of the Text, without shewing the scope and drift of the Spirit of God in it, would make sad work, as I might show from many Scriptures, and has occasioned many abominable Errors, nay Heresies, to abound in the World" (1691a:34 [Appendix]).

Keach's interpretations frequently drew on the Old Testament as a source of types and figures that foreshadowed and helped interpret New Testament passages (1682). From Isaiah, he quoted "Thy Watchmen shall lift up the voice; with the voice together shall they sing" (Isa. 52:7–8) to support his position on congregational singing (1691a:51). In advocating congregational singing, Keach felt he was restoring a lost and neglected ordinance to public worship. The whole church, he thought, ought to sing together in mixed assemblies "as 'tis the Duty of all to hear God's Word and to pray with united Hearts, so to sing together with united Voices." In addition, he argued that unbelievers might also sing. Unbelievers joining with the church was one thing, he said, and the church joining with unbelievers was another (1691a:102, 105).

Most significant, Keach vigorously opposed Marlow's efforts to exclude women from singing in public worship. Keach argued repeatedly for distinctions that Marlow was not making. In singing, he said, "there is a Teaching, but chiefly we speak to our own selves. . . . [T]he matter of the Psalm or Hymn is full of teaching and Admonition, yet tis the Matter sung which teaches, rather than the Singers may be said to do it: nor is it any contradiction to say when I teach others, yet I am thereby taught and admonished my self" (1691a:37 [Appendix]).

As to that teaching which is in Singing, it doth not lie in a Min-
isterial way, and therefore [is] not intended by the Spirit of God
here; Preaching or Teaching is not Singing, nor Singing Preaching or Teaching, though there is a Teaching in it. . . . [H]e or she
that reads the Scripture may be said in some sense to teach, there
is much teaching in it; yet sure a Woman may be suffered to do
this, as a case may present it self [sic], both in the Church, or at
home either, in her Husbands presence, and not be deemed to
usurp Authority over him: for the Usurpation the Apostle speaks
of, respects a Womans own Husband (if not chiefly) as well as
others; and therefore if she must not sing in the Church, so by
your Argument she must not sing nor read the Scripture at home
in the presence of her Husband, because there is a kind of teaching in both those Duties; and if she should, as you intimate, she
would not only break Silence, but usurp Authority over the Man,
i.e. her Head and Husband, which is forbid. The Lord deliver
poor Women, and Men too, from such kind of Doctrine as this.
(1691a:34–35 [Appendix])

Keach argued that singing ought to be with united voices and done
together harmoniously, men and women, children and adults, ministers and congregation, and even believers and unbelievers. He did not,
however, approve of solo singing, which he associated with ballad
singing:

Since we are commanded to sing, and Christ hath given no other Direction about it but that of his own Practice, with his Disciples after the Holy Supper, and that of the Practice of Paul and
Silas, who sung together, we may assure ourselves there is no
other manner of Singing to be brought into the Church but with
united Voices; and he that should set up, or bring in any other
way or manner, doubtless would be guilty of an Innovation.
Should one alone sing in the midst of the Congregation, like a
Ballad-Singer, what Word of God is there to justify any such
practice? (1691a:74–75)

Keach's congregation at Horsley-down voted on the matter of hymn
singing and agreed to sing every Lord's day, but only after the preaching, so that any who did not want to participate would be free to leave
without offending those who wanted to stay and sing. Marlow and a
small group of supporters left the congregation anyway and established
another church, Mayes Pond, which was reported by Crosby to be the
same in every respect with the exception of singing. Joseph Ivimey

(1811–30, 4 vols.), in giving an account of the same event, implies that the doctrine preached at Mayes Pond may have been somewhat less Calvinistic than that at Horsley-down. In any case, a trend was already in motion. Congregational singing became the rule in Particular Baptist churches almost half a century before it was widely accepted among General Baptists. Even the Mayes Pond congregation agreed to sing when its second minister made it a condition of his acceptance that the church practice congregational singing.

The Particular Baptists not only regarded congregational singing more favorably than the General Baptists but had become strong advocates of it by the beginning of the eighteenth century. Some congregations even sang newly composed hymns in addition to psalms. Documentation of this development is scattered and scant. Two important sources of information about these developments are church records and the Confessions of Faith that were adopted and published by the Particular Baptists.

Records for 1671 of the Broadmead Church in Bristol (Hayden, ed., 1974), for example, indicate that some Particular Baptists were practicing congregational singing and were singing as heartily as Primitive Baptists sing now. These records include a reference to a complaint "by old Mr Wright" that the Psalm singing at their meeting place could be heard at his house in Halliers Lane.[7] There are numerous later references in those records indicating that psalm singing was common practice there. A later reference in records of another Particular Baptist church, dated 1 March 1686, reads, "Mr. Kiffin opened his meeting place; and he and others preached at it, and psalms were sung there."

A series of Confessions of Faith reflects a growing consciousness of singing as an important part of public worship. The first of these, the London Confession, was published in 1644. The Particular Baptists had organized later than the General Baptists, not having a congregation of their own until 1633, when a group that did not believe in infant baptism withdrew (with permission) from an Independent congregation of Protestant dissenters in London and established a church. Within ten years, there were seven Particular Baptist congregations in London, and they published their own Confession of Faith, a predestinarian document, apparently in response to the imprisonment of one of their preachers. This confession did not include any statement at all on singing. About thirty years later, however, this changed.

With the renewal of persecution of nonconformists in England in 1673, the Particular Baptists in and near London deliberately presented a united front with Presbyterians and Congregationalists by using the Westminster Confession (1646) as the basis for a new confession of their own. This new confession was prepared by Elder William Collins of the Petty France Church in London, approved at a gathering of representatives from Particular Baptist churches in England and Wales in 1677, and adopted in 1689 by the first English Particular Baptist General Assembly in London. It included the following important statement on singing:

> The [I Tim. 4.13.] reading of the Scriptures, Preaching, and [2 Tim. 4.2. Luk. 8.18.] hearing the word of God, teaching and admonishing one another in Psalms, Hymns and Spiritual songs, singing with grace in our Hearts to [Col. 3.16. Eph. 5.19.] the Lord; as also the Administration [Mat. 28.19,20.] of Baptism, and [I Cor. 11.26.] the Lords [*sic*] Supper are all parts of Religious worship of God, to be performed in obedience to him, with understanding, faith, reverence, and godly fear; moreover solemn humilitation [*sic*] [Esth. 4.16. Joel. 2.12.] with fastings; and thanksgiving upon [Exo. 15.1 etc. Ps. 107.] special occasions, ought to be used in an holy and religious manner.[8]

As Lumpkin points out, this statement is musically significant on two counts: first, it represents a change from the London Confession of 1644 by incorporating a statement on singing; and second, it goes beyond the injunction of the Westminster Confession to sing Psalms (1969:237–38). The new confession approves also hymns and spiritual songs.

The influence of this confession extended to America through the son of Benjamin Keach, Elias, who, in 1688, became pastor of the Pennepack Baptist Church in Pennsylvania, organized in an area that is now within the city of Philadelphia. The Pennepack church was, at first, typical of predestinarian Baptist congregations of that period. A program booklet printed in 1938 for the 250th anniversary celebration of the church described the congregation as having begun with twelve members that included five Baptists from Radnorshire, Wales, one from Kilkenny, Ireland, and six from England. By 1700, membership had increased to forty-six. The church met in members' homes until 1707, when it built a modest meetinghouse, twenty-five feet square, on land given by Samuel Jones, later a pastor of the church (Torbet 1950:228–29).

This church apparently practiced hymn singing, at least after communion, from the time it was established. Church minutes dating from around 1692 reported on the earlier period when Elias Keach was pastor: "The usual Customs observed by Elias Keach at the celebration of the Lord's Supper was to deliver the bread and the Cup to the Deacon and the Deacon delivered it unto the Communicants. Also he usually Concluded with singing A hymn of praise Composed for that purpose, and then with Committing us to god [*sic*] by prayers" (Brackney 1983:121).

Elias Keach was a key figure in the earliest days of the group of churches that were to form the Philadelphia Association in 1707.[9] This association included the Welsh Tract Church to which Primitive Baptists of the Mountain District Association trace their beginnings in America. The congregation had organized in Wales and moved, as a group, to Philadelphia in 1701, settling in the vicinity of Pennepack for two years before purchasing a tract of land in Delaware and moving there to build the Welsh Tract Church. This church is credited by Morgan Edwards, a Baptist historian and the pastor of the Philadelphia church from 1761 to 1771,[10] with being "the principal, if not sole, means of introducing singing . . . among the Baptists in the Middle States" (Spencer 1877:41).

When Elias Keach returned to London and assumed the pastorate of the Tallow Chandler's Hall Church, he published, in 1697, a set of articles of faith in the name of that church which were "almost exactly the Assembly Confession of 1689 with the addition of articles on hymn-singing and the laying on of hands upon baptized believers." It is Keach's confession that was the first generally used Baptist Confession in America (Lumpkin 1969:348–49).

Records of the Welsh Tract Church show that the confession Keach published in London was translated into Welsh in 1716 by Abel Morgan, a Philadelphia minister, and it was signed by members then, though it may never have been published. Attached to the confession was "an article relative to Laying on of hands; Singing Psalms; and Church Covenants." The Philadelphia Association had formally adopted the confession by 25 September 1742, for on that date the association ordered a printing of an edition that included two new articles which were in fact reprints of articles 27 and 28 of the confession Elias Keach published in London in 1697 and which had been incorporated into the confession signed by members of the Welsh Tract Church in 1716 (Lumpkin 1969:349). The article "Of Singing Psalms, &c." reads as follows:

> We believe that "acts 16 25 eph 5 19 col 3 16" singing the praises of God is a holy Ordinance of Christ, and not a part of natural religion, or a moral duty only; but that it is brought under divine

institution, it being injoined on the churches of Christ to sing
psalms, hymns, and spiritual songs; and that the whole church
in their public assemblies, as well as private christians, ought to
"heb 2 12 jam 5 13" sing God's praises according to the best light
they have received. Moreover it was practiced in the great representative church, by "matt 26 30 mat [*sic*, mark] 14 26" our Lord
Jesus Christ with his disciples, after he had instituted and cele-
brated the sacred ordinance of his Holy Supper, as a commemo-
rative token of redeeming love. (Lumpkin 1969:351)

This article, written in London toward the end of the decade during which the controversy about singing reached its height, represents
an explicit acknowledgment of singing as an ordinance established by
Christ, and one in which the "whole church in their public assemblies"
ought to participate. Adoption of this statement by the Welsh Tract
Church, later by the Philadelphia Association, and then by the Kehukee Association in North Carolina, is a clear indication of commitment
to congregational hymn singing in those American churches. The influence of these predestinarian Baptists extended rapidly from Pennsylvania, Delaware, and New Jersey, where they first settled, into eastern North Carolina and directly into the southern mountains.

Though some members of Mountain District Association churches
today would, no doubt, find the accounts of these early controversies about singing interesting, they would reject any explanations of
their own religious song style that were based only on history or tradition. For outside observers also, an account of the historical pro-
cesses that influenced the current Primitive Baptist song style does
not explain the singing, but it does help frame the picture. This background provides a point of access to a practice and style of singing
that Primitive Baptists have long assumed but typically explain only
by brief references to scriptural authority. Historically, however, several differing developments in church music have grown from contrasting interpretations of these same scriptural texts. Also, it is clear
that the interpretation most influential on the development of Primitive Baptist musical practice was similar to Calvin's, one that read the
Scriptures typologically and metaphorically. It was held by predestinarian Particular Baptists in England who carried their practice to
their first settlements in Pennsylvania and Delaware. These accounts
also indicate that by the beginning of the eighteenth century, some
of the basic features of this musical practice—rejection of musical instruments, and an acceptance of congregational hymn singing—were
established among predestinarian Baptists through deliberate efforts

in both England and America. These two features have remained relatively stable and consistent since then among predestinarian Baptists in America.

This historical record implies a stronger relationship between predestinarian doctrine and unaccompanied congregational hymn singing than is generally acknowledged in musicology or cultural studies. The opposing positions on singing taken by General Baptists (with Arminian doctrines) and Particular Baptists (holding Calvinistic doctrines) offer no simple equation, however, for the relation of doctrine to musical practice. For example, it is not clear to what extent differences in doctrine can explain why Baptists with Arminian views have tended to be more open to change in their musical practice than their predestinarian neighbors. It is nevertheless hard to ignore a correlation. Historically, we can see that those Baptists who have increasingly emphasized the human role in salvation have also expanded the role of music in worship, shifting from an extreme of little or no singing in seventeenth- and eighteenth-century churches to current programs of music ministry that, in some churches at least, are administered on a grand scale. These music ministries may support piano and/or organ accompaniment for all singing, several trained choirs of singers and bell ringers, church orchestras, the use of instruments and styles associated with folk revival music and popular music including jazz and rock, interpretive dance, simple to elaborate sound systems for amplifying both instruments and voices, formal concerts of sacred music, and salaried staff members who are professionally trained in church music. On the other hand, Primitive Baptists, while making small changes in their musical practice, continue a practice of singing that would probably still be recognizable to their earliest predecessors.

Related issues surface in the early debates about singing among the English Particular Baptists. Arguments about music occurred among the Particular Baptists themselves as well as between them and other groups in the seventeenth century. Both Keach and Marlow had supporters within the Horsley-down congregation as well as among Particular Baptists in other churches. Pressures to make changes came, then as now, from within the church as well as from outside. These internal arguments reveal similarities between Marlow's position and that of the General Baptists, but, further, they reveal conflicting mindsets or patterns of reasoning in the interpretation of biblical texts. Keach's response to Marlow represents his opposition, not just to Marlow's conclusions, but especially to an approach that interprets a text literally and without attention to the "drift and scope" of the whole Bible. Keach believed that scriptural texts sometimes had to be interpreted figuratively or metaphorically in order to draw out their true meanings, and he appears to speak for the majority of pre-destinarian Baptists at that time. Both types of thinking are present in the churches of the Mountain District Association, coexisting un-easily at times. In subsequent chapters I will explore how each ex-presses itself in a contemporary practice of singing.

Finally, these early debates also frame a discussion of women in the church. I have quoted extensively from historical accounts that concern women, in part, to indicate the lengthy and serious thought that Particular Baptists gave to including women in congregational singing, a practice that is now commonly and widely accepted. More important, however, this historical perspective suggests that a shared practice may carry different meanings for different groups. Without some historical background, for example, even close observers of Primitive Baptist singing would probably not attach much significance simply to the presence of congregational singing in Primitive Baptist churches, and they would see little, if any, significance in women's participation in this singing. Previous studies of Primitive Baptists, in fact, tend to refer to church members as a group, implying that gender makes no difference in religious roles and experience. In light of the extreme male dominance still present in this church, however, that seems unlikely and gender issues naturally arise. Singing appears to be linked in some important way to gender because it is the one place in which women consistently have a voice in the worship ser-vice.[11] Furthermore, women themselves attach significance to their participation in the singing in church meetings. These historical ac-counts prepare us to see this, to question our assumptions, and to explore more fully what Primitive Baptist singing means in these churches today.

3

Religious Identity
and the Sound of Singing

Don't get me wrong, we're the same people, but there's a little
deviation in the tunes.

—Primitive Baptist elder, Virginia, 1982

PEOPLE TRY TO COPY the sound of the Old Baptists, a Primitive Baptist woman told me during my first visit to her home—and, she said,
she believed some of them could come pretty close. She played a recording of "Amazing Grace" from a popular album by Judy Collins
to make her point. The opening stanza held her attention as, slowly
and without accompaniment, the singer interpreted the familiar melody, skillfully elaborating it with Old Baptist–like passing tones and
turns. My hostess listened attentively and indicated her approval until
a background chorus of voices transformed the character of the song
in its second verse. She lost interest when the sound of the song began to change. In midsong she turned off the stereo and motioned
me back toward the master bedroom where she and her husband kept
their tape recorder. Rummaging through a desk drawer full of cas-
sette tapes of Primitive Baptist meetings that they or friends had made
for themselves, she said that she just wanted me to hear something.
She finally found the tape and triumphantly played a second version
of "Amazing Grace" (fig. 1).

Fig. 1. "Amazing grace how sweet the sound" (John Newton, Goble no. 175)
with the tune "New Britain" as sung by the congregation of Little River Primitive Baptist Church, 19 June 1983, Sparta, North Carolina (WI-128).

saved   a   wretch   like   me!   I   once   was   lost,   but

now   am   found,   Was   blind,   but   now   I   see.

1. Amazing grace, how sweet the sound!
   That saved a wretch like me!
   I once was lost, but now am found,
   Was blind, but now I see.

2. 'Twas grace that taught my heart to fear,
   And grace my fears relieved:
   How precious did that grace appear,
   The hour I first believed.

3. Through many dangers, toils, and snares,
   I have already come;
   'Tis grace has brought me safe thus far,
   And grace will lead me home.

4. The Lord has promised good to me,
   His word my hope secures;
   He will my shield and portion be
   As long as life endures.

5. Yes, when this flesh and heart shall fail,
   And mortal life shall cease,
   I shall possess within the vale
   A life of joy and peace.

6. The earth shall soon dissolve like snow,
   The sun forbear to shine,
   But God, who called me here below,
   Will be forever mine.

The voices on this recording sounded familiar, and when I named the song leader and congregation of her own home church, she seemed pleased. But then she wanted to know if I could hear the difference. If she heard me wondering aloud "which difference," she did not acknowledge it. Her question was rhetorical, and the tone of her voice made it clear that she thought the congregational version was the better of the two.

Some weeks later, during the weekend of an annual association meeting, that episode came to mind when two colleagues and I were overnight guests in another Primitive Baptist home. Our elderly host turned on his radio, inviting us to hear the Sunday morning broadcast by a local Primitive Baptist preacher. As he turned the dial searching for the program, a sound caught his ear and he tuned in carefully to a station that was introducing its program with the commercially popular recording of "Amazing Grace." He, too, listened attentively until the second verse began and then abruptly turned off the radio, deciding aloud that he was not going to be able to find what he wanted us to hear that morning. I became curious when he showed a sudden loss of interest in the song, but he shrugged off all questions about singing. He could tell us, he said, about what had not changed in the Primitive Baptist church, and that was the preaching. Later that day, at the association meeting, I mentioned the commercial recording to another Primitive Baptist. It was nice, she said, but it was not the "joyful sound," and then she hurried off to hear the preaching, leaving me to puzzle over what the various responses to that recording might mean.

At the very least, these three lay members were distinguishing between singing in a traditional style that was reminiscent of Primitive Baptists and singing that was authentically Primitive Baptist, and although they were showing an attraction to the first, they were expressing a preference for the latter. But the reference to the joyful sound raised questions about what lay behind the preference. What ideas did Primitive Baptists hold about their singing that were not necessarily evident in the practice itself? What did it mean to them to speak of "the joyful sound," for example, particularly in reference to the slow, minor-sounding tunes that comprised approximately one-fifth of the repertory we heard, ones they themselves even described as "lonesome." This description seems more apt than "joyful" when paired with solemn hymn texts like "Broad is the road that leads to death" (fig. 2) or "Mixtures of joy and sorrow" (see chapter 5, fig. 60).

Fig. 2. "Broad is the road that leads to death" (Isaac Watts, Goble no. 7) with the tune "Windham" (Daniel Read) as sung by the congregation of Union Primitive Baptist Church, 3 July 1982, Whitehead, North Carolina (WI-045).

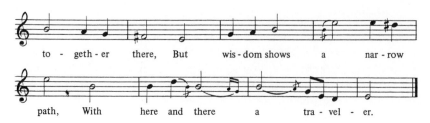

to - geth - er there, But   wis - dom shows   a   nar - row

path,   With   here and there   a   tra - vel - er.

1. Broad is the road that leads to death,
   And thousands walk together there,
   But wisdom shows a narrow path,
   With here and there a traveler.

2. "Deny thyself, and take thy cross,"
   Is the Redeemer's great command;
   Nature must count her gold but dross,
   If she would gain the heav'nly land.

3. The hypocrite, who tires and faints,
   And walks the way of God no more,
   Is but esteemed almost a saint,
   And finds his own destruction sure.

4. Lord, let not all my hopes be vain,
   Create my heart entirely new,
   Which hypocrites could ne'er attain,
   Which false apostates never knew.

Church elders, conscious of their role as spokesmen and often good singers and song leaders themselves, became our primary sources of information about Primitive Baptist singing. Elder Billy Cook, the son of a Primitive Baptist elder and a member of a neighboring association to the Mountain District, offered some of the most extended comments on singing. A war veteran, disabled in Vietnam, he had had a lot of time to think, he said, and had given much thought to Primitive Baptist singing. He often chose narratives and metaphors to talk about singing and to draw out the meanings he saw in it.

Some of his stories were about his own experiences as a soldier but he also told other wartime stories that he believed were true. One of his Vietnam stories illustrated his belief that Primitive Baptist singing has a sound or style so distinctive that it can be recognized even by people who are not themselves Primitive Baptists.

You know, here I was thirteen thousand miles from home and thought no one would ever have known any Primitive Baptist songs or anything, but I was singing the little song [Goble hymn number 268] on guard duty and one of my fellow buddies there come up when I was singing. I didn't know he was there, and as I sang it he approached me, and he said, "Cook," he said, "what is that song you're singing?" I told him it was "Must Jesus bear the cross alone?" And he said, "Well that's the same way that my grandmother sings it, and she was a Primitive Baptist." (WI-106)

Fig. 3. "Must Jesus bear the cross alone" (Thomas Shepherd, Goble no. 268) with the tune "Pisgah" as sung by the congregation of the Little River Primitive Baptist Church, ca. 1960, Sparta, North Carolina. Recorded by Elder Lasserre Bradley. *Old Hymns Lined and Led by Elder Walter Evans*, Sovereign Grace 6444.

1. Must Jesus bear the cross alone
   And all the world go free?
   No; there's a cross for every one,
   And there's a cross for me.

2. How happy are the saints above,
   Who once wept sorr'wing here!
   But now they taste unmingled love
   And joy without a tear.

3. The consecrated cross I'll bear,
   Till death shall set me free,
   And then go home my crown to wear—
   For there's a crown for me.

There was more to the sound of Primitive Baptist singing, however, than simply being distinctive and recognizable. According to El-

der Cook and several other church spokesmen, the singing was the
sound of the Church, a sign of God's chosen people. Elder Cook illustrated this with two narratives of visionary experiences in which
hymn singing played a key role. His brother had recorded one of these
experiences in the last letter he wrote. This happened, the preacher
said, shortly before his brother's death.

> I have a brother that's been deceased since April 1966. . . . Two
> or three days before his death, he was standing in the air termi-
> nal in Travis Air Force Base in the state of California waiting on
> his airlift . . . and he was writing a letter home. And we got the
> letter two days after we got the telegram that the boy was dead.
> But when he wrote that letter, he told this. In the letter, he said,
> "Dad, you and Mom and . . . others of the church was standing
> in . . . church." And he said, "As you stood there, you started
> singing 'There is a fountain filled with blood.'" And he said, "I
> stood and I listened and I seen the expression on the face, and
> feeling in the song." And he said, "When I come to myself, tears
> was running down my face." And he said, "My greatest friend
> there . . . inquired of what was wrong. . . . I told him about the
> little log church and what I'd seen and what I had felt." And he
> said, "My friend now has said that he would love to pay a visit
> to [the church]," unknowing in that within a matter of four
> days . . . they would both be sent back, one deceased and one
> alive. (WI-106)

Fig. 4. "There is a fountain filled with blood" (William Cowper, Goble no.
12) with the tune "Cleansing Fountain" as sung by the congregation of Woodruff Primitive Baptist Church, 10 July 1983, Glade Valley, North Carolina (WI-
144).

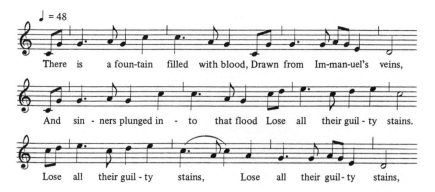

And sin - ners plunged in - to that flood Lose all their guil - ty stains.

1. There is a fountain filled with blood,
   Drawn from Immanuel's veins,
   And sinners plunged into that flood
   Lose all their guilty stains.

2. The dying thief rejoiced to see
   That fountain in his day;
   O may I there, though vile as he,
   Wash all my sins away.

3. Dear, dying Lamb, thy precious blood
   Shall never lose its power,
   Till all the ransomed church of God
   Be saved to sin no more.

4. E'er since, by faith, I saw the stream,
   Thy flowing wounds supply,
   Redeeming love has been my theme,
   And shall be till I die;

5. And when this lisping, stam'ring tongue
   Lies silent in the grave,
   Then, in a nobler, sweeter song,
   I'll sing thy power to save.

6. Lord, I believe thou hast prepared,
   Unworthy though I be,
   For me a glorious free reward,
   A golden harp for me.

7. 'Tis strung and tuned for endless years
   And formed by pow'r divine,
   To sound in God the Father's ears
   No other name but thine.

Elder Cook interpreted the vision as a sign of grace, and he interpreted his brother's response to the vision as an indication that the brother, though not a church member, was indeed a child of God. A church deacon who was also participating in the conversation nodded his agreement as the preacher explained, "As far as a member of the church, my brother wasn't. But as far as a child of God, I believe he was, because that's the [way the] hand of the Lord reveals itself . . . [in] these inspired feelings and that sweet hope" (WI-106).

That hymn singing would figure prominently in a vision did not seem at all surprising to Elder Cook. Instead, he suggested that the vision was not unique and told about a similar experience that the deacon's son had reported.

> Brother Darden has a son . . . who was in flight transit from the United States to Germany. And he wrote a letter home and he said, "Dad, . . . as we were coming across the waters," he said, "I seen you," and I think he said his mom and maybe others come before him, singing "Amazing Grace." And he said, "When I come to myself," he said, "tears was dropping off my face." "But," he said, "I don't care what anybody thinks and what they may have seen, . . . I was greatly inspired of that that I seen, and that that I felt." (WI-106)

Elder Cook told us then that we would find that children of God had these experiences, and that such experiences led Primitive Baptists to believe that people do not have to attach their names to a church book to be children of God. Instead, they had to "be washed and regenerated of Christ . . . and I believe that that's what has occurred with people that has seen this." This belief did not diminish, however, the importance of the Primitive Baptist church.

Using the metaphor of the dove, one of their favorite representations of the church, the deacon and Elder Cook sketched out the relationship between their image of the Primitive Baptist church and the sound of its singing. Brother Darden began by saying that he and his two sons had seen a dove in a tree in their yard for the past several nights and had become curious about its nest.

> One of our old preachers said a dove, which is spoken of in the Scripture, represents the church, [and that it] builds the sorriest nest that ever was. And I said I want to see that, if it's got its nest there yet, and I went. And it is, it's the sorriest nest you ever seen for a bird. . . . It's out of little sticks, just little twigs. It looks to me like the eggs [would] just fall on through. . . . But now you don't find no birds a-mixing and a-mingling with doves. . . . You see blackbirds and all, mixed together. Now you watch doves and see if they ever mix and mingle with them, they just won't do it. (WI-106)

The preacher extended the metaphor to show its relationship to the sound. "Well, another thing too about the dove is the sound that the dove carries. There's no other bird—even a mockingbird cannot mock the sound of a dove. And that's the reason so many apply the representation of the dove to the church, is that the church has that sound which nobody else can" (WI-106).

Although Primitive Baptists indicated general agreement with these ideas, most were not this explicit about the meanings embodied in their metaphors and narratives. One elder, for example, reminded his congregation, "There's been many Daughters, been many of them, but only one Dove." Another Primitive Baptist elder responded to my questions by telling a story about hearing a Primitive Baptist preacher sing. His story implied that he saw extramusical meanings in the singing he heard, and he began by telling me that he was a Missionary Baptist at the time this happened.

> [M]y uncle called me one night and said, "I want you to go hear this [Primitive Baptist] preacher tonight." Said, "He's real good." Said, "He's from Kentucky." I said all right. Well I went. And back then a lot of our churches had two windows at the back, beside the pulpit. And they had the windows raised. . . . While the church was singing, [the preacher] was sitting there smoking. Well, that didn't set good with me at all. . . . And, so I think to myself, now if I've come all this way over here just to hear a *man* preach, I'd be better off to stay at home. And that's the way I felt. And he got up and he said, "Let's sing 'Amazing Grace' the way John the Baptist sang." Well, I didn't know what was coming off then. And he sung it, and I tell you the truth, he made hair stand on your head, and that's a fact. And he sang it so long and so loud, you could hear it for two miles if you had been outside. His voice just rang. (WI-127)

These narratives and comments suggest that some, and perhaps many, Primitive Baptists invest the singing in their churches with meaning related to religious identity, identity not only as Primitive Baptists but even more as children of grace, members of the true church that is separate from the world and that transcends the boundaries set by denominations and nations. On the basis of their comments, an observer could reasonably wonder whether any differences in singing between Primitive Baptist congregations in various regions and associations, or even within associations and neighboring independent congregations, would have any real significance for Primitive Baptists themselves, or would even be apparent to them. But additional comments, from this elder and deacon and from other Primitive Baptists, made clear not only that they acknowledged differences in the singing of their various churches, but also that they considered those differences substantial enough at times to inhibit the participation of visiting Primitive Baptists, and that they held definite preferences in regard to song style.

A visiting preacher's wife made her awareness of differences in Primitive Baptist singing quite clear one night in a service when she leaned over toward me during a hymn and whispered, "I just can't sing with these people." As an outsider trying to participate in the singing, I felt sympathetic. The hymnbook we were using that night contained only texts, and many of the tunes the congregation sang from memory were unfamiliar to me. The rhythms of most of them had no regular beat and the song leader was sitting in the congregation with his back to us, giving no visual cues to help singers stay together. Nevertheless, I was surprised that she, a Primitive Baptist, would have any problems participating in the singing or would comment on it. Even though she was formally a visitor in the association, she had undoubtedly attended services in this particular church many times when her husband came to preach. By her own report, she felt enough at home there that she usually sat in the members' pews. Even so, she still seemed acutely conscious of differences between the singing of her home church, no more than an hour's drive away, and that of the church she was visiting. She told me after the service that she thought I would find that the singing varied greatly from church to church and that she supposed that Primitive Baptists generally thought the singing in their home church the best.

Until then, I had mainly been struck by the differences in singing that set apart Primitive Baptists from other denominations. Even the place of singing in the order of worship differed from that in mainline churches. In all of the Primitive Baptist churches I visited, for example, most of the singing occurred before the meeting formally began. As noted earlier, congregations remained seated to sing for half an hour or more when they first met, and then stood to sing a hymn to formally open the meeting. Next, after a prayer, preachers often requested any of a few short, preparatory hymns that stress the minister's inability to preach without the Lord's help, as for example, "Hungry, and faint, and poor" (see chapter 5, figs. 70–72). At the close of the service, Primitive Baptists stood and sang again—not an altar call or invitation hymn as among Missionary Baptists, but a song for the ritual hand of fellowship with the preachers and other members. A further difference was that although an elder or song leader chose the songs to open and close meetings, any member could make song requests during the first period of singing, and the congregation thus exercised significant control over the repertory sung in each church. All of the singing in public worship was from hymnbooks and was congregational and unaccompanied. The churches permitted no instruments and no choirs, and, unlike the Old Regular Baptists, they permitted no solos apart from the phrases a song leader delivered in occasionally lining out a hymn.[1] Explaining the Primitive Baptist preference for congregational singing, Elder Cook said, "We love to sing with all the people, not with a choir or quartet or duet but . . . all of the people joining together. [We] believe that's what David was referring to when he said, 'Come and let us go up to the house of the Lord together'" (WI-106).

Within this framework of similarities, however, there were differences in the hymn singing in various Primitive Baptist churches, at times even when the churches were fewer than ten miles apart. Sometimes striking and sometimes subtle, these differences were surprising to me because they occurred within a group of churches that had much in common. In their church fellowship network, preachers traveled frequently to preach in all the churches and at association meetings that all the churches attended. Likewise, members also attended services in most churches within the same network. (One preacher remarked that it seemed strange to him sometimes that he could travel so many miles to preach and still look out at the congregation and see the same faces that he saw at home.) Nevertheless, Primitive Baptists themselves acknowledged, and sometimes even pointed out, differences in congregational choices of hymnbooks, in repertories chosen from these books, and in stylistic features ranging from pitch and tempo to choice of melody and textual changes. All these created a distinctive singing tradition in each of these various churches.

The variety of hymnbooks published by and for Primitive Baptists, of course, increases the likelihood that different congregations will make different hymnbook choices. In a nationwide survey, Drummond (1989) found ten books currently in use among Primitive Baptists. Three of these consist only of texts with no musical notation, and seven others contain texts with tunes harmonized for four voice parts printed in shaped notes in a piano-score format. Publishing dates range from 1841 to 1983. Drummond's report on his survey leads one to expect that the choice of hymnal in Primitive Baptist churches would vary with geographical region and with the influence of the compiler. But the actual extent of variation in hymnbook choices we found in the churches of a single mountain association and among its neighboring Primitive Baptists was greater than these survey results suggested. In this relatively small area, mostly within twenty miles in any direction from a central point, churches were using six of the ten hymnals Drummond listed and three editions of one of the six, a total of eight different hymnbooks. All of these were published by and for Primitive Baptists.

The *Primitive Baptist Hymn Book,* a book of texts without musical notation compiled by D. H. Goble in 1887, was used by four North Carolina churches in the Mountain District Association and in some of its neighboring churches outside the association and, until 1984, it was also used by two of the association's five Virginia churches. One of these two churches then changed to the eleventh edition of the *Old School Hymnal,* published in 1983. Another of the Virginia churches used the ninth edition of the *Old School Hymnal* (1963), originally published by Elder J. A. Monsees, which contains some songs that were omitted from the later editions. And still another Virginia church in the association preferred the 1918 edition of the *Primitive Baptist Hymn and Tune Book,* compiled by Elder John R. Daily. Some of the elders and friends who were visiting the Mountain Association came from neighboring associations or from independent churches that use Elder Benjamin Lloyd's *The Primitive Hymns* (texts only), published in 1841; or *The Good Old Songs,* compiled by Elder C. H. Cayce and published in 1913; or Silas H. Durand and P. G. Lester's *Hymn and Tune Book,* published in 1886; or the tenth edition of the *Old School Hymnal* (1980).

Drummond suggested that such choices were sometimes influenced by contacts between a hymnbook compiler and influential members of a particular congregation. Our own fieldwork supported this suggestion. "The use of the Daily hymnal at Galax, for example, is probably owing to the fact that the principal song leader there—a man in his eighties—had personal contact with John R. Daily's sons and that Daily himself had visited and preached in the region. The use of two other books—those of Elder Cayce and Elder Monsees—is also probably due to the fact that these elders traveled through the region preaching and leaving behind affectionate regard for themselves and their books" (D. W. Patterson 1985:6).

Attributing the adoption of a hymnbook simply to a compiler's influence may, however, be somewhat misleading. During our fieldwork, the changing needs of a Virginia congregation coincided with the publication of the *Old School Hymnal* number 11 and with the visit of an elder from Georgia, a member of the editorial committee that prepared that hymnal. The visiting elder had come to fill an appointment to preach, and he brought with him a copy of the newly published hymnbook. He and his wife and I were among the house guests of the song leader (also a deacon) and his wife, influential lay members of the congregation, and one evening after church some other members joined us to sing a few songs from the new book. Two younger singers, both teenagers, gave the book an enthusiastic reception. They could read music and liked having musical notation for the alto, tenor, and bass parts. It was harder, they said, to sing parts when they had to use a book that contained only the song texts.

Before this visiting elder came, the song leader had already been thinking ahead to the time when he would ask a younger singer to take over some of his song-leading duties. He was having to work harder at remembering which tunes fit which texts, and even had to pass over several hymn requests in church meetings when neither he nor anyone he asked could recall the tunes.[2] He and his wife both were cheered to see young people take an interest in the church, and they wanted to nurture that interest. It was clear that the members of this Virginia congregation liked the elder from Georgia who introduced the new hymnbook and that they also enjoyed the preaching visits of an elder from Ohio who was on the board of directors of the publishing company. In addition, the father of the younger singers, a deacon and good singer himself, and a successful businessman, agreed to make a substantial financial contribution toward a set of the new books for the church. That this church eventually changed hymnbooks, then, may certainly be attributed partly to the compiler's (in this case, editorial board member's) influence. Equally important, however, was the coincidence of an opportunity for change and the perception of influential members that the church needed to make a change.

Another factor that influences decisions about hymnbooks, especially a decision to keep the old rather than adopt the new, is an assessment of the doctrinal soundness of the hymn texts collected in those books. Hymnbook compilers, church elders, and members alike share a concern for maintaining consistency between what they believe and what they sing, and they all aim for doctrinal soundness in their religious songs. One of the oldest hymnbooks still in use among Primitive Baptists, *The Primitive Hymns* compiled by Benjamin Lloyd in 1841, one elder felt, contained too many Arminian sentiments to be satisfactory. His personal favorite among the hymnbooks was the *Hymn and Tune Book* compiled by Durand and Lester (1886), and he said of this book, "You won't find one sentence that is pleasing to nature or gives man any credit. [In] the Goble [hymnbook], you'll find just a few. In all the others you'll find many hymns that just apply to nature more than have any spiritual meaning" (WI-185).

Some of the hymnbook compilers, themselves Primitive Baptists, acknowledged giving particular attention to text. In their preface, Durand and Lester (1886) wrote that "our first care has been that every sentiment expressed should be in harmony with the truth of God, believing that 'Christians should never sing what they do not believe to be true.'" The following year D. H. Goble also emphasized that he had taken care "especially that no unsound sentiment be found in any selection. We are fully persuaded that we had as well preach unsound doctrine as to sing it with an attempt at devotion." The favorable reception of his hymnbook was to him a token of "the oneness of mind and feeling existing between us" (1887:3–4). Elder Cayce echoed these sentiments in the preface of the hymnbook he compiled in 1913. "We believe that people should sing the truth, as well as preach it" (1980:3).

Goble was typical of these Primitive Baptist hymnbook compilers in freely altering hymn texts to make them conform to his understanding of doctrine. In the preface to the *Primitive Baptist Hymn Book*, he acknowledged making "numerous small changes" in the texts he selected in order to make them compatible with Primitive Baptist doctrine.[3] A Primitive Baptist preacher who was familiar with both the Goble and Cayce hymnbooks pointed out the difference in a hymn text that was common to the two Primitive Baptist hymnbooks. The text, attributed to William Cole, began "O happy time, long waited for." The hymn text was the same for all six stanzas in both books, except for two lines. The preacher read these two, the final lines of the third verse, from the Goble book (no. 195). "My heart and treasure is above, / And I for heaven bound." He said that he thought this statement was presumptuous, and read aloud the revised lines as Cayce (no. 494) published them. "My heart with Jesus and His saints, / In sweetest union bound." This was the only song he knew of, he said, that Cayce had rendered better than Goble, and he thought the change made it much more beautiful.

There is a general acknowledgment among Primitive Baptists, however, that even the best intentions of the compilers often do not prevent the publication of texts that are flawed doctrinally, and there is agreement also that there are enough differences among Primitive Baptists to make it unlikely that any one collection would suit them all. Furthermore, editions of the *Old School Hymnal*, especially numbers 10 and 11, were designed for Primitive Baptist use in informal settings as well as in public worship. This means that the editorial board did not consider all songs in the hymnbook to be appropriate for worship services. Although not everyone on the editorial board agreed with this policy, said one elder who was a member of the board, they did try to maintain doctrinal accuracy in the texts.

All the hymns [were put forward one at a time] so you could have an opportunity to vote for them or against them. And [one elder] voted against a number that he was outvoted on, because his motive really was that all hymns in the book should be directed strictly towards worship service, and nothing flexible enough for what we might call private devotions at home, or other type of singing. But apparently the other members felt like there should be a little more variety in the book, although they did delete . . . a few. . . . We did have a few hymns in [the number 10 edition] . . . that in some aspects seemed to not really be, in sentiment, sound. They were written by other people, [who] . . . were just not Primitive Baptists at all and they were not writing to blend with what we believed. They were writing as they felt in their hearts about God and heaven and Christ. And sometimes you could tell . . . they knew a lot about God. But there again, doctrinally, they believe differently. They believe there's a condition somewhere met by men, you know, for salvation. And naturally, that's blended into their songs. (WI-139)

The churches themselves may exercise their own informal editorial control by not singing a particular song even though the text appears in their hymnbooks. Even congregations using the same hymnbook demonstrate differences in their repertories that stem from differing perceptions of doctrinal inaccuracies in texts. Elder Evans, in the Mountain Association, pointed out that one hymn, "There is a fountain filled with blood," expressed too much assurance of salvation. He read two lines from the first stanza: "And sinners plunged into that flood / Lose all their guilty stains." He shook his head at such an idea. "That's doubtful," he said. The North Carolina congregations he serves as pastor did not sing that hymn during any of our visits, though a Virginia church in the association did use it, and so did a neighboring independent Primitive Baptist church in North Carolina (see fig. 4, pp. 36–37).

A visiting elder who fills preaching appointments in the Mountain Association saw another problem in some song texts that describe heaven. He said that human emotions come in conflict with church doctrine when a song suggests that the desire to be reunited with loved ones in heaven will be fulfilled.

We definitely do not believe . . . that heaven is . . . going to be a family reunion. . . . Though often we find songs that relate to "I'm going there to see my mother," and those are good songs, but they have that human tie to them. . . . A lot of people are

looking forward to go to heaven to see their family. . . . There *will*
be a family but it'll be a *family of God*. . . . Now there's a lot of
songs that relate to our love for one another, to honor thy father and thy mother, and bring up your children in the nurture
and admonition of the Lord, and songs in the hymnbook that
relate to closer family ties, and a better marriage tie
and . . . there's nothing wrong with it. But if it alludes to [main-
taining these ties in] eternity then it's really going beyond what
the Scripture says. (WI-139)

Sometimes, only part of a hymn text causes problems. Rather than
not sing a song that is well liked and is largely acceptable to a congregation, a song leader may simply ask the congregation to omit an
objectionable stanza in the singing. The visiting elder said that his
churches generally leave out a stanza of "Precious Memories" and that
they always skip a verse in another song "that we sing in the tune of
'Precious Memories.'" Three of its verses "are real good and sound.
But at our church, if you were there, you would notice the song leader
would say we'll sing the first three verses, and he'll never let the congregation sing the last one because it . . . particularly alludes to family relationships in heaven. And so . . . even though it's in the book, . . .
they will be sure to leave that verse out" (WI-139).

Another visiting elder who often preaches in the Mountain Association said that a lot of his people don't like to sing "Just as I am"
(Goble no. 269) and that some refuse to sing "What a friend we have
in Jesus" (Goble no. 308). The line "What a privilege to carry every-
thing to God in prayer" in the latter song, he explained, was not fully in accord with the doctrine of total depravity. "If man is a totally
depraved creature, he'll carry what God wants" (WI-100). Some
Mountain Association churches, however, use both of these songs.
"What a friend we have in Jesus" was one of the most often requested songs in several churches. It seemed to be a particular favorite of
an elder from Virginia, who often requested it when he was called
on to preach the first sermon. From one association to another, then,
and even from one church to another within an association, not only
does the choice of hymnbooks vary but so does the repertory of
hymns sung from those books. These selected repertories help distinguish particular congregations, especially when their songs are the
result of choices based on that group's consensus about the compati-
bility of text and doctrine.

Doctrinal truth, however, is not the only kind of truth Primitive
Baptists consider when choosing hymnbooks and requesting songs.

Particularly important to them is that the hymns be expressive of their personal spiritual experience. A woman, when asked why Goble's *Primitive Baptist Hymn Book* was her favorite, responded, "It's got the prettiest songs in it than any book that's ever been [written]. . . . It's the words to them that makes them pretty—the meaning that they have" (WI-059). One elder alluded to the importance of experience when he compared two doctrinal hymns. One hymn that he often quoted but seldom sang expresses a doctrinal point of view but does not express experience from a first-person viewpoint. "There's one [hymn] in particular [Goble no. 18], I use it quite a bit just to quote. It's a very strong doctrinal hymn. It sums up what the Primitive faith believes . . . [but] we very seldom ever sing it. . . . I like the words of that one better than I like, you know, to sing it" (WI-100). The hymn reads as follows:

1. There is a period known to God,
      When all his sheep redeemed by blood
   Shall leave the hateful ways of sin,
      Turn to the fold, and enter in.

2. At peace with hell, with God at war,
      In sin's dark maze they wander far,
   Indulge their lusts and still go on
      As far from God as sheep can run.

3. But see how heav'n's indulgent care
      Attends their wand'rings here and there,
   Still near at hand, where'er they stray,
      With piercing thorns to hedge their way.

4. When wisdom calls they stop their ear,
      And headlong urge the mad career;
   Judgments nor mercies ne'er can sway
      Their roving feet to wisdom's way.

5. Glory to God—they ne'er shall rove
      Beyond the limits of his love;
   Fenced with Jehovah's "shalls" and "wills,"
      Firm as the everlasting hills.

6. Th' appointed time rolls on apace,
      Not to propose, but call by grace,
   To change the heart, renew the will,
      And turn their feet to Zion's hill.

The preacher valued this hymn for its statement of belief and for its description, in the second stanza, of "a person under conviction." But the second hymn was his favorite for singing. In this text (Goble no. 199), the hymn writer placed belief in a context of personal spiritual experience.[4]

1. Hail, sov'reign Love! that first began
   The scheme to rescue fallen man;
   Hail, matchless, free, eternal grace,
   That gave my soul a hiding-place.

2. Against the God that rules the sky
   I fought with hands uplifted high;
   Despised his rich, unbounding grace,
   Too proud to seek a hiding-place.

3. But thus th' eternal Counsel ran:
   "Almighty Love, arrest the man."
   I felt the arrow of distress,
   And found I had no hiding-place.

4. Indignant Justice stood in view;
   To Sinai's fiery mount I flew;
   But Justice cried with frowning face,
   "This mountain is no hiding-place."

5. Ere long a heav'nly voice I heard,
   And Mercy's angel-form appeared;
   She led me on with gentle pace,
   To Jesus, as my hiding-place.

6. On him almighty vengeance fell,
   That must have sunk a world to hell,
   He bore it for his chosen race,
   And thus became their hiding-place.

7. A few more rolling suns, at most,
   Will land me safe on heaven's coast,
   Where I shall sing the song of grace,
   And see my glorious hiding-place.

Other members spoke of spiritual experience also when asked which songs they liked best. One deacon replied, "Any of them that serve my heart, I like," and one preacher referred to songs that "speak my experience." Another elder elaborated. "These old hymns, well, the reason I love them—when you get down to the facts of them—

they're based on experiences of God's people and on the Scripture. You don't find none of these like, 'Build me a home in the corner of Glory.' That sounds silly to me" (WI-105).

These comments do not necessarily mean that the singers take hymn texts as literal expressions of their experience, however. Like their interpretations of the Bible, Primitive Baptists' interpretations of hymn texts are typically multilayered. A preacher called attention to the following text (Goble no. 277), a hymn sung regularly in several churches we visited (see fig. 57, pp. 146–47, for tune).

1. A home in heav'n! what a joyful thought!
     As the poor man toils in his weary lot;
   His heart oppressed, and with anguish riv'n,
     From his home below to a home in heav'n.

2. A home in heav'n! as the suff'rer lies
     On his bed of pain, and uplifts his eyes
   To that bright home what a joy is giv'n,
     With the blessed thought of a home in heav'n.

3. A home in heav'n! when our pleasures fade,
     And our wealth and fame in the dust are laid,
   And our strength decays, and our health is riv'n,
     We are happy still with our home in heav'n.

4. A home in heav'n! when the sinner mourns,
     And with contrite heart to the Savior turns;
   O then what bliss in that heart forgiv'n,
     Does the hope inspire of a home in heav'n!

5. A home in heav'n! when our friends are fled
     To the cheerless home of the mould'ring dead;
   We wait in hope of the promise giv'n,
     We will meet again in our home in heav'n.

Members of one association knew that this song was a favorite of an elderly member whose health was rapidly deteriorating, and they sang it anytime he was able to attend church services. The preacher in another association explained that the text held deep spiritual meanings.

You know, it doesn't matter what tune it's sung in, there are so many things in the words that a lot of people tend to overlook. Like that one, "on his bed of pain"—that doesn't [mean] lying in bed, you know, with suffering. But there's . . . suffering in life, and through the suffering in life, it is a bed of pain at times. Then you can joyously look to something that's beyond what the earth has to offer. . . . A lot of these songs are very deep if you really penetrate into them to see what the author is trying to bring about. (WI-100)

Differences in singing between congregations extend beyond preferences for particular hymnbooks and songs to preferences for different ways of singing those songs, and these seem particularly important to members in identifying the churches where they feel most at home. Singers sometimes showed marked differences in their preferences for how high or low the singing pitches should be, for singing in unison or in harmony, for how fast or slowly songs should be sung, and for different versions of a melody.

Elder Cook interpreted for us, without being asked, some of the singing we had heard in one of the churches in his association. His comment revealed a sensitivity to pitch and its implications as he tactfully pointed out that the singing we had heard earlier in his church— singing led by a visiting preacher from Michigan (originally from Kentucky)—was not representative of the North Carolina and Virginia churches we were visiting. "I know you took notice here that Saturday afternoon with Elder Farrow and his wife, they're much more aggressive people than what we are. They sing their songs higher, they're harder for people to sing. . . . It was really too high to get the parts in there, the alto, you could sing bass with it but it would be hard, or the tenor, you couldn't have sang that with him because it was just entirely about three or four notes higher than what it should have been" (WI-106).

Elder Cook said that Primitive Baptists disagreed among themselves about whether hymns could be sung best in parts or in unison. His father-in-law served as an elder, he said, in a neighboring association to the west. "And a lot of people in that little body doesn't [like part singing]. They go back to the Scripture that states this, 'Come you out from the world and be ye a separate people.' And they say, 'Well now, how can we be separate and sing the parts that the world sings?'" (WI-106).

He and several other elders, however, liked having singers add their alto, tenor, or bass harmonies to the melody or "lead." Elder Cook preferred singing in parts because he believed that helped keep people together when they tried to sing. It was hard, he thought, to sing with people who were not singing parts.

You can take all men and all women singing lead . . . and I can't sing with them, and I'm sure you couldn't either. They're hard to sing with . . . this man out in front of you and the one behind you. Either they're trying to get ahead of you or they're trying to drag the tune out, one of the two. . . . Back when I first joined the church in '59, when the older generation was yet present, . . . there were people who did sing in unity, even though they all sang . . . lead. And they sang together, no one was out in front, no one was behind dragging their feet. But in the last twenty to twenty-five years, it's changed much in that part of the country. (WI-106)

Tempo—how fast or how slow to sing—was another facet of singing that prompted Primitive Baptist comment. Differences in tempo sometimes appear between churches in an association, but they tend to be more notable between associations. Two churches in the Mountain Association, for example, showed a consistent preference for tempos that were slightly faster than one beat per second while their sister churches often sang at speeds slower than one beat per second. In general, though, the singing in this association was not as fast as the singing in a piedmont association to the east, nor as slow as the singing in a neighboring mountain area association to the north. In the piedmont association, said an elder who pastored churches there, we sing "one-third or twice again as fast as in the Mountain Association. I don't like a draggy song."

I would have dismissed some variations in tempo as too slight to be of any importance if Primitive Baptists themselves had not mentioned it. On one occasion, a North Carolina woman singing beside me in a service in a Virginia church remarked that the song was moving a little fast, a change that had seemed of no consequence to me. But before the next hymn, the song leader confirmed her perception by saying to the congregation, "We might be singing the hymn just a little bit faster than some of you are used to, but that way we'll be able to get in more songs." It was clear, then, that even a small change in tempo would no more be overlooked by the singers in that church meeting than it would be by professional musicians in a concert hall, for whom tempo is a critical element in interpretation, nor would it be a change without purpose.

How fast a song is sung affects the number of songs that can be included in a meeting, since the time allotted to singing remains about the same. The length of the song is also a factor, of course, but the

congregation that sings faster will usually sing more songs in a giv-
en service. Elder Cook, whose churches used some of the slowest tempos we heard, said that his churches would usually sing only three
songs, or perhaps four, in the first half hour. Most of the churches we
visited sang four to six hymns during a normal meeting, but a few
sang eight to twelve songs in the same time. Singing faster can have
other consequences also, especially if the beat of the song becomes
fairly regular. A regular pulse is more likely to engage bodily responses such as keeping time with the foot, and the vocal elaboration of
the melody is likely to decrease.

To Elder Cook, though, a more significant problem of singing faster was that faster tempos made it difficult, or impossible, to line out
hymns (see fig. 69, pp. 161–62, for a musical example).[5] Lining out is
an old style of responsorial singing of psalms and hymns that is still
practiced in a few Primitive Baptist churches, but it is no longer common. Song leaders who line out hymns start by singing the hymn tune
with the congregation. Then, after the tune is well established, the
song leader begins to sing the text ahead of the congregation, one or
two lines at a time, in a stylized solo chant. The congregation responds
with the hymn tune for each segment of chanted text, and song leader and congregation alternate in this call-response pattern for the re-
mainder of the hymn. Elder Cook noted with some pleasure that
churches in a West Virginia association still called on him to line out
hymns for them when he visited. "Their singing is much, much faster than ours. . . . Same tunes basically, but it's faster and they—I don't
reckon there's a minister in [that] association that I could even think
of that lines a song. But every time we go and visit, they're on to us,
all the people and the ministers, to sing, you know, a song, and line
it in the way we sing it here, not there. You can't sing a song fast and
try to line it at all" (WI-106).

Historically, this practice enabled those who did not have hymnbooks, or who could not read, to participate in the singing. But there
is no clear need now to continue the practice of lining out hymns.
There is no shortage of hymnbooks in these churches and almost all
of the current church members are literate. However, because the
practice of lining out hymns was traditional in the church, Elder Cook
thought there was some biblical reason to continue even if there was
no practical need to do so. He noted quickly that not everyone shared
this opinion.

And you'll find that most of the people love the lining of the
songs. And you'll go places, though—and I have an uncle who

is a Primitive Baptist minister out in West Virginia and an uncle that lives here in Abingdon that goes to his church—and they don't like the songs to be lined at all. They said now that is supposed to have been in the older days and we are supposed to change with the time. But really, if one reads the Scriptures closely and pays attention to them, it really don't tell us to change, does it? Again there falls that Scripture, "Mark ye well her bulwarks and keep her ways, that the generations after you may be taught." (WI-106)

Even more important to Elder Cook than the sense of continuity with past generations of Primitive Baptists was a feeling of spiritual movement that he thought sometimes carried over from the hymn singing into the lining out, an experience that elevated all of the singers together in his churches and elsewhere. "Now when a song is sung with great movement [of the spirit] . . . it will be lined the same way. . . . When a song is really sung together, and I'm saying now all of the people in unity and putting forth their voices, being magnified together . . . it really causes the man who's [lining] it to be as magnified as the people are in the singing. And you'll find a difference" (WI-106).

Another way that singing differed in these churches was in the tunes themselves. Within the Mountain District Association, a given tune was remarkably consistent in its melodic patterns from one congregation to the next. Melodic differences within the association seemed confined to small points here and there, such as the beginning of a tune, which might vary from one song leader to another. In one church, for example, a tune began by approaching the key tone from below (fig. 5a). In another church, the same tune began on the key tone followed by a rise of a third (fig. 5b and 5c), before repeating the key tone. Also, a melody would be rendered more elaborately (fig. 6a) by one congregation and less elaborately by another (fig. 6b).

Fig. 5. Examples: Beginning a tune.

(a) (b) (c)

Fig. 6. Examples: Melodic elaboration.

(a) (b)

One elder compared the singing of churches he visited in the Mountain Association to singing in those he pastored in the piedmont. His churches sang from a different hymnbook (Lloyd 1978 [1841]) and they sang a number of songs we did not hear in the mountain churches, but he did not talk about hymnbooks or repertory. Instead, he stressed differences in the tunes themselves. Some of the tunes in the two areas were very similar, he thought, but "we sing it just a little different." Another elder responded similarly. When asked how a particular tune went, he replied, "different ways in different places," and sang for us the version he liked best. A brief comparison of the tune "Conflict" as sung in two neighboring associations offers an example of this melodic variation. "Conflict," which is printed in most Primitive Baptist hymn-and-tune books,[6] is itself a variant of "Bourbon," a tune published in shape-note tunebooks.[7]

The tune we recorded from congregational singing in the Mountain Association was clearly the same skeletal tune even though it was not quite like either of the published versions. Our recordings included congregational singing in nine services at four different churches. In these recordings, the tune served as a setting for three different hymn texts.[8] We had one additional recording, made some years earlier, of Elder Walter Evans singing the hymn during an interview. These ten recordings of "Bourbon" spanned a period of thirteen years, and in each one the tune was essentially the same.

Fig. 7. "Awake, my soul, in joyful lays" (Samuel Medley, Goble no. 4) with the tune "Conflict" or "Bourbon" as sung by the congregation of Little River Primitive Baptist Church, 18 July 1970, Sparta, North Carolina (WI-027).

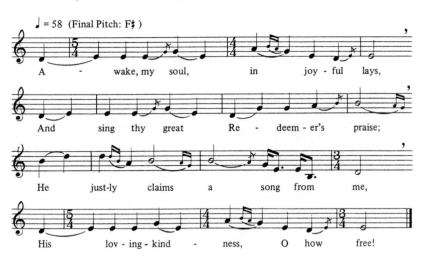

1. Awake, my soul, in joyful lays,
       And sing thy great Redeemer's praise;
   He justly claims a song from me,
       His loving-kindness, O how free!

2. He saw me ruined in the fall,
       Yet loved me notwithstanding all;
   He saved me from my lost estate,
       His loving-kindness, O how great!

3. Though num'rous hosts of mighty foes,
       Though earth and hell my way oppose,
   He safely leads my soul along,
       His loving-kindness, O how strong!

4. When troubles, like a gloomy cloud,
       Have gathered thick and thundered loud,
   He near my soul has always stood,
       His loving-kindness, O how good!

5. Often I feel my sinful heart
       Prone from my Jesus to depart,
   But though I have him oft forgot,
       His loving-kindness changes not.

6. Soon shall I pass the gloomy vale,
       Soon all my mortal pow'rs must fail,
   Oh! may my last expiring breath
       His loving-kindness sing in death.

7. Then let me mount and soar away
       To the bright world of endless day,
   And sing with rapture and surprise
       His loving-kindness in the skies.

A second version of the tune came from the singing of an elder who occasionally visits, preaches, and holds membership in a neighboring mountain association. He learned the tune from his grandfather, who was also a Primitive Baptist elder, he said, and he sang the tune to demonstrate how it is sung in his churches (fig. 8).

Differences are clearly present in these tunes but the singers think of them simply as different ways of singing the same tune. In both versions of "Bourbon," the tune follows the same basic pattern or structure for its four phrases: AAvBA. In each tune, that is, the melody for the first phrase is repeated for the last phrase (A), it is very

Fig. 8. "Awake, my soul, in joyful lays" (Samuel Medley, Goble no. 4) with the tune "Conflict" or "Bourbon" as sung by Elder Eddie Lyle, 24 July 1982, West Jefferson, North Carolina (WI-100).

similar for the second phrase (Av), and it is different for the third phrase (B). The main difference in the two songs occurs in the tones of the melody, not in its phrase structure. In the first example, for instance, the singers used only five tones and sang a minor-sounding tune. In the second example, the singer used nine tones and produced a more major-sounding tune.

In the case of another hymn, "House of the Lord," the differences in the tune sung by members of the two associations were even greater. These differences were not confined to the tones in the melody but extended to the phrase structure. The reader can note that, in this version of the song from the Mountain District Association, the first two lines of the tune are exactly alike and the last two lines are different from the first two but they are similar to each other, an AABBv phrase structure:

Fig. 9. "House of the Lord" (Daily no. 136) as sung by the congregation of Galax Primitive Baptist Church, 13 August 1983, Galax, Virginia (WI-198).

But the place most de - light - ful this earth can af - ford,

Is the place of de - vo - tion—the house of the Lord.

1. You may sing of the beauty of mountain and dale,
    Of the silvery streamlet and flow'rs of the vale;
    But the place most delightful this earth can afford,
    Is the place of devotion—the house of the Lord.

2. You may boast of the sweetness of day's early dawn,
    Of the sky's softening graces when the day is just gone;
    But there's no other season or time can compare
    With the house of devotion—the season of prayer.

3. You may value the friendships of youth and of age,
    And select for my comrades the noble and sage;
    But the friends that most cheer me on life's rugged road,
    Are the friends of my Master—the children of God.

4. You may talk of your prospects of fame or of wealth,
    And the hopes that oft flatter the fav'rites of health;
    But the hope of bright glory—of heavenly bliss!
    Take away every other, and give me but this.

5. Ever hail, blessed temple, abode of my God,
    I will turn to thee often to hear from His word;
    I will walk to the altar with those that I love,
    And delight in the prospect revealed from above.

When the preacher from the neighboring association sang his version of the song, he again used a somewhat different set of tones. However, he also sang the two phrases of the melody in a different pattern than we heard in the Mountain Association. The reader can see that, in his tune (fig. 10), the first, second, and fourth lines are almost identical, and the third line is different (AABAv).

Elder Cook, whose association has not always been in fellowship with the Mountain Association, acknowledged differences in singing among the Primitive Baptist churches, but he cautioned that differences in singing did not necessarily mean differences in belief. "Now as you've noticed among our people, here [in Virginia] and down [in

Fig. 10. "You may sing of the beauty" (Goble no. 218) with the tune "House of the Lord" as sung by Elder Eddie Lyle, 24 July 1982, West Jefferson, North Carolina (WI-100).

North Carolina] where you were at, don't get me wrong, we're the same people, but there's a little deviation in the tunes, and their speaking, and the pace of it. They sing it faster and we sing it slower. Now they would sing . . . much faster down there than we do here" (WI-106).

Clearly, then, Primitive Baptists find differences in singing among their own churches. They are often conscious of even subtle changes as they visit from church to church. Differences in books, hymn texts, selections, melody, harmony, pitch, and tempo appear to affect how comfortably they participate in meetings outside their own home church or association. Inevitably, members compare any congregational singing they hear in the churches they visit with the particular sound of singing in their home church, and at the same time they recognize underlying similarities in most Primitive Baptist singing.

Both sides of this paradox, however, have their foundations in Primitive Baptist belief and practice. On the one side, it is through the general sound of Primitive Baptist singing that a child of grace may recognize his or her own spiritual home. Elder Evans, speaking to an annual meeting of the Mountain Association, described this in his own experience as he traveled from the Union Baptists to a home with the Primitives.

[I was] . . . out in the cornfield . . . one day, husking corn in the fall of the year, by myself. . . . I was away from home and I was restless. I didn't believe things where I was at, with no disrespect to those people. My dad belonged to them, my mother did,

and all of her people. . . . And while I was there husking corn,
lonesome, restless, without a home—almost like the man without a country—all of a sudden, I heard singing somewhere. I
couldn't describe it to save my life. I don't know—it was above
me, somewhere in the air. I don't know where it was at, how
high it was . . . no man's particular voice. And I don't mean no
harm by this, but all I did know is that it was the voice of Old
Baptists. Pardon me for just saying it that plain. I didn't know
who it was. And I wasn't with them. They were singing songs.

And on one snowy third Saturday in November 1951, he said, he
found his way to the source of that singing, a Primitive Baptist church
where he joined the family of Old Baptists and found it "a home to
me" (WI-204, WI-155).

What is the nature of this church community? "I don't think the
church is set up to populate heaven," said Elder Dewey Roten, "it is
set up as a home. It serves God's people as Canaan land served the
Israelites, as long as we behave ourselves. It's a home, it's a place
where we get spiritual food, and spiritual blessings, and it's the most
wonderful place I know about here on earth" (WI-019).

Being excluded from the church and that fellowship is a serious
matter. A deacon talked about this issue. "If you get out here and . . .
carry on like the world does," he said, "the first thing [Old Baptists]
do, they bring you before the church and if you're not willing to quit
that and repent from that, somebody'll make a movement and a second to exclude you and you're on the outside" (WI-106).

It is this Primitive Baptist practice that illuminates the importance
of the distinctive sound of each congregation's singing. For if you are
put out of your own home church, you have little chance of being
admitted to any other Primitive Baptist congregation. Its distinctive
singing, then, is the voice of your home church. The unique sound
affirms the principle that has marked one entire dissenting wing of
the British Reformation: the autonomy of the individual congregation.
Thus the constitution of the Mountain Association openly states that
delegates appointed by individual congregations to the association
"shall have no power to lord it over God's heritage, nor shall they
have any ecclesiastical power over the churches, nor shall they in-
fringe on any of the internal rights of any church in the union."[9]

In its singing, each congregation gives life and voice to this principle. So the diversity in Primitive Baptist song traditions—differences
in hymnbooks, text and tune repertoires, and performance styles—
implies much more than just random historical happenstance. These

differences subtly affirm the Primitive Baptist heritage of congregational autonomy. They are the distinguishing sounds of an individual's spiritual home. Elder Cook implied as much when he said, "These
Old Baptists have a peculiar nature about them. They can't sing these
songs just anywhere." If you have lost your place—your particular
church, your spiritual home—you may still be a "child of grace" but
you have suffered some loss of identity. As the Primitive Baptist deacon significantly put it, "You've lost your voice" (WI-106).

4

Woman as
Singer and Symbol

You may have noticed that even small words carry
great meanings.

—Primitive Baptist woman, North Carolina, 1982

WHEN I ASKED a deacon's wife what role women had in the Primitive Baptist church, she said flatly that women did not have a "role" in the church and "that's all there is to that!"[1] She was one of the most active and highly respected people in the church. Another woman told me that women "take their places, and they sing"—as if these were two very important actions by which women maintain a presence and voice in the church. She regarded church attendance as a religious duty that gave great satisfaction. To observers, this can seem quite puzzling.

Primitive Baptist women and men practice an old-time predestinarian religion that, on the surface, delegates to women not only a separate but also an unequal place in all formal church matters. The church's separation of male and female, marked by two entrances in some of the older churches and by some degree of separate seating in virtually all of the churches I visited, is carried further by a total male dominance in the formal church polity, a dominance that Primitive Baptists believe is founded on Scriptures. As Elder Evans explained, "Sarah obeyed Abraham. . . . Of course that didn't mean that she called him lord in heaven, but she recognized him as her authority, you know, over her" (WI-165).

The preacher spoke respectfully of women—who make up 55 percent to 65 percent of Primitive Baptist congregations—and he quickly acknowledged that some of the women in his churches were very perceptive. "And I'm not saying that [women] don't have a certain knowledge of the Scripture, and things of that sort. Maybe sometimes even more than some men, as far as that's concerned. I talk to sisters and members of the church that's very well blessed to understand some things in the Scripture. Sometimes even more than some men you talk to, for that matter" (WI-165). One deacon confessed that after ten years as a church member, "I still can't understand a lot I read, in the Bible, I mean. I can read it and not understand it. My wife can understand it better than I can. I mean she can explain it better than I can" (WI-094).

The same deacon told also about another deacon's wife who had successfully helped revitalize one of the association's churches. When her husband's death and a dwindling membership had threatened the existence of her home church, she began representing that church at association meetings and was eventually successful in securing a pastor for it. "I think she feels like she wants to carry on where [her husband] left off, and she does a lot of things that a lot of other women doesn't do. I mean, as far as that goes, she . . . won't try to take the lead in church when she gets to church, but she will go as a messenger to association and such" (WI-094).

These men recognized that women in their churches had abilities, but the preacher nevertheless maintained that ability in itself did not qualify women to be leaders of men. "Men," he declared flatly, "oughtn't to be governed by them." Men are clearly dominant in these churches. Women participate in the singing, but otherwise they remain deliberately silent during church meetings as a conscious acknowledgment that men are in charge.[2]

Men are in charge in other denominations, of course, but there is a difference with Primitive Baptists in the degree to which men have authority. Congregations call on their most able men to lead the church in prayer and to introduce the worship services, even though the men themselves may find this task difficult.[3] The deacon who had acknowledged struggling to understand the Bible also found it difficult to introduce the worship services. "They call on me a lot of times to maybe open services . . . but sometimes it's awful hard. Sometimes you feel like that . . . or I do—I'm sure everybody don't feel that way—but I feel like that the Lord just don't give you anything to say. And if he don't, as far as I'm concerned, you're not going to say much" (WI-094). Congregations may even invite these men to preach if they show some evidence of having spiritual gifts. At the very least, men of the church are permitted to make announcements and contribute to business meeting discussions.

Women, however—even the most able and articulate among

them—expect to sit quietly and listen. Occasionally, preachers publicly commend women on their silence in church, reminding them that they are expected to ask their husbands or another spokesman to communicate their concerns to the church. The strictness with which this rule of decorum is enforced varies somewhat from one congregation to another, but members generally believe that church elders would and should correct any woman who speaks out and thus exceeds appropriate limits. Situations that require this kind of intervention were rare in Elder Evans's experience. "I've never had no problem with [women speaking] here in my churches but . . . back over through the years they ventured [twice] to speak in conference [the business meeting of the church], and when . . . they'd get sort of run down where I could get in a word, . . . I just ask them to be seated" (WI-165).

Women often told me that they share this view of decorum and referred to scriptural authority to support their opinion. A deacon's wife, when asked how she felt about the rule of silence, simply stated, "That's exactly the way I believe, that [women] are supposed to keep quiet. And if they have any questions, or anything that's worrying them, and bothering them, they're to ask their husbands, at home. And it says in the Bible, I don't remember just where it's at, for the women to keep silent. And I firmly believe that they should" (WI-159).

Mrs. Toler, a widow whose husband had never been a Primitive Baptist, spoke in favor of complete male authority in the church:

> We're not allowed to bring up any policy, or change policy, or offer things of that sort, because we think we have Scripture to oppose that. You know St. Paul says if a woman would know anything, to ask her husband, and if she doesn't have a husband, then she can ask one of the brethren, but for her to be quiet in the church. . . . It all boils down to the fact that the man is the head of the woman the same as Christ is head of the church . . . and so to put a woman up and let her be in authority over the men, in any capacity, would be . . . going against . . . the man as the head of the woman the same as Christ is head of the church. . . . We like it this way. (WI-109)

Another widow confessed feeling some ambivalence about having to keep silent in church meetings. She supported the practice, nevertheless, because it was traditional. "Back when [my mother] was younger, if [women] wanted something said [in church], they got around to their daddy or a deacon or somebody and talked to them before preaching time. . . . Really, if I hadn't been brought up that way,

I'd say I didn't like it. But my mother was real strong about that. And there've been times when out here in my home church that I would have spoke up and said something when I didn't because of that" (WI-147).

That contemporary American women cheerfully uphold and strongly support the traditions of a church in which their participation is so limited and narrowly defined is a remarkable feature of Primitive Baptist life and one not easily understood. At a practical level, it is not surprising that the practice of separate seating for men and women is strictly observed during the annual communion and foot-washing services. Men do not wash the women's feet nor do women wash the men's feet, and naturally when men sit together they can serve each other easily and women can do the same. But men and women continue to maintain their distance from one another during the regular worship services in the absence of a clear need to do so. If women must accept subordinate roles and receive few compensations in terms of privilege or personal recognition for their contributions, why do they continue to ask for, and find, a home in this particular church?

Answers that rely on stereotypes of southern mountain folk as ignorant, poverty stricken, and culturally isolated fail to acknowledge the realities of these churches and of the lives of these women. The members of these churches are none of those things. One gains some initial insight into the complex nature of the question from observing and listening to women in the church community, and from the accounts they give of their own religious experience.

Women actively participate in the life of the church, but since there are no Sunday schools, choirs, musical instruments, missionaries, or women's societies in the church, their actions are less visible than one sees in other churches. The communication network among women in the church, for example, is not directly observable but members reported that it is both active and effective. A deacon suggested that the telephone is instrumental in maintaining this network, although he said that he "couldn't tell you, really, what the women do. I think they visit more on the telephone than anything. Because I'm sure that there's certain ones that, during the week, will call. There's a few of them I know do, will call most of the other women [in the church] and they'll talk on the telephone" (WI-094).

Mrs. Toler confirmed that the informal communication is so effective in the church community that even last-minute changes in services would be possible, either through announcements on a local Primitive Baptist radio program that aired on Sunday mornings, or "with the telephone service that was through the communities, you know, the word could get around. You could change it quickly, you know . . . just friends calling . . . from one to another" (WI-109). Women, then, would not be directly responsible for making the decisions about changes, but they would be the primary means of implementing them.

Actions that could have higher visibility are downplayed by the women who perform them, but congregations know the contributions their women have made. Deacons' wives launder the cloths and sterilize the pans that their husbands distribute for foot washing; they bake the unleavened bread and may even make the wine for the communion table that the deacons set once a year at each church. Without calling attention to themselves, women decorate family graves in the cemeteries. Assuming a traditional division of roles, the men usually do the maintenance work, new construction, and repairs on their churches, while women undertake the cleaning chores. One church member reported, "Now you take at our church, I'm sure nobody's told you this, but one of the ladies cleans it. And she will not let nobody know when she's going or nothing else. I mean she don't care if you know when she's there, but she don't tell nobody when she's going to clean it. . . . She'll say she don't want any help. And they'll try to pay her and she don't want any pay" (WI-094).

Hospitality is another traditional role that Primitive Baptist women take seriously. Although many of these women have full-time jobs in local businesses, textile industries, and schools, some regularly open their homes to traveling preachers and other out-of-town church visitors. These women are conscious of a long tradition of hospitality among Primitive Baptists, and they make every effort to house and feed church friends who have come from out of town to attend weeklong special meetings or annual association meetings. Several women showed long lists of visitors' names in guest registers they have kept over the years. Elder Evans spoke fondly of one woman who, he said, had fed more Old Baptist preachers than any woman he knew.

Aside from attending church meetings, preparing and serving food is the most visible and substantial service that all women perform for the church. Both women and men take the traditional view that food preparation is the woman's duty. After citing a passage of Scripture to support his view, Elder Evans interpreted one of its phrases to make his point about this duty: "This word 'faithful in all things' don't just mean being a faithful wife to a husband. . . . 'In all things' here is pertaining to the church. . . . [Women] do the cooking, in other words" (WI-165).

"Doing the cooking" is no small job. Two refrigerators, a large freezer, and a well-stocked pantry were familiar sights in the Primitive Baptist homes I visited. In homes occupied by only two people, some kitchens or dining rooms are still furnished with cloth-covered tables that will seat twelve, and two homes I visited even had two kitchens. Although only deacons' wives prepare the bread and homemade wine used in annual communion services, every woman who is able cooks a generous family-style meal to share during the noon break at these all-day meetings.[4] Women who have house guests cook even more, sometimes setting the table a fourth time daily for their guests to have sandwiches or snacks after evening church services. Mrs. Toler explained that not every woman is able to do this much, but they all make substantial contributions.

> We do help one another, you know, and especially when there's going to be an association meeting . . . [at one of the churches], the other churches take food. . . . No one church is big enough to supply all the food for three days of meetings . . . Now, [she names a member] . . . well, of course her husband is real good to help her . . . and sometimes she has help—hires somebody to help—and she has a good friend . . . that comes always and she's helped her a lot, too. But to have guests, and as many as she has sometimes, and then to carry up food for three days, and have food at home to eat, it's a big thing. I mean, it would be big if I were to do it. . . . But to her it's worth it . . . and she handles it very well. . . . [Women] want to do everything that they can, but you wouldn't say that they're all alike exactly. I think everybody wants to help some, but it won't be to the same degree. (WI-109)

In the summer when most churches are having their annual meetings, women put many hours into food preparation for church gatherings, often at times when they are already tired from a day's work or not feeling well. They do not deny this, and yet they speak persuasively of cooking for these meetings as a pleasure. "No one minds" one woman insisted. "It's worth it for the fellowship." She, like most of the women, spoke of fellowship as the most rewarding feature of these communal meals. I heard variations of this sentiment from both men and women.

Food has important consequences in strengthening the fellowship that women value so highly in the church, but food also has symbolic significance and women are reluctant to accept too much credit for their contributions. Mrs. Toler redirected my attention from the ma-

terial to the spiritual by advising me that the food women prepared
was not as important as the kind of food that people really want when
they come to church. "In our church here we're strict . . . and people
come to be fed. It's spiritual food you go for, it's not to be entertained. . . . And of course you have to have this desire, you've got to
be hungry, you've got to be thirsting after righteousness before you
are satisfied, before this has any meaning for you. . . . If this were tak-
en away from me, I'd be of all people most miserable, really I would"
(WI-109).

Implicit in her statement is the idea that "spiritual food" strength-
ens one's understanding, that women who think and reason can find
more food for thought in the Primitive Baptist church than in other
churches. And these Primitive Baptist women do show intellectual
energy. Mrs. Jordan, who works for a clothing manufacturer, has kept
a notebook for years, recording data from every service she attended—names of preachers present, hymns sung, Scriptures read or quoted, sermon topics, and quotations from sermons. At first she kept
these records as references for family discussions with an elderly par-
ent at home who could not attend services, but later she continued
the practice for her own benefit. She says it helped her to pay attention during the service and also to recall things she wanted to think
more about later.

Mrs. Toler, the owner of a small business, expressed a strong preference for doctrinal sermons that offer detailed explication of Scriptures rather than less weighty, anecdote-filled sermons. She says that
"stories" in sermons interest her only when they clearly illustrate a
point of doctrine. If a preacher gets off the familiar doctrinal track,
or stops in midjourney, she is among the first to notice. She recalled
directing my attention to the sermon when we first met:

> I was real excited, I felt like that I'd really heard a good sermon
> that night. And, you know, when [the preacher's wife] intro-
> duced you, and she said you were interested in our music, and
> I said, "Well maybe we could interest you in our doctrine too."
> Well, I meant that . . . I could think of two or three passages that
> I wanted [the preacher] to quote to substantiate his point, I mean
> to really confirm it real good, and he never did. But he made
> his point anyway. But there were other things that he could have
> used, and I kept hoping that he'd use them. (WI-109)

These two women represent many who have found an intellectual
stimulation in their church that appears to be grounded in an expec-
tation that individuals will think for themselves. Although explica-

tion of Primitive Baptist doctrine is a male responsibility, judging how thoroughly a preacher has interpreted and explicated that doctrine is the responsibility of each individual. Some women have acquired a confidence in their own beliefs and in their ability to defend them thoughtfully that, they feel, sets them apart from members of other churches. A Primitive Baptist woman who works in an office with local women of various denominations says that, although she and her coworkers occasionally talk about religion, the others "don't seem to think for themselves, just accept whatever the preacher says." Mrs. Toler reported having similar impressions:

> You know, it's the hardest thing to ever get a subject going with anybody, well, outside of the Primitive Baptists, that I can talk doctrine to. I don't. I try to bring people out and find out what they're thinking, what their beliefs are, and it's awfully hard. They just don't—I don't know whether they're that interested in doctrinal things. I don't much believe they are. You know, some churches just aren't as concerned about doctrine as we are. Like [the man] who used to have the service station up here, he said he just was a Methodist and whatever they advocated he just went along with what they said. And I said, "Don't you ever read for yourself, or study for yourself at all?" He said no, he didn't. (WI-109)

Casual acceptance of a preacher's ideas is unlikely in the Primitive Baptist church, where members are quick to notice if a preacher says something they cannot support. A retired schoolteacher told me that if a preacher starts talking about something she did not believe, she just turns her hearing aid off. This did not happen often with Primitive Baptists, she said, "but I've heard some others put up some pretty weak stuff" (WI-174). Men are the ones who take direct action, however. A deacon explained, "Well now, you'll find some of our preachers that'll get in and they'll stumble at things. . . and of course we have to look over them. They ain't perfect. If a man's not blessed to reason it out, why he's just not blessed. Well now, if you get him out like we are, talking, why we tell him, 'Brother, we don't believe that, because you can't prove it. Ain't no way you can prove that.' But for most of the modern world, it don't matter what the man preaches when he gets into the stand, because they don't know" (WI-106).

Although some women freely discussed church practices, their own church-related activities, or their interest in doctrine, almost all were more reticent when talking about their religious experience or how they came to join the church. In their brief comments, however, they revealed something of the emotional dimension of their place in the church. Like Primitive Baptist men, women wait for some evidence of God's grace to be manifested in their lives before they ask the congregation for a home in the church. They often wait for years and endure long periods of self-doubt and feelings of unworthiness, having both a great desire and a great reluctance to join the church. Their spiritual struggles occasionally reveal themselves in vivid dreams or visionary experiences. The women found some of these reassuring. For example, a vision of Jesus, with his arms outstretched, appeared briefly to one woman as she looked at the bedroom wall in her home after going to bed one night. She found the experience puzzling at first, but with the encouragement of a friend, she eventually came to see it as a sign of grace.

Mrs. Toler had seen no visions, but she did have vivid memories of a spiritual experience during which she felt a wind blowing through her body:

Whether I was asleep or awake, I don't know, but . . . I felt the wind blowing, you know. In the Scriptures it says . . . "the wind bloweth and listeth, and thou hearest the sound thereof but cannot tell . . . from whence it cometh and to whither it goeth. So is everyone that is born of the spirit." Well this wind blowing, this sensation that I had that this wind had gone completely through my entire person, and that I was awakened, or I was conscious, and I thought this is my regeneration. This is "the wind." This is what is meant by the Scriptures, you know. And I remembered it, certainly, and it's been meaningful, but I didn't take too much stock in it. I mean it didn't trouble me or excite me all that much for a time. But after that . . . I wanted to go to church. I went everywhere I could. But I wasn't happy with where I was . . . because I just wasn't hearing what I wanted to hear, what was in keeping with my experience. Because I felt like the Lord had done this for me and I had no part in it. . . . But, as I was saying, I went everywhere I could find a church to go to, and most of the time when I felt that I had heard the gospel I couldn't help but shed tears . . . I felt so good that I just shed tears. And, of course, I didn't join the church for a good long, I mean . . . I didn't come back to the [Primitive Baptist] church for, I guess, oh, a couple of years, or three maybe. But I kept on going and enjoying myself very much. And the morning that I decided, well, I didn't decide here [at home] but after I got to church. And it was even after the preacher had preached and we, you know how we go around and shake hands. Well . . . I thought, oh I want to go, I wanted to get up there so quickly I felt like [the people in front of me] were in my way. And of course I asked for a home in the church and I was received and I've never been sorry, of course. (WI-109)

Other women told of religious experiences that disturbed them, such as the following warning dream that an elderly woman, a retired schoolteacher, recalled having in her youth:

Now you know a lot of people say there's no hell, but I've seen that. I guess it was in a dream, it don't seem like to me it was. But I seen my soul and it looked like just a black . . . crow or something, you know, just a-flying around. And this smoke was coming up out of that pit, and there was just a lot of them birds a-flying around, and once in a while one would go down in there. And I was one in the crowd now, I just knowed I was. And it just . . . bothered me to death. . . . And I woke up and I got up and went out on the porch, and it still yet seemed like to me that I could just see that, you know. (WI-174)

Their religious experiences often begin during childhood, but Primitive Baptist women, like men, do not usually join the church until they are adults, and often not until after marriage. Some join late in life, and a few attend all of their lives without ever joining. Even after going through years of spiritual doubts and struggles, women say that when they finally present themselves to the congregation and request "a home in the church," they do it spontaneously.

I had wanted to go ahead and join when my husband did, but I was backward I guess. And I just kept putting it off. I had thought about it, and went a time or two planning to join. And [I'd] come back, and I'd study on it, and talk to [my husband] about it. . . . So the day that I joined I didn't have any intentions of joining when I went. I sure didn't. And it just seemed like there was just the awfulest burden on me, after I got in the church, you know, it was just, I can't explain it to you. But after I went up there and joined, seemed like that lifted that burden, but it wasn't gone until after I was baptized. Now that was my experience. And after I was baptized then it just all left me, seemed like, and I just felt relief. (WI-159)

Other women remembered experiencing similar feelings, especially that of carrying some burden until the moment of baptism. One said, "You've heard people say a great burden was lifted after they were baptized. That's how it was for me. And I immediately began to feel at home among Primitive Baptists."

In addition to feeling relieved of a burden upon joining the church and being baptized, women also feel they have become part of a larger, loving family. For many of these Primitive Baptists, the concept of "family" properly belongs only to life in this earthly, physical world. Only here can family life exist and here it must be nurtured, for women, like men, believe there will be no recognition of one's family members in heaven.

Family life is not necessarily limited to one's kinship group, however. Seeing and experiencing the church itself as a family in its ideal form is one of the more pervasive themes in women's accounts of their religious experience. Underlying these accounts is a belief that when they can recognize and experience the church as a family, they have some evidence that it is the true church. One woman said, "I would go [to church] and seemed like I just felt like I was one of them . . . all the members there . . . felt just like they was one of my family. I just felt so relieved and good with them. And seemed like they just loved me, and just wanted to be with me. I don't know if all, if anybody else has that experience like I did or not" (WI-159). For another woman, the feeling of being among family seemed to develop more slowly after joining the church: "Well, I'll be honest, I didn't notice people until I joined the church. To me life was to get rich, to get ahead, to progress. . . . People didn't mean that much to me. . . . But after I joined the church, they became my family . . . and as time goes on you know more about them, and you understand them, and . . . they just become closer" (WI-062).

Mrs. Toler stressed the acceptance and trust she feels within her church family, and she summarized her feelings by characterizing the church as a "resting place":

And I think of myself back prior to my being involved in the Primitive Baptists. . . . And at that time I thought to myself, if I needed to confide in somebody . . . that I could respect and know that my confidence . . . was respected, I couldn't think of many people that I could turn to, if any. And now, there are so many, so many people that I could turn to and would feel . . . that I'd be understood and loved for it, even if it was something that

was bad. I think I'd be understood . . . there's so many that I feel
I could go to within the ranks of this association. . . . It's a sense
of kindredship, brothers and sisters in Christ Jesus. That's what
we're supposed to be. You know if I feel that my sins have been
forgiven, and you feel that yours have been forgiven . . . well
then, aren't we kindred, don't I belong in the family of God? . . .
To me, this is what it's all about. It's a . . . resting place. . . .
There's a definite saving in this time-world for me, in the gospel church, as I believe the Primitive Baptist to be. (WI-109)

June Hawks Goins, a Primitive Baptist poet and hymn writer
whose work has found wide acceptance in the church, spoke for many
when she too described the church as a resting place (1968:7):

> Come be with those who understand
> The trials you must face,
> Oh, bring your burdened, weary heart
> Unto its resting place.

A woman who had been active in the Methodist church before joining the Primitive Baptists also found the church restful in this emotional and spiritual sense. But her description of the church as a resting place also had a literal and practical meaning: she found it a great
relief, she said, to have no obligations to teach Sunday School, work
on committees, sing in the choir, and attend planning meetings.

Primitive Baptist women's own reports of their experience in the
church make clear, then, that they find satisfaction in their church.
They are in general agreement with men that this church is a "resting place," a "home," a "family," and a place of true "fellowship" for
them. Like men, women have experienced delays in joining the
church, feelings of unworthiness and uncertainty that accompany a
desire to join the church, and relief from burdens when they are finally
baptized.

However, it still is not clear how these modern American women
could feel at home and supported in a church where they appear to
be so disempowered. One approach to the question is a more focused
exploration of how this church views women. These views are suggested in the performance and texts of hymns, and further revealed
in the religious rhetoric practiced chiefly by men—in the choice and
explication of frequently quoted Scriptures, in the elevated language
of sermons, and even in the conversational language and practice of
daily life.

Not surprisingly, a search through the hymn texts yields far more male than female images, particularly those referring to God, such as Father, Jehovah, Savior, King, and Redeemer. Of the 321 texts in *The Primitive Baptist Hymn Book*, only 26 contain direct references to female figures, and these references occur either in the form of the nouns "woman," "Mary," "bride," "mother," "sister," and "daughter," or the pronouns "she" and "her." Of the 26 hymns that contain these references, fewer than 10 are actually being sung now, making any inferences about women from texts alone highly speculative. Nevertheless, the existence and approval of such references makes them possible indexes to Primitive Baptist views of women and to women's images of themselves and to women's experience in the Primitive Baptist church.

In keeping with the doctrinal view of the human as sinful and unworthy, the few hymn texts that refer to women present them as unfortunate and/or unhappy (a "weeping widow"), or as subject to human failings ("Mary's stains," "doubting sister"). There is not a single reference to the Virgin, and there is no sentimentalization of the mother in the hymn repertory. These are telling omissions in a culture that tends to elevate both virgins and mothers. Primitive Baptists see the world as fallen and themselves living in it, and this doctrine of total depravity even finds expression in a hymn text (Goble no. 185) that quite unsentimentally emphasizes a mother's weakness rather than her strength.

> Can a woman's tender care
> Cease toward the child she bare?
> Yes! She may forgetful be,
> Yet will I remember thee!

Primitive Baptists honor mothers in sentimental songs they write and sing, but they keep this repertory separate from that used in the church. An elder explained that they do not use songs about mothers or other kin in worship because the church must avoid any appearance of placing mothers above God. However, men often speak of their mothers as the persons who usually brought them to church services when they were children. It is not unusual to hear singers attribute their love of music and singing, as well as their extensive knowledge of hymns, to their mothers, who often sang at home.

Preachers sometimes include stories about their mothers in their sermons, and such stories can move a whole congregation to tears—men and women alike. One preacher told of his mother's devotion to the church and of her strength and courage shortly before she died. He confessed to a sympathetic congregation, "I'd rather have an old mother in Israel praying for me than anything else in this world, I'll tell you that, brother. I'll tell you their prayers goes a long way." And then he spoke directly to the women. "So you mothers in Israel, don't think that you're not needed in the church" (WI-207).

The preacher's comment brought into view a more complex picture of both men and women in the church. He addressed the congregation first as Primitive Baptists, with the implicit understanding that women and men alike experienced the doubt and uncertainty that accompany the church's consciousness of human failings, and that all members had also experienced the hope that gave some relief from the dark and difficult times in their lives. His comment further implied that women's experience of the church was different in some ways and that women could naturally have ambivalent feelings about being confined to the traditional domestic, nurturing role that the church expects. Women rarely suggested this themselves, however. They invariably reported finding satisfaction in preparing food for the church and in participating in the fellowship of the church.

The role that preachers in the Mountain Association advocated for women in the church, the symbolic one of "mothers in Israel," seemed to acknowledge women's power and simultaneously hold it in check since the church interpreted this role as fully consistent with its rule of silence for women. For example, when women engaged in public prayer, they sat quietly with their heads bowed, as did all members of the congregation, while an elder or deacon knelt and voiced an extemporaneous prayer on behalf of all present. For women's prayers to have particular spiritual power, then, women themselves must be conceptualized in some way that transcended their human failings, as an ideal that was not completely detached from women in the congregation even though it appeared to be detached from their experience. The rhetoric that illuminates the church's symbolization of women offers one way to explore these puzzling aspects of women's roles.

There is some evidence that the woman, traditionally a symbolic figure for the Christian church, remains a powerful and active symbol for Primitive Baptists. What effect this has on women is not clear since women do not directly comment on it when asked to talk about their own experience. Retention of the symbol of woman as a type of church is too pervasive to ignore, however, and the rhetoric used in the sermons and songs of the church offers an alternative avenue for exploring ideas about gender that could give a more complete picture of the role of women in the Primitive Baptist church.

This approach gains validity when we see how much attention Primitive Baptists give to the feminine pronouns they read in Scriptures and sing in hymns. Elder Evans, for example, exercising habits of thinking that attend to the smallest details, unraveled a passage from the book of Revelation for his congregation in the following manner:

> "And he showed me a pure river of water of life, clear as crystal, proceeding out of the throne of God and of the Lamb." Here's the very origin of it now. "And in the midst of the street of it, and on either side of the river, was there the tree of life, which bare twelve manner—" And it wasn't thirteen, if you please, and it wasn't eleven . . . I'll just leave it there. "Twelve manner of fruit and she yielded her fruit every month." And you thought that was "his," didn't you? That word's "her." Go back and check it. Go back and double check it. "Yielded HER fruit every month." . . . I'm not saying that Christ is not interwoven in this, by no means, he certainly is. But still, that word's *her*, in the feminine gender. (WI-070)

Apparently deriving their language from the King James translation of the Bible, hymn writers used, and Primitive Baptists have retained, feminine pronouns to assign gender to some words that we may no longer think of as feminine. Not only do earth and nature take on a feminine gender in these hymn texts, but so do moon, hand, soul, love, mercy, faith, conscience, reason, wisdom, Zion, and church.[5] Some of these associations are simply suggestive. The concept of soul as feminine, for instance, is loosely supported in hymn texts. Out of numerous references to the soul, only a few assign to it any gender at all, but these designations are all feminine.[6] In the hymn that follows, for example, the reader will note these lines:[7] "My soul stands trembling while she sings / The honors of her God."

Fig. 11. "Keep silence, all created things" (Isaac Watts, Goble no. 3) with the tune "Hicks Farewell" as sung by the congregation of Union Primitive Baptist Church, 6 June 1982, Whitehead, North Carolina (WI-009).

while   she sings   The   hon - ors   of   her   God.

1. Keep silence, all created things,
       And wait your Maker's nod;
   My soul stands trembling while she sings
       The honors of her God.

2. Life, death, and hell, and worlds unknown
       Hang on his firm decree;
   He sits on no precarious throne,
       Nor borrows leave to be.

3. Chained to his throne, a volume lies,
       With all the fates of men,
   With ev'ry angel's form and size,
       Drawn by th' Eternal pen.

4. His providence unfolds the book,
       And makes his counsels shine;
   Each op'ning leaf, and ev'ry stroke,
       Fulfills some deep design.

5. Here he exalts neglected worms
       To scepters and a crown;
   And there the foll'wing page he turns,
       And treads the monarch down.

6. Not Gabriel asks the reason why,
       Nor God the reason gives;
   Nor dares the fav'rite angel pry
       Between the folded leaves.

7. My God, I would not long to see
       My fate with curious eyes,
   What gloomy lines are writ for me,
       Or what bright scenes may rise.

8. In thy fair book of life and grace,
       O may I find my name
   Recorded in some humble place,
       Beneath my Lord the Lamb!

Comments in interviews and conversations do not affirm that the
Primitive Baptist concept of soul is necessarily feminine, but they do
suggest this as a possibility. Mercy and wisdom likewise had tenta-

tive gender associations in both hymn and biblical texts used by Primitive Baptists. Elder Roten alluded to the feminine nature of mercy in an interview when he was asked, "Which [hymns] do you think speak the experience most truly?" He noted that there were "a whole lot of them" and then quickly found and read the full text of one he thought fit his experience.[8] That hymn included the following lines: "And Mercy's angel-form appeared; / She led me on with gentle pace."[9]

This same elder reminisced about "one of the most glorious times" he experienced in the pulpit. He could not recall his sermon, he said, but he remembered his text clearly: "Wisdom hath builded her house, she has hewn out her seven pillars, she's killed her beast, she's mingled her wines, she's furnished her table" (WI-004, WI-019). Although none of the several hymn texts that mentions wisdom assigns to it any gender identity, one text (Goble no. 123) does speak of a role for wisdom that, among Primitive Baptists, is clearly feminine:

> Come all ye hungry starving souls,
>   That feed upon the wind,
> And vainly strive with earthly toys
>   To fill an empty mind.
>
> Eternal wisdom has prepared
>   A soul-reviving feast,
> And bid your longing appetites
>   The rich provision taste.

Any tentativeness in gender associations rapidly diminishes when the language shifts to images of the church. Here the identification with the feminine becomes strong and pervasive. For example, Zion, the city of God and church of the heavenly world, is feminine according to hymn texts, Scriptures, and sermons. At least one hymn about Zion, "Glorious things of thee are spoken," is a congregational favorite:

Fig. 12. "Glorious things of thee are spoken" (John Newton, Goble no. 163) with the tune "Ripley" as sung by the congregation of Cross Roads Primitive Baptist Church, 18 July 1982, Baywood, Virginia (WI-087).

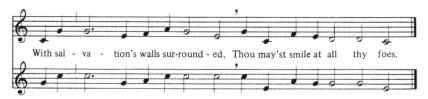

With sal - va - tion's walls sur-round - ed, Thou may'st smile at all thy foes.

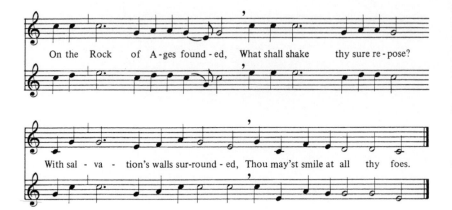

On the Rock of A - ges found - ed, What shall shake thy sure re - pose?

With sal - va - tion's walls sur-round - ed, Thou may'st smile at all thy foes.

1. Glorious things of thee are spoken,
   Zion, city of our God!
   He, whose word can not be broken,
   Formed thee for his own abode:
   On the Rock of Ages founded,
   What shall shake thy sure repose?
   With salvations's walls surrounded,
   Thou may'st smile at all thy foes.

2. See! the streams of living water
   Springing from eternal love,
   Well supply thy sons and daughters,
   And all fear of want remove:
   Who can faint while such a river
   Ever flows thy thirst t' assuage;
   Grace, which like the Lord, the giver,
   Never fails from age to age.

3. Round each habitation hov'ring,
   See the cloud and fire appear!
   For a glory and a cov'ring,
   Showing that the Lord is near;
   Thus deriving from their banner
   Light by night and shade by day;
   Safe they feed upon the manna
   Which he gives them on the way.

4. Blessed inhabitants of Zion,
   Washed in the Redeemer's blood;
   Jesus, whom their souls rely on,

> Makes them kings and priests to God;
> 'Tis his love his people raises
> Over self to reign as kings,
> And as priests, his solemn praises
> Each for a thank-offering brings.

> 5. Savior, if of Zion's city,
> I, through grace, a member am,
> Let the world deride or pity,
> I will glory in thy name:
> Fading is the worldling's pleasure,
> All his boasted pomp and show,
> Solid joys and lasting treasures
> None but Zion's children know.

Preachers reinforce the feminine nature of Zion in their sermons. In his explication of one scriptural text, Elder Evans brought together past and present, earthly world and heavenly world, reminding his congregation once more of Zion's meaning for them:

> This particular spot was in the southwestern part of Jerusalem—Zion. . . . And David the king took possession, and actually lived there himself. . . . But in spite of David's, you might say prestige, or wanting to be honored by having it named . . . the "City of David," the word "Zion,"—[used by] the old poets, the songs we sing here [at church] many times, the Old Testament writers—seemed like "Zion" somehow held on. . . . And so it describes here . . . a type of sacred capital. . . . She's the city of the great king. . . . She's exalted there, the house of God. (WI-027)

But it is in the self-image of the local church network that the most pervasive feminine references appear. In identifying the church as feminine, Primitive Baptists are not unique. They share with many churches this traditional image and hymns that stress that image, such as "I love thy kingdom, Lord" (Goble no. 266), which includes the following lines:

> I love thy church, O God;
> Her walls before thee stand,
>
> . . . .
>
> For her my tears shall fall;
> For her my prayers ascend;
> To her my cares and toils be giv'n
>
> . . . .

> I prize her heav'nly ways;
> Her sweet communion, solemn vows,
> Her hymns of love and praise.[10]

If Primitive Baptists are not alone in identifying the church as feminine, however, they do appear to be unique in the strength with which men, in particular, weight the identity of the church as feminine. This identity is reinforced not only in hymns, but more specifically in daily language, Scripture, sermons, and narratives of personal experience. Virtually all lay members and elders talk informally among themselves about their "sister" churches, at once revealing and underlining their strong sense of the church here in this world as feminine. Elders strengthen that identity in their sermons. Elder Evans consistently used feminine pronouns when paraphrasing and explicating Scriptures that referred to the church. An example is his interpretation of a passage from Ezekiel 16: "'And I saw thee polluted in thine own blood, and I said unto thee . . . "Live." And he placed a skirt on her and washed her . . .' There's a mutual love here between Christ and his church. He condescended because of God's eternal love for her" (WI-042).

Another preacher wove into his sermon an account of his experience of seeing the church for the first time.

> I can remember . . . sitting in that church pew one day as a little
> child, and that preacher began to preach about the church and
> about this woman and the jewel that was in her forehead and
> all those things. And I believe—I'm serious beloved. I'm not say-
> ing this to boast—if I hadn't restrained my very little frame, I'd
> have leaped through that building. From that day forward, I'll
> tell you this, there was nothing the same about the church. Be-
> cause then I could see her, high and lifted up, above the things
> of this earth. (WI-207)

The bride, another traditional Christian symbol of the church, is particularly visible in contemporary Primitive Baptist expression. Among the older hymns, only two refer to the church as bride. One of these references is indirect and simply mentions Christ as the "Bridegroom of your souls," but the other (Goble no. 244) is more descriptive and contains the following lines:

> Then, in his love and his decrees,
>   Christ and his bride appeared as one,
> Her sin, by imputation, his,
>   Whilst she in spotless splendor shone.

This symbol is shared by many churches, of course, but it appears to be unusually active in the thought and experience of Primitive Baptists. Elder Evans, for example, refers to the church as bride in an original poem that includes the following verses:

> Then out of Adam's poor fallen race
> The Father gave his son a bride,
> He promised to save her by his grace,
> He then agreed for her to die.
>
> He found her polluted in her own blood,
> In the ruins of the fall did lay,
> He raised her up from where she fell,
> By his loving hand was raised to stay.[11]

During an interview, another elder told about receiving the image of the church as bride in a dream. "I had a dream or a vision one night and I saw the most beautiful woman that I've ever saw. She was up in the sky, just up above the earth. I thought she was dressed like a bride adorned for her husband. I think the Lord revealed that to me, that that was his church, she's above the world, she's not of the world" (WI-020).

More surprising is yet another elder's account of a vision in which he saw the church for the first time. In this account, he uses the bride as a symbol of the church but also acknowledges that, doctrinally speaking, he has a husband. "I remember the first time that I saw the church, the bride of Christ. And the most beautiful bride—one of the most beautiful women that I ever looked upon or ever expect to look upon. At that time I didn't even know I had a husband. Brethren, we have a husband—the Lord Jesus Christ. He's the husband of the bride. And how wonderful to look upon these things" (WI-207).

Although Primitive Baptists may have abandoned the two older hymns that refer to the church as bride, they have not abandoned the symbol in their singing. A newer hymn, "The Bride of Christ (fig. 13)," is frequently requested in churches that sing from the *Old School Hymnal.*

In their comments, personal experience narratives, and songs, Primitive Baptist elders and poets reveal to their congregations the extraordinary power with which traditional symbols of the church act in their lives. This public elevation of feminine images operates freely alongside, and in sharp contrast to, women's own private religious experiences and the public restriction on women's participation in the church. Often, however, only the restrictions are visible to an outside

Fig. 13. "The Bride of Christ" (hymn no. 226) from *Old School Hymnal* No. 11. Words and music by J. F. Parker. Reproduced by permission.

observer, who may simply see women in this church as inappropri-
ately submissive. Primitive Baptist women may seem unduly bound
by religious traditions that encourage or even require them to sit sep-
arately from the men, to serve the church in the traditional womanly
activities of cooking and cleaning, and to keep silence in the church—
recipients of scriptural exegesis but never themselves allowed to interpret Scripture publicly, pray aloud publicly, preach, or hold any
prominent leadership roles. Primitive Baptist women are conscious
of being seen in this limited way.

Nevertheless, this is not how these women see themselves and it
is not how they experience their church. The Primitive Baptist woman typically finds in her church a scripturally grounded religion, re-
plete with human imperfections but firm and predictable in doctrines.
She is aware of negative views held by outsiders but she finds practices in this church that are compatible with her interpretation of the
Bible, with her religious beliefs, and with her sense of order. She has
often looked for a church home in other denominations, but the Primitive Baptist church is the one that best satisfies her emotionally as
well as intellectually. One woman reflected on the drawing power of
the church in the following way. "There was a time that I wouldn't
have told anyone that I was a Primitive Baptist, and I felt a little em-
barrassed over those things. But . . . I don't suppose there was ever a
time that I saw my mother, you know, humbling herself to wash somebody's feet, or they hers, that I wasn't moved, even as a child" (WI-
109).

Where formal structures are restrictive, a Primitive Baptist woman often sees and uses informal channels to exert her influence and
thus avoids a sense of social powerlessness. Through listening to the
Scriptures and sermons, singing the hymns of the church, and ground-
ing her actions in her own religious beliefs and experience, a Primitive Baptist woman realizes her power to affect the course of church
life and fellowship. She is modest but sees a vital place for women
in the church and finds significance and meaning in participating in
those activities that nurture her church family. In turn, she finds—
and may claim—support. One elder's report of his response to a Primitive Baptist woman's call is representative. "I went up to Pennsylvania by the special request of . . . [a friend's] wife . . . and baptized
them. . . . His wife requested me to come and said 'if you don't come
I'll never be satisfied.' So that put me on the spot. . . . And so [it]
looked like I about had to go" (WI-070).

A Primitive Baptist woman may criticize the preacher in her pro-
tectiveness of church doctrine, but she listens attentively when he re-

minds her and the rest of his congregation that women are not just a part of the church, that they are, in fact, a type of the church. She hears the language of the King James version of the Bible carried over into songs and sermons as the congregation articulates its experience, and that sound becomes a powerful affirmation of the female as the chosen and beloved. Even the existence of the Bible itself can be a reminder of this care, according to one elder, who says, "I call it a love letter—from Jesus to his bride."

In their speech and experience then, men not only identify the church as feminine, but they identify themselves as part of that church. And their behavior is generally consistent with this identity. Instead of seizing the power that their dominant role suggests would be available to them in church, men, like women, yield to the authority of the Bible. That authority places leadership responsibilities on them but does not empower them to lord it over anyone, including women.

Primitive Baptist women are silent in church meetings, I contend, not only because they believe that is the right thing to do, but also because their silence is part of a system that works for them and for the church. Leaving the public sphere to the men who are charged with defending the faith, women are free to devote their energies to deepening the fellowship that has almost certainly been crucial to the survival of these churches in recurring periods of conflict and stress over the past three hundred years. When elders speak of the woman as a type of church and of the church as the bride of Christ, they are not elevating Primitive Baptist women into a sense of helpless perfection—their doctrine of total human depravity prevents that—but they are expressing again the hope that all of these men and women share of being among the elect, the chosen, members of the true church.

The practice and sound of their hymn singing expresses that hope. Calling out requests for hymns is the one part of public worship open to all members, and hymn selections represent women's choices as well as men's. Usually women sing more softly than men, but their higher voices always carry easily over the lower voices of men and their occasional alto harmonies add texture to the sound. The distinctive sound of their singing—different from the sound of ballads, country music, or string band and other instrumental music they enjoy outside of church—is deeply rooted in a predestinarian theology that stresses particular election. With that sound, Primitive Baptists deliberately separate themselves from the secular world and assert their equality as children of God.

Rock Creek Primitive Baptist Church, near Independence, Virginia. An old-style meeting house with separate entrances for women and men. Photo by Beverly Bush Patterson.

Little River Primitive Baptist Church, Sparta, North Carolina, rebuilt in brick with an added shelter for dinner on the grounds. Photo by Daniel W. Patterson.

Peach Bottom Primitive Baptist Church near Independence, Virginia, remodeled with an addition that extends the front beyond the original separate entrances. Photo by Tom Davenport.

Cross Roads Primitive Baptist Church in Baywood, Virginia. Its congregation has adopted extensive renovations inside and outside the building and recently replaced its Goble hymnbook with the newest Primitive Baptist shape-note hymnal. Courtesy of the American Folklife Center, Library of Congress.

PRIMITIVE BAPTIST

HYMN BOOK

FOR

ALL LOVERS OF SACRED SONG

COMPILED BY

D. H. GOBLE

"PRAISE YE THE LORD"

PRINTED AND FOR SALE BY
THE D. H. GOBLE PRINTING COMPANY
GREENFIELD, IND.

Title page from D. H. Goble's *Primitive Baptist Hymn Book,* published in 1887 and still in use. The actual size is 5 x 4 inches.

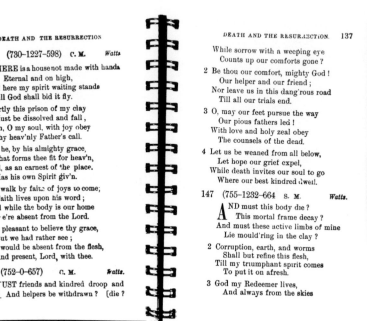

145 (730–1227–598) C. M. *Watts*

THERE is a house not made with hands
Eternal and on high,
And here my spirit waiting stands
Till God shall bid it fly.

2 Shortly this prison of my clay
Must be dissolved and fall,
Then, O my soul, with joy obey
Thy heav'nly Father's call.

3 'Tis he, by his almighty grace,
That forms thee fit for heav'n,
And, as an earnest of the place,
Has his own Spirit giv'n.

4 We walk by faith of joys to come;
Faith lives upon his word;
And while the body is our home
We're absent from the Lord.

5 'Tis pleasant to believe thy grace,
But we had rather see;
We would be absent from the flesh,
And present, Lord, with thee.

146 (752–0–657) C. M. *Watts.*

MUST friends and kindred droop and
And helpers be withdrawn? [die?

While sorrow with a weeping eye
Counts up our comforts gone?

2 Be thou our comfort, mighty God!
Our helper and our friend;
Nor leave us in this dang'rous road
Till all our trials end.

3 O, may our feet pursue the way
Our pious fathers led!
With love and holy zeal obey
The counsels of the dead.

4 Let us be weaned from all below,
Let hope our grief expel,
While death invites our soul to go
Where our best kindred dwell.

147 (755–1232–664) S. M. *Watts.*

AND must this body die?
This mortal frame decay?
And must these active limbs of mine
Lie mould'ring in the clay?

2 Corruption, earth, and worms
Shall but refine this flesh,
Till my triumphant spirit comes
To put it on afresh.

3 God my Redeemer lives,
And always from the skies

Sample hymn texts from D. H. Goble's *Primitive Baptist Hymn Book.*

Men in members' pews at Cross Roads Primitive Baptist Church, singing from Goble's *Primitive Baptist Hymn Book* before the preaching service. Courtesy of the American Folklife Center, Library of Congress.

Singing during the hand of fellowship at the close of the service at Cross Roads Primitive Baptist Church. Courtesy of the American Folklife Center, Library of Congress.

Congregational singing at Galax Primitive Baptist Church in Galax, Virginia, using hymnbooks with shape-note notation, now the common practice in most Primitive Baptist churches. Courtesy of the American Folklife Center, Library of Congress.

Primitive Baptists gathered to sing hymns on the banks of the New River while candidates for church membership prepare for baptism. Photo by Beverly Bush Patterson.

Church elders baptizing new members after leading them into the river. Photo by Beverly Bush Patterson.

Elder Walter Evans displaying his grandfather's Bible at his home in Sparta, North Carolina. Photo by Tom Davenport.

Elder Walter Evans playing his fiddle at home. Photo by Tom Davenport.

5

Creativity in the Old Way of Singing

You know, that's the secret in not having the notes to these
[hymns]: a fellow can just sing it . . . however his heart feels.

—Primitive Baptist deacon and
song leader, Virginia, 1982

ELDER BILLY COOK represents a declining number of Primitive
Baptists who defend the use of a hymnbook without tunes and an
old way of singing. His preference for tunes "that's been passed down
from generation to generation" suggests that he believes the tunes
sung by his and other congregations using Goble's *Primitive Baptist
Hymn Book* (1887) are from a long and unbroken oral tradition. On
the surface, the congregations themselves seem to support this image, singing all of their tunes from memory.

A close look, however, reveals a much more active situation in
which churches have drawn on a variety of musical sources over the
years and have exercised congregational autonomy in making their
choices about singing. In field and historical research with the singing of absolutist Primitive Baptists in Virginia, Brett Sutton (1982)
found beneath the surface of the singing a mixed and complex relationship between oral and written song traditions. In my research
among conditionalist congregations further west, I found the same.
Many of the hymn tunes I heard Primitive Baptists singing from memory had appeared in nineteenth-century tunebooks such as William
Walker's *The Southern Harmony* (1835) and *The Christian Harmony*
(1867). At least half of the tunes had been published by 1850 in tunebooks once used widely in singing schools in the rural South, and a
great many continue in print in recent editions of B. F. White's 1844
tunebook, *The Sacred Harp,* and in Primitive Baptist tunebooks as well.

Some of the older church members, in fact, report having partici-
pated as young people in singing schools at their own churches. Two
senior members of a Virginia congregation that used the Goble book,
an eighty-five-year-old woman and an eighty-eight-year-old man, remembered attending a singing school at their home church. The
preacher who taught the school was paid in wheat and corn, and
maybe meat, recalled the woman. "He didn't ask for pay," she said,
but "out of the goodness of their hearts" people gave what they had
or could afford. The preacher taught the singing school for two weeks
during the summer, they said, and he used note books. Then they
showed us a favorite photograph—a picture of the singing-school
class taken outside the church around 1910.

A music-reading member of another church in the association said
that he had gone to singing schools at his church five or six times
in his youth. He remembered schools being taught three or four
hours a week for four to six weeks in the fall. Daily's *Primitive Baptist Hymn and Tune Book* (1902, 1918), which has been in use in his
church since it was founded in 1913, was the book he studied (WI-
088).

Elder Evans, who regularly lined out hymns for his congregations
in a completely traditional style, had also learned to read music written in shape notes when he was a young man. He could read just
about any music, he told us, as long as it was written in shape notes.
He recalled attending several singing schools, one at a Primitive Baptist church he later served as preacher.

> I was about eighteen years old ... in 1927. Paul B. Collins was
> the singing teacher ... taught for two weeks here. . . . My voice
> was just strong in them days. I didn't have to strain, you know,
> it was just natural. And he spotted me singing—I liked to sing
> [either] soprano or tenor then. He called me out. . . . Says, "You,
> back there singing with that strong voice." Says, "Come up here
> a minute" ... gave me his baton. Said, "You lead a song or two,
> let me help on a weak place." . . . He could sing anything, that
> fellow could. (WI-168)

Evans believed that some of the hymns and ballads he learned as
a child from his mother had been influenced by print. She had attended singing schools, he said, and he sang "Beset with snares" (fig. 14)
to a tune he thought she had learned there. He remembered hearing
her sing this when he was a "kid boy" (WI-026).

Fig. 14. "Beset with snares on ev'ry hand" (Philip Doddridge, Goble no. 69) with the tune "Frozen Heart" as sung by Elder Walter Evans, 18 November 1980, Sparta, North Carolina. Recorded by Tom Davenport (WI-026).

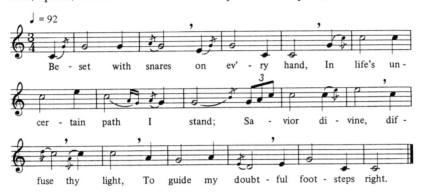

1. Beset with snares on ev'ry hand,
     In life's uncertain path I stand;
   Savior divine, diffuse thy light,
     To guide my doubtful footsteps right.

2. Engage this roving, treach'rous heart,
     To fix on Christ the better part;
   To scorn the trifles of a day,
     For joys that none can take away.

3. Then let the wildest storms arise;
     Let tempests mingle earth and skies;
   No fatal shipwreck shall I fear,
     But all my treasures with me bear.

4. If thou, my Jesus, will be nigh,
     Cheerful I live, and joyful die;
   Secure, when mortal comforts flee,
     To find ten thousand worlds in thee.

Elder Evans also recognized the tunebook tradition behind some of the congregational songs. In one worship service he called for the hymn text "I am a stranger here below" and reminded the congregation of a former member, now deceased, who had always requested singing that hymn in the "old tune" for "High o'er the hills the mountains rise." Talking about that later, Evans revealed his awareness that the source of his tune was a piece printed in William Walker's *Southern Harmony* (fig. 15).

When we came to close, I thought of an old member of that church. . . . Had one particular seat, that's where he'd sit—on the second bench from the front, right next to the wall. That's his place. . . . That's why I mentioned it Sunday, you could almost see him. Well he'd say, "Brother Walt, let's sing 'I'm a stranger here below,' number 200 in our little book. . . ." He said, "Sing it in that old tune." Now this comes out of the old *Southern Harmony* . . . and we'd sing it in that tune. That's why we sang that last Sunday . . . because I just remembered . . . that was one of his favorite songs. (WI-112)

Fig. 15. "I am a stranger here below" (Goble no. 200) with the tune "French Broad" as sung by the congregation of Antioch Primitive Baptist Church, 25 July 1982, Stratford, North Carolina (WI-097).

1. I am a stranger here below,
    And what I am 'tis hard to know,
   I am so vile, so prone to sin,
    I fear that I'm not born again.

2. When I experience call to mind,
    My understanding is so blind,
   All feeling sense seems to be gone,
    Which makes me fear that I am wrong.

3. I find myself out of the way;
    My thoughts are often gone astray;

Like one alone I seem to be:
  Oh! is there any one like me?

4. So far from God I seem to lie,
    Which makes me often weep and cry;
  I fear at last that I shall fall,
    For if a saint the least of all.

5. I seldom find a heart to pray,
    So many things step in my way;
  Thus filled with doubts, I ask to know
    Come, tell me, is it thus with you?

6. So, by experience, I do know
    There's nothing good that I can do;
  I can not satisfy the law,
    Nor hope nor comfort from it draw.

7. My nature is so prone to sin,
    Which makes my duty so unclean,
  That when I count up all the cost,
    If not free grace, then I am lost.

The links between the orally transmitted tunes in congregational singing and the tunebook tradition, however, are multilayered. Some of the Primitive Baptist hymn-and-tune books continue the old tune-book practice of identifying hymns by the name of the tune instead of the text. "New Britain," for example, appears as the title of the hymn "Amazing Grace" in Cayce's *The Good Old Songs*. But the situation is more complicated than that because tunes in the old song-books themselves bore a complex relationship to oral tradition. For example, in the *Southern Harmony* that "old tune" requested by Elder Evans's church member bears the title "French Broad." William Walker, in a headnote, attributed it to himself.

Such claims of authorship can have a variety of meanings and have to be interpreted carefully. As George Pullen Jackson has pointed out (1953 [1937]:122), the compilers of these shape-note tunebooks were themselves often acting as tune collectors and arrangers rather than creators. Although they self-consciously composed some of the tunes they published, they adapted many others from oral tradition. Walker's claim, then, did not necessarily mean that "French Broad" was an original composition or would even be a tune new to his readers. Jackson reasoned that Walker must have been referring simply to the

Fig. 16. "High o'er the hills the mountains rise" (William Walker) with the tune "French Broad" from William Walker's *The Southern Harmony*, 265.

3. Although I walk the mountains high,
Ere long my body low must lie,
And in some lonesome place must rot,
And by the living be forgot.

4. There it must lie till that great day,
When Gabriel's awful trump shall say,
Arise, the judgment day is come,
When all must hear their final doom.

5. If not prepared, then I must go
Down to eternal pain and wo,
With devils there I must remain,
And never more return again.

6. But if prepared, oh, blessed thought!
I'll rise above the mountain's top,
And there remain for evermore
On Canaan's peaceful, happy shore.

7. Oh! when I think of that blest world,
Where all God's people dwell in love,
I oft-times long with them to be
And dwell in heaven eternally.

8. Then will I sing God's praises there,
Who brought me through my troubles here
I'll sing, and be forever blest,
Find sweet and everlasting rest.

words when he took credit for the song, not only because he was "melodizing in beaten paths," but also because Walker declared after publishing the tune that he had learned it from his mother when he was only five years old (around 1814). In addition, Jackson pointed out that British-derived tunes similar to "French Broad" circulated widely in the secular repertory of singers in the Appalachians. Cecil Sharp transcribed one of these, the ballad "Macafee's Confession," in 1918 from the singing of a woman in western North Carolina (fig. 17). "French Broad," then, shows that tunebook publications and oral song traditions in Primitive Baptist churches have long influenced each other, so that the music of even the oldest oral style of lined-out congregational hymn singing is not a purely oral tradition.

Fig. 17. "Macafee's Confession" as sung by Mrs. Mary Gibson at Marion, North Carolina, 4 September 1918, from Cecil Sharp's *English Folk Songs from the Southern Appalachians*, 2:16. Copyright © 1932 Oxford University Press. Reproduced by permission.

Moreover, the southern tunebooks that influenced Primitive Baptist tradition were themselves heterogeneous in content, drawing on a diverse range of printed and oral sources. Most of those tunebooks popular in the nineteenth-century South included European compositions—for example, psalm tunes such as "Old Hundred"—and American imitations of those models, such as "Windham." The fuging tunes in these books also imitated British and European models. Intermixed with these pieces were late-eighteenth- and early-nineteenth-century hymns influenced by German standards of musical composition, and also numerous spiritual songs recorded—as proven by compilers' statements or by comparison with early manuscripts and modern field collections—directly from American oral traditions. The tunebooks included additional songs imitating that folk style.

Also appearing in them were genteel compositions, such as those of Lowell Mason, that reacted to this developing American tradition of church music by looking back to Europe for melodic and harmonic ideas. By 1867, these tunebooks had added gospel songs, a popular form developing out of the old camp-meeting spirituals. Even performance pieces such as anthems were part of the mix.

The materials in these tunebooks always show some tension between the repertories imitating literate British and European models and those influenced by oral American models. Despite this mixture of influences from the tunebook legacy, however, Primitive Baptist congregations have put their own stamp on the singing. One way to see this is to compare transcriptions of oral performances with tune analogues from the printed tradition.

We recorded approximately 100 different tunes that Primitive Baptists sang from memory with 120 (or approximately one-third) of the texts in Goble's *Primitive Baptist Hymn Book*. Some of these recordings were taped in church services, others during interviews with church members. While the recordings doubtless do not include the entire tune repertory of these churches or the exact repertory of any one congregation, they do represent a group of tunes known to most, if not all, of the members of those churches we visited. They include all the most frequently sung melodies. Notation does not, of course, record significant features of the sound such as tone color and volume, and it cannot fully capture the melodic graces and rhythmic accents and patterns of movement. Even with such limitations, though, my transcriptions of a sample of these tunes illustrate oral features of the singing with which Primitive Baptists produce a homogeneous repertory out of diverse traditions of religious song. After demonstrating this, I will offer an additional tune sample to show in more detail the creativity with which Primitive Baptist singers adapt and select from these diverse traditions to form their own song style.

The congregational performance of a tune may vary either subtly or markedly from the form of the tune printed in tunebooks. In tunes such as "Balerma" (fig. 18) and "Sacred Throne" (fig. 19) that the Primitive Baptist oral tradition took from a repertory of standard hymn tunes, basic melodic structures remain unchanged. (Compare fig. 18 with fig. 23, below; the latter shows the use of a different tune for the same text.) When singing these melodies, the congregations do, however, draw on a rich tradition of ornamentation in the style earlier used in ballad singing in the region. At a minimum, they embellish notes with accented and unaccented passing tones, with melodic turns, and with tones that anticipate or prepare the note that follows.

Fig. 18. "O for a closer walk with God" (William Cowper, Goble no. 59) with the tune "Balerma" (François A. Barthelemon, adapted by Robert Simpson), as sung at the Mountain District Primitive Baptist Association meeting, 5 September 1982, Sparta, North Carolina (WI-103).

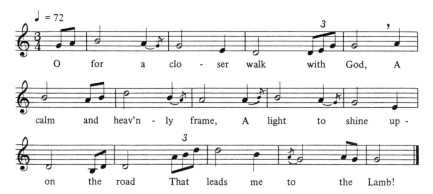

1. O for a closer walk with God,
     A calm and heavenly frame,
   A light to shine upon the road
     That leads me to the Lamb!

2. Where is the blessedness I knew
     When first I saw the Lord?
   Where is the soul-refreshing view
     Of Jesus and his word?

3. What peaceful hours I then enjoyed!
     How sweet their mem'ry still!
   But now I find an aching void
     The world can never fill.

4. Return, O holy Dove, return,
     Sweet messenger of rest;
   I hate the sins that cause my mourn,
     And so disturb my breast.

5. The dearest idol I have known,
     Whate'er that idol be,
   O come and tear it from its throne,
     I'll worship only thee.

6. So shall my walk be close with God,
     Calm and serene my frame;

So purer light shall mark the road
That leads me to the Lamb.

Fig. 19. "Ye pilgrims that are wandering home" (Goble no. 236) with the tune "Sacred Throne" or "Martyrdom" (Hugh Wilson) as sung by the congregation of Union Primitive Baptist Church, 5 June 1982, Whitehead, North Carolina (WI-008).

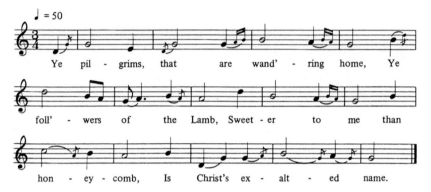

1. Ye pilgrims, that are wand'ring home,
     Ye foll'wers of the Lamb,
   Sweeter to me than honey-comb,
     Is Christ's exalted name.

2. Let us with undissembled love,
     Like children in one band,
   March to our Father's house above,
     And to the promised land.

3. My little flock, I bid adieu,
     Our parting is to-day;
   O may we all to Christ prove true,
     And try to watch and pray.

4. There is one thing that wounds my heart,
     And grieves my soul full sore:
   To think we must in body part,
     Perhaps to meet no more.

5. We need not wait but few more days,
     Then he will call us home,
   Where fear of parting ne'er will come,
     In that bright world above;

6. Where we'll surround the throne of God,
   And sing redeeming love;
   And there I hope to see your face,
   And join to praise the Lord.

Approximately 20 percent of the tunes I heard in Primitive Baptist services were standards in many Protestant hymnals. "Laban" (figs. 20–21), for example, appears in almost all of the hymnals published for Primitive Baptists and, according to a tune index by Katharine Diehl (1966), in at least thirty-five additional hymnals from other denominations. Such tunes were often composed by genteel, formally trained American nineteenth-century musicians, such as Lowell Mason. Primitive Baptists sing at least five of Mason's tunes—"Bethany,"[1] "Boylston" (see fig. 72), "Cleansing Fountain" (see fig. 4), "Ripley" (see fig. 12), and "Laban." Other well-known tunes in their repertory are William Bradbury's "Sweet Hour of Prayer" (for the hymn of the same name, fig. 24), "Woodworth" (as the setting for "Just as I am," fig. 25), and "Brown" (with "Love is the sweetest bud that blows" and "I love to steal awhile away" [fig. 26]). They also sing "Maitland," the familiar setting by George Allen for "Must Jesus bear the cross alone" (fig. 74). Over the years, these popular devotional hymns became as familiar to Primitive Baptists as they did to Southern and Missionary Baptists, Methodists, Presbyterians, and others. Their presence in the *Primitive Baptist Hymn Book* (1887) suggests that the tunes associated with them probably entered the Primitive Baptist repertory about the same time they became popular among other denominations.

Although Primitive Baptists adopted a dozen or more melodies attributed to Mason and his colleagues, they were selective, usually choosing the tunes that reflected American influences. And they did not at all accept the performance style these musicians tried to inculcate. Concerning keeping the proper rhythm, for example, Bradbury and Root instructed "Teachers of Music, Choristers, Singers, and all interested in American Church Music" that "in the performance of a piece of music, the time should be computed with the same accuracy and regularity as by a Metronome or a clock" (1853:3,9). Two years later, Thomas Hastings earnestly advised Presbyterians that "the best ornaments of style in church music, are a fine voice, and exact time, connected with a distinct, chaste, free, polished, and impassioned enunciation" (1855:25).

Even a casual look at the rhythmic irregularities in the following

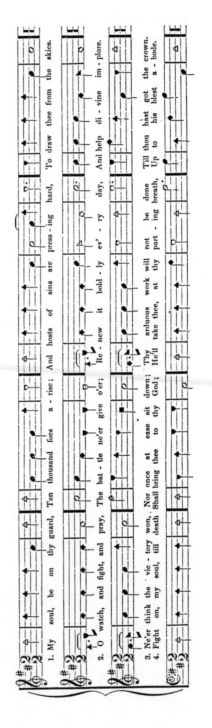

Fig. 20. The tune "Laban" (on the third staff from the top) by Lowell Mason from Thomas Hastings's *The Presbyterian Psalmodist*, 191.

transcriptions of Primitive Baptist singing (see especially figs. 21, 22, 23, and 26) will show that the congregations do not follow such mechanistic practices. Some of the transcriptions have no meter signatures because, more often than not, congregations do not sing with regular, predictable beats. In these tunes, the rhythmic freedom introduces subtle emphases—especially at the ends of phrases—that bond the text and tune naturally, instead of attempting an artificial bonding with "chaste, free, polished, and impassioned enunciation."

Fig. 21. "Blest be the tie that binds" (John Fawcett, Goble no. 72) with the tune "Laban" (Lowell Mason) as sung by the congregation of Cross Roads Primitive Baptist Church, 18 July 1982, Baywood, Virginia (WI-087).

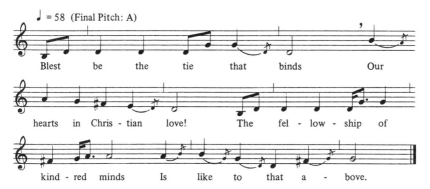

1. Blest be the tie that binds
    Our hearts in Christian love!
   The fellowship of kindred minds
    Is like to that above.

2. Before our Father's throne
    We pour our ardent prayers;
   Our fears, our hopes, our aims are one—
    Our comforts and our cares.

3. We share our mutual woes;
    Our mutual burdens bear:
   And often for each other flows
    The sympathizing tear.

4. When we asunder part
    It gives us inward pain;
   But we shall still be joined in heart,
    And hope to meet again.

> 5. This glorious hope revives
>   Our courage by the way;
>   While each in expectation lives,
>   And longs to see the day.
>
> 6. From sorrow, toil, and pain,
>   And sin we shall be free;
>   And perfect love and friendship reign
>   In blessed eternity.

Fig. 22. "Rock of Ages, cleft for me" (Augustus M. Toplady, Goble no. 40) with the tune "Toplady" (Thomas Hastings) as sung by the congregation of Little River Primitive Baptist Church, 18 July 1970, Sparta, North Carolina. Recorded by Daniel Patterson and Blanton Owen (WI-027).

> 1. Rock of Ages, cleft for me,
>   Let me hide myself in thee;
>   Let the water and the blood,
>   From thy wounded side which flowed,
>   Be of sin the double cure;
>   Cleanse me from its guilt and pow'r.
>
> 2. Not the labor of my hands
>   Can fulfill thy law's demands;
>   Could my zeal no respite know,
>   Could my tears forever flow,
>   All for sin could not atone;
>   Thou must save, and thou alone.

3. Nothing in my hand I bring,
   Simply to thy cross I cling;
   Naked, come to thee for dress;
   Helpless, look to thee for grace;
   Black, I to the fountain fly;
   Wash me, Savior, or I die.

4. While I draw this fleeting breath,
   When my eye-strings break in death,
   When I soar to worlds unknown,
   See thee on thy judgment throne—
   Rock of Ages, cleft for me,
   Let me hide myself in thee.

Fig. 23. "O for a closer walk with God" (William Cowper, Goble no. 59) with the tune "Elizabethtown" (George Kingsley) as sung by the congregation of Little River Primitive Baptist Church, 18 July 1982, Sparta, North Carolina (WI-089). For full text, see fig. 18.

Fig. 24. "Sweet hour of prayer" (William W. Walford, Goble no. 220) with the tune "Sweet Hour of Prayer" (William B. Bradbury) as sung by the congregation of Peach Bottom Primitive Baptist Church, 9 July 1983, near Independence, Virginia (WI-143).

at my Fa - ther's throne, Make all my wants and

wish - es known. In sea - sons of dis - tress and

grief, My soul has of - ten found re -

lief, And oft es - caped the tempt - er's

snare By thy re - turn, sweet hour of prayer.

1. Sweet hour of prayer, sweet hour of prayer,
   That calls me from a world of care,
   And bids me at my Father's throne,
   Make all my wants and wishes known.
   In seasons of distress and grief,
   My soul has often found relief,
   And oft escaped the tempter's snare
   By thy return, sweet hour of prayer.

2. Sweet hour of prayer, sweet hour of prayer,
   Thy wings shall my petition bear
   To him whose truth and faithfulness,
   Engage the waiting soul to bless:
   And since he bids me seek his face,
   Believe his word and trust his grace,
   I'll cast on him my ev'ry care,
   And wait for thee, sweet hour of prayer.

3. Sweet hour of prayer, sweet hour of prayer,
   May I thy consolation share,
   Till from Mount Pisgah's lofty height,
   I view my home and take my flight:
   This robe of flesh I'll drop, and rise
   To seize the everlasting prize,

And shout while passing through the air,
Farewell, farewell, sweet hour of prayer.

Fig. 25. "Just as I am, without one plea" (Charlotte Elliott, Goble no. 269) with
the tune "Woodworth" (William B. Bradbury) as sung by the congregation
of Cross Roads Primitive Baptist Church, 25 June 1982, Baywood, Virginia
(WI-033).

1. Just as I am, without one plea,
    But that thy blood was shed for me,
   And that thou bid'st me come to thee,
       O Lamb of God, I come!

2. Just as I am, and waiting not
       To rid my soul of one dark blot,
    To thee, whose blood can cleanse each spot,
       O Lamb of God, I come!

3. Just as I am, though tossed about
       With many a conflict, many a doubt,
    Fightings within, and fears without,
       O Lamb of God, I come!

4. Just as I am—poor, wretched, blind;
       Sight, riches, healing of the mind,
    Yea, all I need, in thee to find,
       O Lamb of God, I come!

5. Just as I am—thou wilt receive,
       Wilt welcome, pardon, cleanse, relieve;
    Because thy promise I believe,
       O Lamb of God, I come!

6. Just as I am—thy love unknown
   Hath broken every barrier down;
   Now, to be thine, yea, thine alone
   O Lamb of God, I come!

Fig. 26. "I love to steal awhile away" (Mrs. Phoebe Brown, Goble no. 267) with the tune "Brown" (William B. Bradbury) as sung by the congregation of Antioch Primitive Baptist Church, 25 July 1982, Stratford, North Carolina (WI-097).

1. I love to steal awhile away
   From every cumb'ring care,
   And spend the hours of setting day
   In humble, grateful prayer.

2. I love in solitude to shed
   The penitential tear,
   And all his promises to plead
   Where none but God can hear.

3. I love to think on mercies past,
   And future good implore,
   And all my cares and sorrows cast
   On him whom I adore.

4. I love by faith to take a view
   Of brighter scenes in heav'n;
   The prospect doth my strength renew
   While here by tempest driv'n.

5. Thus, when life's toilsome day is o'er,
   May its departing ray
   Be calm as this impressive hour,
   And lead to endless day.

Primitive Baptist oral traditions and publications have also retained melodies composed in the style of early British and European psalm tunes under titles like "Windham" (see fig. 2), "Cookham," "Primrose," "Davis," and "Devotion"—pieces that have passed from use in most other denominations. First published in tunebooks during the late eighteenth and early nineteenth centuries, these tunes were among the first flowerings of American psalm-and-hymn tune compositions. Primitive Baptists continue to sing these older and less familiar tunes with the rhythmic and melodic freedom that often characterizes hymns that move them deeply. I heard Elder Evans lead "Windham" once, for example, with a testimony to the congregation that although "hard to sing," the melody is one of the old "lonesome" tunes that are among his favorites.[2] Since these tunes are readily accessible to the reader in modern editions of *The Sacred Harp*, I offer here only one comparative example—"Cookham"—to illustrate how one congregation embellishes the tune. Four additional transcriptions will confirm such elaboration as standard practice.

Fig. 27. "'Tis religion that can give" (Mary Masters, Goble no. 169) with the tune "Cookham" as sung by the congregation of Union Primitive Baptist Church, 4 June 1983, Whitehead, North Carolina (WI-122).

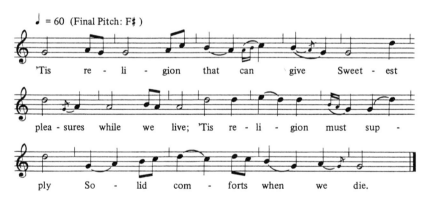

1. 'Tis religion that can give
    Sweetest pleasures while we live;
    'Tis religion must supply
    Solid comforts when we die.

2. After death its joys will be
    Lasting as eternity!
    Be the living God my friend,
    Then my bliss shall never end.

Fig. 28. "Cookham" from William Walker's *The Southern Harmony*, 8.

Fig. 29. "God moves in a mysterious way" (William Cowper, Goble no. 1) with the tune "Primrose," "Twenty-Fourth," or "Melody" (Amzi Chapin) as sung by the congregation of Little River Primitive Baptist Church, 28 July 1983, Sparta, North Carolina (WI-162).

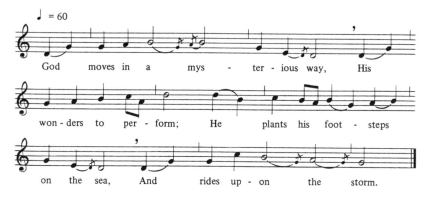

1. God moves in a mysterious way,
    His wonders to perform;
    He plants his footsteps on the sea,
    And rides upon the storm.

2. Deep in unfathomable mines
    Of never-failing skill,
    He treasures up his bright designs
    And works his sov'reign will.

3. Ye fearful saints, fresh courage take,
    The clouds you so much dread
    Are big with mercy, and shall break
    In blessings on your head.

4. Judge not the Lord by feeble sense,
    But trust him for his grace;
    Behind a frowning Providence
    He hides a smiling face.

5. His purposes will ripen fast,
    Unfolding ev'ry hour;
    The bud may have a bitter taste,
    But sweet will be the flower.

6. Blind unbelief is sure to err,
    And scan his work in vain;
    God is his own interpreter,
    And he will make it plain.

Fig. 30. "O Thou in whose presence" (Joseph Swain, Goble no. 229) with the tune "Davis" (Freeman Lewis) as sung by the congregation of Cross Roads Primitive Baptist Church, 23 June 1983, Baywood, Virginia (WI-137).

1. O Thou in whose presence my soul takes delight,
      On whom in affliction I call;
   My comfort by day, and my song in the night,
      My hope, my salvation, my all.

2. Where dost thou at noontide resort with thy sheep,
      To feed on the pastures of love?
   Say, why in the valley of death should I weep,
      Or alone in the wilderness rove?

3. O why should I wander an alien from thee,
      Or cry in the desert for bread?
   Thy foes will rejoice when my sorrows they see,
      And smile at the tears I have shed.

4. Ye daughters of Zion, declare, have ye seen
      The Star that on Israel shone?
   Say, if in your tents my Beloved has been,
      And where with his flock he has gone?

5. This is my Beloved, his form is divine,
      His vestments shed odors around;
   The locks on his head are as grapes on the vine,
      When autumn with plenty is crowned,

6. As roses of Sharon, as lilies that grow
   In vales, on the banks of the streams,
   On his cheeks does the beauty of excellence glow,
   And his eyes are as quivers of beams.

7. His voice, as the sound of the dulcimer sweet,
   Is heard through the shadows of death;
   The cedars of Lebanon bow at his feet,
   The air is perfumed with his breath.

8. His lips as a fountain of righteousness flow,
   That waters the garden of grace,
   From which their salvation the Gentiles shall know,
   And bask in the smiles of his face.

9. Love is in his eye-lids, and scatters delight
   Through all the bright mansions on high,
   Their faces the cherubim veil in his sight,
   And praise him with fullness of joy.

10. He looks, and ten thousands of angels rejoice
    And myriads wait for his word;
    He speaks, and eternity, filled with his voice,
    Re-echoes the praise of the Lord.

Fig. 31. "O happy day when saints shall meet" (Goble no. 234) with the tune "Devotion" (variously attributed to Amarick [or Amariah] Hall, most recently to Alexander Johnson) as sung by the congregation of Little River Primitive Baptist Church, 16 May 1982, Sparta, North Carolina (WI-082).

1. O happy day, when saints shall meet,
   To part no more! the thought is sweet!
   No more to feel the rending smart,
   Oft felt below when Christians part.

2. O happy place! I still must say,
   Where all but love is done away;
   All cause of parting there is past,
   Their social feast will ever last.

3. Such union here is sought in vain,
   As there in ev'ry heart shall reign;
   There separation can't compel
   The saint to bid the sad farewell.

4. On earth, when friends together meet,
   And find the passing moments sweet,
   Time's rapid moments soon compel
   With grief to say, Dear friends, farewell.

5. The happy season soon will come,
   When saints shall meet in heav'n, their home;
   Eternally with Christ to dwell,
   Nor ever hear the sound, Farewell.

A bolder revision of a tunebook piece appears in the Primitive Baptist adaptation of the fuging tune "Ninety-fifth" (fig. 32). The fuging tune is a form developed from British and European models by eighteenth-century New England tunesmiths for use in American singing schools. Such a tune normally has a short opening section of two phrases in which all of the voices sing simultaneously in harmony followed by a longer closing section in which voices overlap, entering in succession like a round but singing parts that are only somewhat imitative. Fuging tunes are still popular with southern shapenote singers, many of whom are Primitive Baptists, but the pieces are not well suited to public worship and are not commonly sung then.

Once, however, at an association meeting of churches in the piedmont that are in fellowship with the Mountain Association, I heard "Ninety-fifth." The pastor, who also preaches in the mountain churches, invited the congregation to stand for a moment as a break between sermons. He then called for one verse of "When I can read my title clear" and led the congregation in singing "Ninety-fifth" from memory. They sang in unison a version that reduced the imitative phrases of "Ninety-fifth" to a single melodic line (fig. 33).[3]

Fig. 32. "When I can read my title clear" (Isaac Watts) with the fuging tune "Ninety-fifth" (third staff) from William Walker's *The Southern Harmony*, 27.

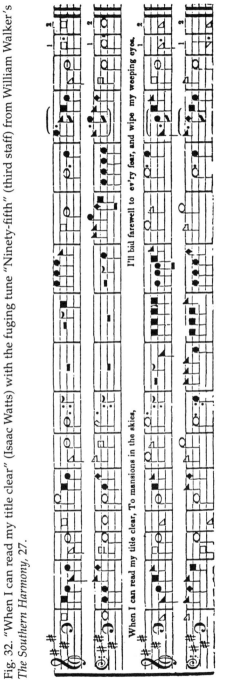

Fig. 33. "When I can read my title clear" (Isaac Watts, Goble no. 161) with the tune "Ninety-fifth" as sung at the Original Little River Primitive Baptist Association meeting, 25 September 1983, near Coats, North Carolina (WI-207).

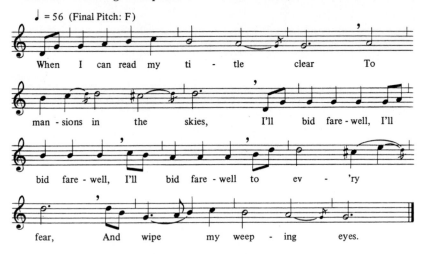

1. When I can read my title clear
   To mansions in the skies,
   I'll bid farewell to ev'ry fear,
   And wipe my weeping eyes.

2. Should earth against my soul engage,
   And hellish darts be hurled,
   Then I can smile at Satan's rage,
   And face a frowning world.

3. Let cares like a wild deluge come,
   And storms of sorrow fall,
   May I but safely reach my home,
   My God, my heav'n, my all.

4. There shall I bathe my weary soul
   In seas of heav'nly rest,
   And not a wave of trouble roll
   Across my peaceful breast.

The tunes discussed and transcribed above clearly originated as compositions for early tunebooks, and Primitive Baptists vary them chiefly by taking small liberties with ornamentation and rhythm. We find bolder creativity in a much larger class of Primitive Baptist tunes that seem to have had an independent existence in oral tradition. These are old American vernacular tunes that rarely, if ever, appear now in the hymnals of other denominations, although they are printed in one or more current Primitive Baptist hymnals. For example, "Detroit" (fig. 34)—a tune from Ananias Davisson's *A Supplement to the Kentucky Harmony* (1820) and one that Jackson associates with the folksong "The Irish Emigrant's Lament" (1981 [1952]:20)[4]—appears in at least three Primitive Baptist hymnbooks.[5] "Imandra" (fig. 35), for which Jackson (1981 [1952]:109–10, 200) finds secular parallels in the British Isles, is another of the old minor tunes still published and sung by Primitive Baptists.[6] "A Sacred Spot" (fig. 36), a variant of "An Address for All," which is credited to William Walker in mid-nineteenth-century tunebooks, is related to the ballad tune "Locks and Bolts." William Walker also claims "Faithful Soldier" (fig. 37), but Jackson thinks it derives from an old tune recorded in Kilrush, Ireland (1953 [1937]: 91–92).

Fig. 34. "How sweet, how heavenly is the sight" (Goble no. 129) with the tune "Detroit" as sung by the congregation of Union Primitive Baptist Church, 5 June 1982, Whitehead, North Carolina (WI-008).

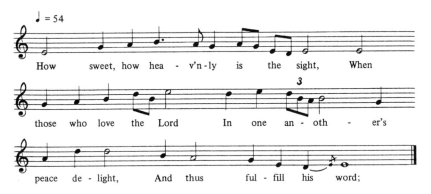

1. How sweet, how heav'nly is the sight,
       When those who love the Lord
   In one another's peace delight,
       And thus fulfill his word;

2. When each can feel his brother's sigh,
       And with him bear a part;
   When sorrows flow from eye to eye,
       And joy from heart to heart;

3. When free from envy, scorn, and pride,
    Our wishes all above,
   Each can his brother's failings hide,
    And show a brother's love;

4. When love in one delightful stream
    Through ev'ry bosom flows,
   And union sweet, and dear esteem
    In ev'ry action glows!

5. Love is the golden chain that binds
    The happy souls above;
   And he's an heir of heav'n that finds
    His bosom glow with love.

Fig. 35. "The voice of the Shepherd" (Goble no. 172) with the tune "Imandra" as sung by the congregation of Little River Primitive Baptist Church,
ca. 1960, Sparta, North Carolina. Recorded by Elder Lasserre Bradley, *Old
Hymns Lined and Led by Elder Walter Evans*, Sovereign Grace 6444.

1. The voice of the Shepherd his flock shall convene,
    And lead them to pastures all fertile and green,
    But unto the stranger they will not draw near,
    Who calls to deceive them, "Lo here, and lo there."

2. The blood of the Shepherd his flock did redeem;
    Grace, mercy, and peace came to sinners by him;

'Tis he who hath told them of such to beware,
Who cry like deceivers, "Lo here, and lo there."

3. He calls them by name, and before them he goes,
    To guide, guard, and succor his lambs from their foes;
    And, glory to Jesus, his church is his care,
    Though oft they do halt 'twixt "Lo here, and lo there."

4. Those gospel pretenders the wall will leap o'er,
    And enter the sheep-fold, though not by the door;
    And fraught with delusion, and hardened to fear,
    Shall cry in confusion, "Lo here, and lo there."

5. The Scriptures declare that deceivers shall come,
    And thousands to final destruction shall run;
    But saints by their calling shall still persevere,
    While hirelings are bawling, "Lo here, and lo there."

6. The way to the Father is Jesus the Son,
    In all that he suffered, in all that he's done;
    And this shall the heralds of Jesus declare,
    Till folded in Zion his sheep shall appear.

Fig. 36. "There is a spot to me more dear" (William Hunter, Goble no. 275) with a variant of the tune "An Address for All" as sung informally during a hymn sing at home, 24 June 1982, Baywood, Virginia (WI-038).

But where I first my Sa - vior found,

And felt my sins for - giv - en.

1. There is a spot to me more dear
   Than native vale or mountain,
   A spot for which affection's tear
   Springs grateful from its fountain.
   'Tis not where kindred souls abound
   Though that on earth is heaven,
   But where I first my Savior found,
   And felt my sins forgiven.

2. Hard was my toil to reach the shore,
   Long tossed upon the ocean;
   Above me was the thunder's roar,
   Beneath, the waves' commotion.
   Darkly the pall of night was thrown
   Around me, faint with terror;
   In that dark hour how did my groan
   Ascend for years of error!

3. Sinking and panting as for breath,
   I knew not help was near me,
   And cried, "O save me, Lord, from death!
   Immortal Jesus, hear me!"
   Then, quick as thought, I felt him mine
   My Savior stood before me;
   I saw his brightness round me shine,
   And shouted, "Glory, glory!"

4. O, sacred hour! O, hallowed spot!
   Where love divine first found me!
   Wherever falls my distant lot,
   My heart shall linger round thee!
   And when from earth I rise to soar
   Up to my home in heaven,
   Down will I cast my eyes once more,
   Where I was first forgiven.

Fig. 37. "I need thee, precious Jesus" (Frederick Whitfield, Goble no. 270) with the tune "Faithful Soldier" as sung by the congregation of Antioch Primitive Baptist Church, 23 July 1983, Stratford, North Carolina (WI-156).

1. I need thee, precious Jesus,
     For I am full of sin;
   My soul is dark and guilty,
     My heart is dead within.

2. I need the cleansing fountain,
     Where I can always flee—
   The blood of Christ most precious,
     The sinner's only plea.

3. I need thee, precious Jesus,
     For I am very poor;
   A stranger and a pilgrim,
     I have no earthly store.

4. I need the love of Jesus
     To cheer me on my way;
   To guide my doubting footsteps;
     To be my strength and stay.

5. I need thee, precious Jesus;
   I need a friend like thee;
   A friend to soothe and pity;
   A friend to care for me.

6. I need the heart of Jesus,
   To feel each anxious care,
   To tell my every trouble,
   And all my sorrows share.

7. I need thee, precious Jesus,
   For I am very blind;
   A weak and foolish wand'rer,
   With dark and evil mind.

8. I need thy cheering presence,
   To tread the thorny road;
   To guide me safe to glory;
   To bring me home to God.

One familiar tune, "Holy Manna," appears in Primitive Baptist hymnals, as elsewhere, with the text "Brethren we have met to worship." Although congregations rarely sing this text, they continue to use the tune, and they sing it in remarkably varied forms (figs. 38–40).

Fig. 38. "Come, thou Fount of every blessing" (Robert Robinson, Goble no. 164) with a variant of the tune "Holy Manna" as sung by the congregation of Little River Primitive Baptist Church, 19 June 1983, Sparta, North Carolina (WI-128).

1. Come, thou Fount of ev'ry blessing,
   Tune my heart to sing thy grace;
   Streams of mercy never ceasing
   Call for songs of loudest praise.
   Teach me some melodious sonnet,
   Sung by flaming tongues above;
   Praise the mount,—O, fix me on it!
   Mount of God's unchanging love.

2. Here I raise my Ebenezer,
   Hither by thy help I'm come;
   And I hope by thy good pleasure
   Safely to arrive at home.
   Jesus sought me when a stranger,
   Wand'ring from the fold of God;
   He, to save my soul from danger,
   Interposed his precious blood.

3. Oh! to grace how great a debtor
   Daily I'm constrained to be!
   Let that grace, Lord, like a fetter,
   Bind my wand'ring heart to thee.
   Prone to wander, Lord, I feel it,
   Prone to leave the God I love—
   Here's my heart, Lord, take and seal it,
   Seal it for thy courts above.

Fig. 39. "How sweet to reflect on the joys that await me" (W. C. Tillou, Goble no. 305) with a variant of the tune "Holy Manna" as sung by the congregation of Little River Primitive Baptist Church, ca. 1960, Sparta, North Carolina. Recorded by Elder Lasserre Bradley. *Old Hymns Lined and Led by Elder Walter Evans*, Sovereign Grace 6057-6058.

In yon bliss - ful re - gion, the ha - ven of rest,

Where glor - i - fied spir - its in rap - tures will greet me,

And lead me to man - sions pre - pared for the blessed.

En - cir - cled with light and with glo - ry en - shroud - ed,

My hap - pi - ness per - fect, my mind's eye a - bove,

I'll bathe in the o - cean of mer - cies un - bound - ed,

And range with de - light through the E - den of love.

1. How sweet to reflect on the joys that await me,
   In yon blissful region, the haven of rest,
   Where glorified spirits in raptures will greet me,
   And lead me to mansions prepared for the blessed.

2. Encircled with light and with glory enshrouded,
   My happiness perfect, my mind's eye above,
   I'll bathe in the ocean of mercies unbounded,
   And range with delight through the Eden of love.

3. While angelic legions with harps tuned celestial,
   Harmoniously join in the concert of praise,
   And saints as they flock from the region terrestrial,
   In loud hallelujahs their voices shall raise.

4. This song of redemption is echoed in heaven:
   [My soul would respond to Immanuel's love:]

"All glory, all honor, all might and dominion,
To him who brought us to the Eden of love."

5. Then hail, blessed state, hail, ye songsters of glory,
   Ye harpers of bliss, soon I'll meet you above,
   To join your full choir in rehearsing the story,
   Salvation from sorrow through Jesus' love.

6. Though prisoned on earth, yet by anticipation,
   Already my soul tastes the sweets from my Love,
   Of joys that await me when freed from this station—
   My heart's now in heaven, the Eden of love.

Fig. 40. "Hail, ye sighing sons of sorrow" (Goble no. 104) with a variant of the tune "Holy Manna" as sung by the congregation of Antioch Primitive Baptist Church, 24 July 1982, Stratford, North Carolina (WI-222).

♩ = 66

Hail, ye sigh - ing sons of sor - row,

View with me th' au - tum - nal gloom,

Learn from thence your fate to - mor - row;

Dead per - haps, laid in the tomb.

See all na - ture fad - ing, dy - ing,

Si - lent, all things seem to mourn,

Life from veg - e - ta - tion fly - ing,

Brings   to   mind   the   mould - 'ring   urn.

1. Hail, ye sighing sons of sorrow,
      View with me th' autumnal gloom,
   Learn from thence your fate tomorrow;
      Dead perhaps, laid in the tomb.
   See all nature fading, dying,
      Silent, all things seem to mourn,
   Life from vegetation flying,
      Brings to mind the mould'ring urn.

2. Oft when autumn's tempest rising,
      Makes the lofty forest nod,
   Scenes of nature how surprising,
      Read in nature nature's God.
   See the sov'reign, sole Creator,
      Lives eternal in the skies,
   Whilst we mortals yield to nature,
      Bloom awhile, then fade and die.

3. Lo! I hear the air resounding,
      With expiring insects' cries;
   Ah! their moans to me how wounding,
      Emblems of my age and sighs.
   Hollow winds about me roaring,
      Noisy waters round me rise,
   Whilst I sit my fate deploring,
      Tears fast streaming from my eyes.

4. What to me is autumn's treasure,
      Since I know no earthly joy?
   Long I've lost all youthful pleasure,
      Time must youth and health destroy.
   Pleasures once I fondly courted,
      Shared each bliss that health bestows,
   But to see where then I sported,
      Now embitters all my woes.

5. Age and sorrow since have blasted
      Ev'ry youthful, pleasing dream;
   Quiv'ring age with youth contrasted,
      O, how short their glories seem!

    As the annual frosts are cropping
        Leaves and tendrils from the trees,
    So my friends are yearly dropping,
        Through old age and dire disease.

6. Former friends, O, how I've sought them!
        Just to cheer my drooping mind;
    But they're gone like leaves in autumn,
        Driv'n before a dreary wind.
    Spring and summer, fall and winter,
        Each in swift succession roll,
    So my friends in death do enter,
        Bringing sadness to my soul.

7. Death has laid them down to slumber;
        Solemn thought to think that I
    Soon must be one of that number!
        Soon—ah, soon with them to lie!
    When a few more years are wasted,
        When a few more scenes are o'er,
    When a few more griefs are tasted,
        I shall fall to rise no more.

8. Fast my sun of life declining,
        Soon will set in endless night:
    But my hope, pure and refining,
        Rests in future life and light.
    Cease this fearing, trembling, sighing,
        Death will break the sudden gloom;
    Soon my spirit, flutt'ring, flying,
        Must be borne beyond the tomb.

Even more deeply embedded in oral tradition are camp-meeting songs that appear in the Primitive Baptist repertory. Congregations use them with even greater liberty than tunes like "Holy Manna." Typically these nineteenth-century songs, many of them recorded in shape-note tunebooks of the period, have either choruses added to well-known hymn stanzas or refrains inserted between the lines of a hymn stanza. In most cases, such additions do not appear in the *Primitive Baptist Hymn Book* and congregations sing them spontaneously. However, when Mountain Association congregations add choruses to the hymns they sing, they do not alter their solemn style of singing nor do they consistently alternate stanzas with the chorus. In one service, for example, we heard the chorus, "And I'll sing hallelujah," only

Fig. 41. The tune "Hallelujah" (second staff) from William Walker's *The Southern Harmony*, 1854, 107.

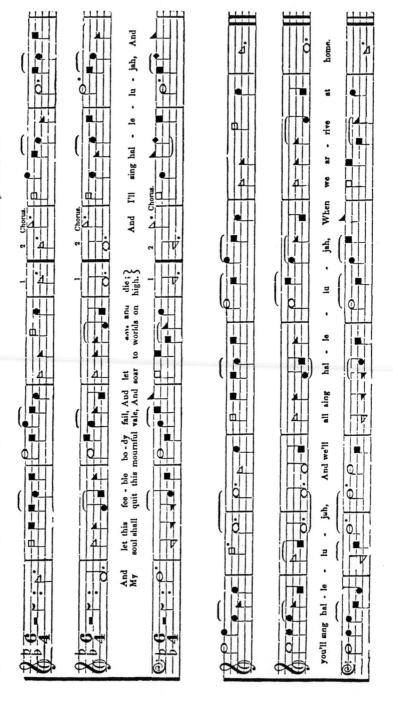

after the congregation had sung all four verses of the hymn, "In all my Lord's appointed ways." The congregation sang this "chorus" with the same slow tempo and deliberate manner that had characterized its singing of the hymn. A casual listener probably would not have noticed the presence of a chorus because it sounded like another stanza, even though its repetitive text reflected a clearly different source and its tune was completely different from that of the hymn to which it was attached.

Fig. 42. "In all my Lord's appointed ways" (John Ryland, Goble no. 256) with the tune "Hallelujah" as sung by the congregation of Little River Primitive Baptist Church, 19 June 1982, Sparta, North Carolina (WI-030).

1. In all my Lord's appointed ways,
   My journey I'll pursue;
   Hinder me not, ye much-loved saints,
   For I must go with you.

2. Through floods and flames, if Jesus lead,
   I'll follow where he goes;

Hinder me not, shall be my cry,
    Though earth and hell oppose.

3. Through duty, and through trials, too,
    I'll go at his command;
   Hinder me not, for I am bound
    To my Emmanuel's land.

4. And when my Savior calls me home,
    Still this my cry shall be:
   Hinder me not; come, welcome, death,
    I'll gladly go with thee.

CHORUS:
    And I'll sing hallelujah,
    And you'll sing hallelujah,
    And we'll all sing hallelujah,
    When we arrive at home.

Often, choruses such as "And I'll sing hallelujah" have contrasting tunes that help distinguish them from the hymn stanzas, but not always. The Goble hymnbook prints one song, "O beautiful hills of Galilee," with a chorus of "We're traveling home," for which congregations employ another camp-meeting practice of singing the same tune for both stanza and chorus. This tune, like the repetitive use of it for both verse and chorus, draws on the oral tradition of camp-meeting songs.[7]

Fig. 43. "O beautiful hills of Galilee" (T. B. Ausmus, Goble no. 281) with a variant of the tune "Pisgah" as sung by the congregation of Antioch Primitive Baptist Church, 27 June 1982, Stratford, North Carolina (WI-048).

1. O beautiful hills of Galilee!
    Amid whose scenes the Savior dwells,
  Your flow'rs that bloom so beautifully,
    Of heaven's lasting beauties tell.

CHORUS:
    We're traveling home, we're traveling home,
      One by one we're traveling home;
    Across death's river our friends are gone,
      And we are following, one by one.

2. "Then, O poor soul, if you would be
    Thus clothed in robes as pure as they,
  Lay all else down, come, follow me;
    My love shall last through endless day."

CHORUS

3. My soul replies, "'Tis not for me,"
    With tears fast streaming from mine eyes;
  That voice still calls, "Come, follow me,
    We're going home beyond the skies.

CHORUS

4. "I come your maladies to heal,
    I left my Father's home on high;
   His wondrous love I thus reveal,
    And thus are trembling souls brought nigh.

CHORUS

5. "I go away—I'll come again,
    My Holy Spirit hov'ring round,
   To show that for you I was slain,
    And guard you till the trump shall sound."

CHORUS

Primitive Baptist congregations have also absorbed into their performance style a gospel song that appears in Goble's *Primitive Baptist Hymn Book*. Gospel songs, unlike hymns, have evolved mostly since the Civil War and are more likely to be cast in the form of testimony, exhortation, or narrative than in the form of praise, prayer, and thanksgiving. Gospel songs typically have a chorus that repeats between stanzas and an easy-to-harmonize tune in the major mode. By 1887, when the *Primitive Baptist Hymn Book* was published, evangelicals had incorporated gospel songs into their worship. Goble adopted this form for "Dear Redeemer, keep me free" (fig. 44). It is the last text in his hymnbook and the only one that he himself wrote. In writing a gospel song rather than a hymn, Goble revealed his own readiness—and correctly predicted that of other Primitive Baptists—to absorb another new song type into the old tradition.

Fig. 44. "Dear Redeemer, keep me free" (D. H. Goble, Goble no. 321) as sung by the congregation of Cross Roads Primitive Baptist Church, 23 June 1983, Baywood, Virginia (WI-137).

hour, By thy Spir - it's, Spir - it's heal - ing power.
Cho.
Sav - ior, hear, draw me near, Keep me
in thy ten - der care, Safe from ev - ery chill - ing
blast, Then I'll rest in, rest in thee at last.

1. Dear Redeemer, keep me free,
   Precious Jesus, Jesus, free in thee,
   From all evil every hour,
   By thy Spirit's, Spirit's healing power.

CHORUS:

   Savior, hear, draw me near,
   Keep me in thy tender care,
   Safe from every chilling blast,
   Then I'll rest in, rest in thee at last.

2. O, the comfort and the joy,
   Of thy presence, presence, nor alloy!
   Then to thee how sweet to sing!
   Dearly blessed, blessed Lord and King.

CHORUS

3. Yea, with contrite heart each day
   Sing thy praise in, praise in richest lay;
   And when life on earth is done,
   May I dwell with, dwell with thee at home.

CHORUS

4. There to join th' angelic throng,
   And the blood-washed, blood-washed saints in song,
   And in richest diadem,
   Singing, "Glory, glory and Amen";

CHORUS

5. "Glory to the great I AM,
   Highest honor, honor to the Lamb;
   Halleluia and amen,
   Praises, glory, glory, yea, amen."

CHORUS

Congregations in the Mountain Association request this song often and know it well. The tune is not available in any of their hymn-and-tune books, but it is similar in style to many that are. The singers adapt the tune to their own rhythmic style with shortened phrase endings that produce alternating measures of three and four beats. Their improvised harmony—parallel to the melody at an interval of a sixth most of the time, with occasional thirds or fifths—conforms to regional patterns.

Other hymn tunes that congregations continue to sing in their regular worship services seem to have no obvious source or parallel in the tunebook traditions. They often have phrases or motifs in common with one or more published tunes, but they have assumed lives of their own and remain distinctive in the minds of the singers. The presence of such songs in the repertory is strong evidence of the vitality of oral tradition in these churches (figs. 45–49).

Fig. 45. "I love thee, my Savior" (Goble no. 315) as sung by Elder Walter Evans, 18 November 1980, Sparta, North Carolina. Recorded by Tom Davenport (WI-026).

1. I love thee, my Savior, I love thee, my Lord,
   I love thy dear people, thy ways and thy word;
   With tender emotion I love sinners too,
   Since Jesus has died to redeem them from woe.

2. Thy Spirit first taught me to know I was blind,
   Then taught me the way of salvation to find;
   And when I was sinking in gloomy despair,
   Thy mercy relieved me, and bid me not fear.

3. My Jesus is precious—I can not forbear,
   Though sinners despise me, his love to declare;
   His love overwhelms me, had I wings I'd fly,
   To praise him in mansions prepared in the sky.

Fig. 46. "Come, my heart, and let us try" (Joseph Hart ["Come my soul"], Goble no. 173) as sung by the congregation of Union Primitive Baptist Church, 5 June 1982, Whitehead, North Carolina (WI-008).

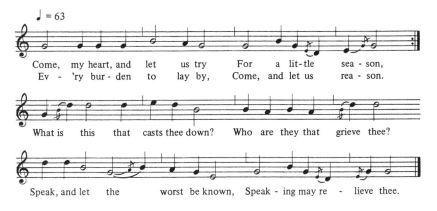

1. Come, my heart, and let us try
     For a little season,
   Ev'ry burden to lay by,
     Come, and let us reason.
   What is this that casts thee down?
     Who are they that grieve thee?
   Speak, and let the worst be known,
     Speaking may relieve thee.

2. Christ by faith at times I see,
     And he doth relieve me;
   But my fears return again,

Those are they that grieve me;
Troubles like the raging seas,
Feeble, faint, and fearful,
Plagued with such a sore disease,
How can I be cheerful?

3. Think on what your Savior bore
   In the gloomy garden,
Sweating blood from ev'ry pore
   To procure thy pardon.
View him hanging on the tree,
   Bleeding, groaning, dying;
See, he suffers this for thee,
   Therefore, cease from crying.

4. Joseph took his body down,
   Wrapped it in linen,
Laid it in the silent tomb,
   And returned mourning.
Soon he rises from the tomb,
   Angels fly from glory:
See how glory shines around;
   He has gone before you.

5. Brethren, don't you feel the flame?
   Mourners, come, behold him!
Let us join to praise his name,
   Let us never grieve him.
Soon we'll join to sing above,
   Soon we'll be in heaven;
There we'll swim in seas of love,
   And forever praise him.

Fig. 47. "Poor and afflicted, Lord, are thine" (Thomas Kelly, Goble no. 257) as sung by the congregation of Antioch Primitive Baptist Church, 23 July 1983, Stratford, North Carolina (WI-156).

But though the world may think it strange,

They would not with the world ex - change.

1. Poor and afflicted, Lord, are thine;
   Among the great unfit to shine;
   But though the world may think it strange,
   They would not with the world exchange.

2. Poor and afflicted, yet they trust
   In God, the gracious, wise, and just;
   For them he deigns this lot to choose,
   Nor would they dare his will refuse.

3. Poor and afflicted, oft they are
   Sorely oppressed with want and care;
   Yet he who saves them by his blood,
   Makes every sorrow yield them good.

4. Poor and afflicted—yet they sing,
   For Christ, their glorious, conq'ring King,
   Through suff'rings perfect, reigns on high,
   And does their every need supply.

5. Poor and afflicted—yet ere long,
   They'll join the bright celestial throng,
   And all their suff'rings then shall close,
   And heav'n afford them sweet repose.

6. Poor and afflicted, filled with grief—
   O Lord, afford us kind relief,
   To cheer the heart that heaves a sigh,
   And wipe the tears from every eye.

Fig. 48. "My gracious Redeemer I love" (Benjamin Francis, Goble no. 226) as sung by the congregation of Little River Primitive Baptist Church, 19 June 1983, Sparta, North Carolina (WI-128).

♩ = 66

My gra - cious Re - deem - er I love,

His prais - es a - loud I'll pro - claim,

And join with the ar - mies a - bove,

To shout his a - dor - a - ble name:

To gaze on his glo - ries di - vine

Shall be my e - ter - nal em - ploy,

And feel them in - ces - sant - ly shine,

My bound - less, in - ef - fa - ble joy.

1. My gracious Redeemer I love,
   His praises aloud I'll proclaim,
   And join with the armies above,
   To shout his adorable name:
   To gaze on his glories divine
   Shall be my eternal employ,
   And feel them incessantly shine,
   My boundless, ineffable joy.

2. He freely redeemed with his blood
   My soul from the confines of hell,
   To live on the smiles of my God,
   And in his sweet presence to dwell;
   To shine with the angels of light,
   With saints and with seraphs to sing;
   To view with eternal delight
   My Jesus, my Savior, my King.

3. O when shall my spirit exchange
    This cell of corruptible clay
For mansions celestial, and range
    Through realms of ineffable day?
Oh, when wilt thou bid me ascend,
    To join in thy praises above,
To gaze on thee, world without end,
    And feast on thy ravishing love?

4. Nor sorrow, nor sickness, nor pain,
    Nor sin, nor temptation, nor fear,
Shall ever molest me again—
    Perfection of glory reigns there—
This soul and this body shall shine
    In robes of salvation and praise,
And banquet on pleasures divine,
    Where God his full beauty displays.

Fig. 49. "Thou, dear Redeemer, dying Lamb" (John Cennick, Goble no. 111) as sung by the congregation of Union Primitive Baptist Church, 6 June 1982, Whitehead, North Carolina (WI-009).

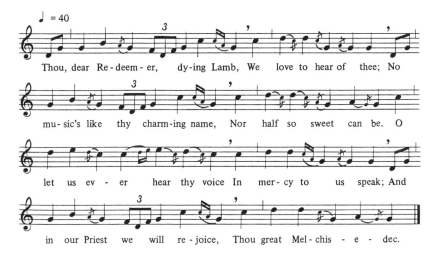

1. Thou, dear Redeemer, dying Lamb,
    We love to hear of thee;
No music's like thy charming name,
    Nor half so sweet can be.

2. O let us ever hear thy voice
    In mercy to us speak;
    And in our Priest we will rejoice,
    Thou great Melchisedec.

3. Our Jesus shall be still our theme,
    While in this world we stay;
    We'll sing our Jesus' lovely name
    When all things else decay.

4. When we appear in yonder cloud,
    With all thy favored throng,
    Then we will sing more sweet, more loud,
    And Christ shall be our song.

   This overview of the hymn tune repertory shows that despite the diversity of historical contexts and musical traditions represented in the songs, what one hears in the actual singing is a single style. The manner of singing produces a sound that both Primitive Baptists and their observers hear as homogeneous. How are congregations achieving this stylistic consistency? It comes partly from oral practices already discussed, such as melodic graces that add both rhythmic and melodic interest to a tune. These, of course, are an essential part of Appalachian traditional singing. Even the occasional nonstandard harmonizations reflect regional preferences. Other rhythmic irregularities seem to arise naturally in singing a text unaccompanied by instruments and detached from any associations with dance. These characteristics have all developed within a long tradition of hymnody that prefers slow tempos and unaccompanied, mostly unharmonized singing. However, the stylistic homogeneity also results from a range of tune choices made within the congregation. The best way to see this is to look closely at how singers themselves select and shape tunes in their religious song repertory. This exploration will lead to an interpretation of the importance of orality in their practice of singing.

   One aesthetic opportunity offered Primitive Baptists when they sing from Goble's *Primitive Baptist Hymn Book* is the chance to select tunes for the texts they sing. Goble followed a long-standing practice—and the lead of his immediate predecessors in hymnbook compiling, Elders Wilson Thompson, Gilbert Beebe, and Benjamin Lloyd—in simply indicating the poetic meters of each text as a guide to choosing tunes. The most common of these are common meter ("C. M."), short meter ("S. M."), and long meter ("L. M."). Song leaders know, for example, that a common-meter text has stanzas of four lines with eight syllables in the first and third lines and six syllables in the second and fourth lines, as follows:

> A-maz-ing grace, how sweet the sound [8 syllables]
> That saved a wretch like me, [6 syllables]
> I once was lost, but now am found, [8 syllables]
> Was blind, but now I see. [6 syllables]

This pattern, 8.6.8.6., is indicated by "C. M." at the beginning of the text. Song leaders are aware that, generally speaking, any tune that fits one common-meter text will fit all common-meter texts. Knowing the meters of the texts and knowing a few tunes that fit those meters, they can choose a tune for any of the hymns in the book.

Some tune-and-text combinations, however, appear to be fixed by custom. For about half of the hymns we recorded, song leaders paired the same tune and text each time we heard the hymn. One combination remained consistent even though the tune we heard was not in the tunebooks published by Primitive Baptists. Congregations sang that hymn, "How lost was my condition" (fig. 50), with the same tune on all six occasions we recorded it: five services in three different churches and a song session in a private home. The tune is similar to "Balm in Gilead," which Jackson found paired with "How lost was my condition" in an 1868 publication.[8]

Fig. 50. "How lost was my condition" (John Newton, Goble no. 224) with a tune related to "Balm in Gilead" as sung by the congregation of Cross Roads Primitive Baptist Church, 20 June 1983, Baywood, Virginia (WI-131).

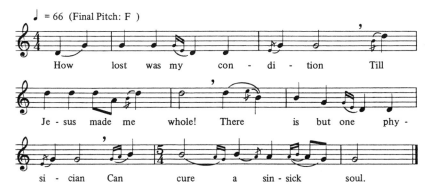

1. How lost was my condition
Till Jesus made me whole!
There is but one physician
Can cure a sin-sick soul.

> Next door to death he found me,
>   And snatched me from the grave,
> To tell to all around me
>   His wond'rous pow'r to save.

2. The worst of all diseases
     Is light compared with sin;
   On ev'ry part it seizes,
     But rages most within:
   'Tis palsy, plague, and fever,
     And madness—all combined;
   And none, but a believer,
     The least relief can find.

3. From men, great skill professing,
     I sought a cure to gain;
   But this proved more distressing,
     And added to my pain:
   Some said that nothing ailed me,
     Some gave me up for lost;
   Thus ev'ry refuge failed me,
     And all my hopes were crossed.

4. At length this great Physician,
     How matchless is his grace!
   Accepted my petition,
     And undertook my case:
   First, gave me sight to view him,
     For sin my eyes had sealed—
   Then bid me look unto him;
     I looked, and I was healed.

5. A dying, risen Jesus,
     Seen by the eye of faith,
   At once from danger frees us,
     And saves the soul from death:
   Come, then, to this Physician,
     His help he'll freely give,
   He makes no hard condition—
     To Jesus look and live!

In other cases, congregations or their song leaders varied their choices, singing almost half of the tunes we heard with more than one text. Not surprisingly, they used a favorite, "New Britain," as the setting for six different texts—all in common meter. In addition to its familiar pairing with "Amazing grace how sweet the sound," they used it with "Love is the sweetest bud that blows," "Let death dissolve my body now," "Not to control the church of God," "God moves in a mysterious way," and "Ye pilgrims that are wandering home."

However, "New Britain" (see fig. 1) was only one of three different tunes they used for these same hymns. The alternate tunes are not in the published hymn-tune repertory, but they are related to traditional lyric songs known in the region. The first of these is very similar to "In the Pines," which the collectors Cecil Sharp and Leonard Roberts both transcribed from singers in Kentucky.[9] The two phrases of the tune they collected generally correspond to the first and last phrases of a hymn tune sung by a North Carolina Primitive Baptist congregation (fig. 51). The same church sang a third tune for "Amazing Grace" at the close of its annual communion service. Using a camp-meeting–style verse-and-chorus structure for the text, the congregation repeated the same four-line tune for each stanza of the hymn and also for each repetition of the added chorus (fig. 52):

> I want to live a Christian here,
> I want to die rejoicing,
> I want to feel my savior's near,
> When soul and body's parting.[10]

Fig. 51. "Amazing grace how sweet the sound" (John Newton, Goble no. 175) with a tune related to "In the Pines" as sung by the congregation of Little River Primitive Baptist Church, ca. 1960, Sparta, North Carolina. Recorded by Elder Lasserre Bradley, *Old Hymns Lined and Led by Elder Walter Evans,* Sovereign Grace 6057–6058.

A - maz - ing grace, how sweet the sound!

That saved a wretch like me!

I once was lost, but now am found,

Was blind but now I see.

Fig. 52. "Amazing grace how sweet the sound" (John Newton, Goble no. 175) with the tune "I want to live a Christian here" as sung by the congregation of Little River Primitive Baptist Church, 20 June 1982, Sparta, North Carolina (WI-031).

Some of the tune choices actually required adjusting melodies to accommodate shorter or longer lines of text. Common-meter texts were the most numerous in the hymn repertory we recorded, but Primitive Baptist congregations also sang texts written in at least twenty-five other metrical patterns. After common meter, the most typical patterns were long meter (L. M., or 8.8.8.8.), short meter (S. M., or 6.6.8.6.), 8s 7s (8.7.8.7.), and 11s (11.11.11.11.). While the metrical patterns guided song leaders in selecting tunes, they did not necessarily dictate that common-meter texts had to be limited to a particular group of tunes. Some song leaders had the skill and musical sensitivity to adapt a given tune to texts of different meters.

With some songs these adaptations may have been unintentional. For example, Goble described two separate texts as "8s6s" even though the actual syllable pattern of 8s and 6s was slightly different in each one. "A few more days on earth to spend" has stanzas of eight lines with a syllable pattern of 8.8.8.6.8.8.8.6. The other text, "How happy's every child of grace," also has stanzas of eight lines, but it has a syllable pattern of 8.6.8.6.8.6.8.6. Congregations easily sang both hymns with the same tune by making a small adjustment in the tune at the end of the second and sixth phrases (fig. 53).

Fig. 53. "A few more days on earth to spend" (Goble no. 223) and "How happy's every child of grace" (Charles Wesley, Goble no. 177) as sung by the congregations of (A) Peach Bottom Primitive Baptist Church, 9 July 1983, near

Independence, Virginia (WI-143), and (B) Antioch Primitive Baptist Church, 23 July 1983, Stratford, North Carolina (WI-156).

A.
1. A few more days on earth to spend,
And all my toils and cares shall end,
And I shall see my God and Friend,
   And praise his name on high:
Nor more to sigh or shed a tear,
No more to suffer pain or fear,
But God, and Christ, and heav'n appear
   Unto the raptured eye.

2. Then, O my soul, despond no more,
   The storm of life will soon be o'er,
   And I shall find the peaceful shore
       Of everlasting rest.
   O happy day! O joyful hour!
   When freed from earth my soul shall tow'r
   Beyond the reach of Satan's pow'r,
       To be forever blest.

3. My soul anticipates the day;
   I'll joyfully the call obey
   Which comes to summon me away
       To seats prepared above:
   There I shall see my Savior's face,
   And dwell in his beloved embrace,
   And taste the fullness of his grace,
       And sing redeeming love.

b. ♩ = 60

How hap - py's ev - 'ry child of grace

Who feels his sins for - giv'n;

This world, he cries, is not my place,

I seek a place in heav'n;

A coun - try far from mor - tal sight,

Yet O by faith I see,

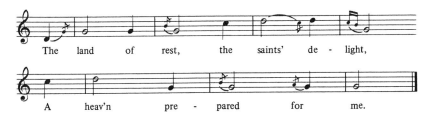

The land of rest, the saints' de - light,

A heav'n pre - pared for me.

B.

1. How happy's ev'ry child of grace
   Who feels his sins forgiv'n;
   This world, he cries, is not my place,
   I seek a place in heav'n;
   A country far from mortal sight,
   Yet O by faith I see,
   The land of rest, the saints' delight,
   A heav'n prepared for me.

2. A stranger in this world below
   I calmly sojourn here,
   Nor can its happiness or woe
   Provoke my love or fear;
   Its evils in a moment end,
   Its joys as soon are passed;
   But O, the bliss to which I tend,
   Eternally shall last!

3. What is there here to court my stay
   And keep me back from home,
   When angels beckon me away,
   And Jesus bids me come?
   Shall I regret to leave my friends
   Here in this world confined?
   To God himself my soul ascends;
   Farewell to all behind.

4. O what a blessed hope is ours
   While here on earth we stay,
   We more than taste the heav'nly pow'rs
   And antedate that day;
   We feel the resurrection near,
   Our life in Christ concealed,

And with his glorious presence here
Our earthen vessel's filled.

5. O would he more of heav'n bestow,
    And let this vessel break,
    And let my ransomed spirit go
    To see the God I seek;
    In rapt'rous love on him to gaze
    Who gives that sight to me,
    And shout and wonder at his grace
    In vast eternity.

Some tune changes were more clearly deliberate when song leaders used the same tune for hymns that had different meters. One elder asserted, in fact, that the short meter (6.6.8.6.) and common meter (8.6.8.6.) were "all the same," and he demonstrated that he could sing the same tune first with a short-meter text (fig. 54) and then with a common-meter text (fig. 55). To accommodate the longer first line of the common-meter text, he simply added two beats to the end of the line by repeating the last note of the melody.

Fig. 54. "I would, but can not sing" (John Newton, Goble no. 159) as sung by Elder Eddie Lyle, 24 July 1982, West Jefferson, North Carolina (WI-100).

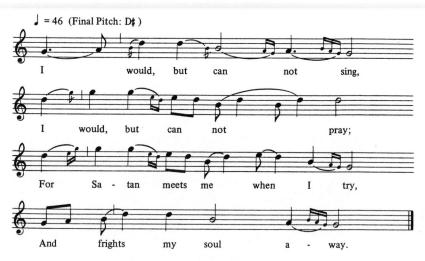

1. I would, but can not sing,
    I would, but can not pray;
    For Satan meets me when I try,
    And frights my soul away.

2. I would, but can't repent,
    Though I endeavor oft;
  This stony heart can ne'er relent
    Till Jesus makes it soft.

3. I would, but can not love,
    Though loved by love divine;
  No arguments have pow'r to move
    A soul so base as mine.

4. I would, but can not rest
    In God's most holy will;
  I know what he appoints is best,
    Yet murmur at it still.

5. O could I but believe!
    Then all would easy be;
  I would, but can not—Lord, relieve,
    My help must come from thee!

6. But if indeed I would,
    Though I can nothing do,
  Yet the desire is something good,
    For which my praise is due.

7. By nature prone to ill,
    Till thine appointed hour
  I was as destitute of will
    As now I am of pow'r.

8. Wilt thou not crown at length
    The work thou hast begun?
  And with the will afford me strength
    In all thy ways to run?

Fig. 55. "Time like a fleeting shadow flies" (Elder Wilson Thompson, Goble no. 190) as sung by Elder Eddie Lyle, 24 July 1982, West Jefferson, North Carolina (WI-100).

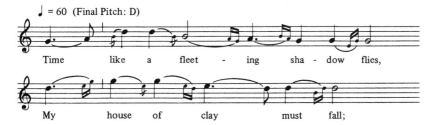

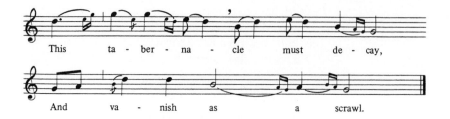

This ta - ber - na - cle must de - cay,

And va - nish as a scrawl.

1. Time like a fleeting shadow flies,
   My house of clay must fall;
   This tabernacle must decay,
   And vanish as a scrawl.

2. My youth and age, my months and years
   Like grass and flow'rs, decay;
   Before the mower's scythe of death
   They soon will pass away.

3. But far beyond death's gloomy vale
   A heav'nly building stands;
   Prolific streams of glory flow
   In those celestial lands.

4. To that bright world, that house above,
   My longing spirit soars,
   Where God, my heav'nly Father, lives,
   And ev'ry saint adores.

5. Then let this earthly mansion fall
   And set my spirit free;
   Why should I wish to stay below,
   And stay so long from thee?

6. I'm but a pilgrim far from home,
   While here on earth I stay;
   My brightest moments are but night,
   Compared with endless day.

7. Then let me wait, and live by faith,
   Till I am called away;
   And to that brighter world ascend,
   That house which can't decay.

8. Let all my fleeting moments pass;
   Earth's painted toys may fade:

> O, Jesus, my eternal life,
>   Support me through the shade.
>
> 9. Then to that world of light and love,
>   Immortal and divine,
>   Bring this poor pilgrim from the tomb,
>   This trembling soul of mine.

Musically gifted song leaders are not alone in making subtle adjustments in remembered melodies. Whole congregations with ease follow the lead singer's variations. How can we explain their skill? The tune itself—a ballad-related tune—offers one clue. It has secular parallels in ballads collected in Kentucky and Virginia by Cecil Sharp in 1917 and 1918. And ballad singing, one of the dominant older song traditions in the southern mountains, requires a comparable flexibility in adapting tune and text. Ballad texts, unlike hymn texts, do not conform to uniform patterns in which all stanzas have a fixed number of syllables and accents in each line. Instead, ballad texts exhibit a form of accentual verse in which the lines may contain varying numbers of syllables while only the pulse, or pattern of musical beats, remains stable from verse to verse. Ballad singers, then, have to be flexible enough to fit, from stanza to stanza, varying amounts of text into the tunes. They do this not just from one song to the next, but from one verse to the next within the same song. At the same time, they have to maintain the same pattern of beats in the musical phrase.[11]

Adapting a tune to different ballad texts is not necessarily like adapting a tune to hymn texts of different meters. The hymn singer, of course, was actually shortening or lengthening the tune by two beats to accommodate the different meters of his texts, whereas the ballad singers were incorporating more or less text into the tune without changing the number of beats. Nevertheless, both adaptations, however effortless the singing sounds, are testimonies to musical skill and to a structural grasp of melodies that allows for almost endless variation.

Hymn singers sometimes adapt tune to text by simply changing the ratio of notes per syllable. On two different occasions the same congregation sang the tune "Idumea" (see fig. 70), once for a hymn with the metrical pattern 8.8.11.8, and once as the setting for a short-meter (6.6.8.6.) hymn. The following comparison of the third lines of each hymn shows that although there was no change in the tune, an increase (or decrease) in wordiness affected how much of the tune was given to each syllable:

Fig. 56a and b. Congregations can adapt a tune to texts of different lengths—without changing the tune—by varying the number of notes sung per syllable of text.

Over time, one might expect to see melodies differentiating even more as singers adapt them to texts of different stanza forms. Several groups of songs in this repertory suggest such a possibility. One group of three hymn tunes, for example, bore some resemblance to a large set of tunes that the ballad scholar Bertrand Bronson associated with the ballad "Wife of Usher's Well," calling the group "one of the most memorably beautiful of all our melodic 'Gestalten.'"[12] The first of the related Primitive Baptist tunes opens with a melodic phrase similar to that of the ballad, as congregations sing "A home in heaven! what a joyful thought" (fig. 57). Although the hymn tune draws from the same stock of melodic phrases as the ballad tune, the phrases of the hymn tune are sequenced differently. For example, the phrase pattern for this tune as a hymn is usually AABA, while the tune as a ballad setting is more typically ABBA.

Fig. 57. "A home in heav'n! what a joyful thought" (William Hunter, Goble no. 277) as sung by the congregation of Cross Roads Primitive Baptist Church, 24 June 1983, Baywood, Virginia (WI-138).

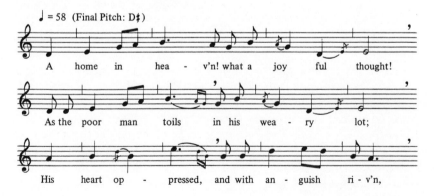

From his home be - low   to a   home   in   hea - v'n.

1. A home in heav'n! what a joyful thought!
   As the poor man toils in his weary lot;
   His heart oppressed, and with anguish riv'n,
   From his home below to a home in heav'n.

2. A home in heav'n! as the suff'rer lies
   On his bed of pain, and uplifts his eyes
   To that bright home what a joy is giv'n,
   With the blessed thought of a home in heav'n.

3. A home in heav'n! when our pleasures fade,
   And our wealth and fame in the dust are laid,
   And our strength decays, and our health is riv'n,
   We are happy still with our home in heav'n.

4. A home in heav'n! when the sinner mourns,
   And with contrite heart to the Savior turns;
   O then what bliss in that heart forgiv'n,
   Does the hope inspire of a home in heav'n!

5. A home in heav'n! when our friends are fled
   To the cheerless home of the mould'ring dead;
   We wait in hope of the promise giv'n,
   We will meet again in our home in heav'n.

Congregations sing the second and third ballad-related hymn tunes of this group to "Come, thou long-expected Jesus" and "Mixtures of joy and sorrow I daily do pass through" (figs. 58, 59). To an outsider, both tunes sound reminiscent of "Wayfaring Stranger." To the singers, however, they are two separate and unrelated tunes. Although both texts appear in several Primitive Baptist hymn-and-tune books, these tunes do not.

Fig. 58. "Come, thou long-expected Jesus" (Charles Wesley, Goble no. 304) as sung by the congregation of Woodruff Primitive Baptist Church, 10 July 1983, Glade Valley, North Carolina (WI-145).

♩ = 54

Come, thou   long - ex - pect - ed   Je - sus!

Born to set thy peo-ple free;

From our fears and sins re-lease us,

Let us find our rest in thee:

Is-rael's strength and con-so-la-tion,

Hope of all the saints thou art;

Dear De-sire of ev-ery na-tion—

Joy of ev-ery long-ing heart.

1. Come, thou long-expected Jesus!
   Born to set thy people free;
   From our fears and sins release us,
   Let us find our rest in thee:
   Israel's strength and consolation,
   Hope of all the saints thou art;
   Dear Desire of every nation—
   Joy of every longing heart.

2. Born, thy people to deliver;
   Born a child, and yet a king;
   Born to reign in us forever;
   Now thy gracious kingdom bring:
   By thy own eternal Spirit,
   Rule in all our hearts alone;

By thy all-sufficient merit,
Raise us to thy glorious throne.

Fig. 59. "Mixtures of joy and sorrow" (author unidentified, Goble no. 225) as sung by the congregation of Union Primitive Baptist Church, 3 July 1982, Whitehead, North Carolina (WI-045).

1. Mixtures of joy and sorrow I daily do pass through,
   Sometimes I'm in the valley—then sinking down with woe;
   Sometimes I am exalted—on eagles' wings I fly;
   Rising above Mount Pisgah, I almost reach the sky.

2. Sometimes my hope is little—I almost lay it by;
   Sometimes it is sufficient if I were called to die;
   Sometimes I am in doubting, and think I have no grace;
   Sometimes I am a shouting, and Bethel is the place.

3. Sometimes I shun the Christian, for fear he'll talk to me;
   Sometimes he is the neighbor I long the most to see;
   Sometimes we meet together—in seasons dry and dull;
   Sometimes I find a blessing of joy that fills my soul.

4. Sometimes I read my Bible—it seems a sealed book;
   Sometimes I find a blessing wherever I do look.
   Sometimes I go to meeting, and wish I'd staid [sic] at home;
   Sometimes I find my Jesus, and then I'm glad I come.

5. O how I am thus tossed—thus tossed to and fro;
   How are my hopes thus crossed wherever I do go!
   O Lord, thou never changes—it is because I stray;
   Lord, guide me by thy Spirit, and keep me in the way.

A logical result of long experience with tune adaptations is that melodic motifs and phrases become separate and distinct in the memory, where they can be recalled and sequenced in new ways. Grasping a new use for these melodic units can be a powerful and spontaneous experience that enables Primitive Baptist singers to see and understand themselves as creators, even when the tunes they create are based in the stock of traditional melodic phrases that are familiar to the whole community. Elder Evans told us about a tune that came to him while he was out in the field working. He went to the house and looked through Goble's hymnbook, he said, "and turned . . . two-hundred-eighty-nine pages before I came to [hymn] 290, and this fit my tune." The text he found was "Love divine, all love excelling," and Elder Evans said that now they sing that tune "all around over this country without knowing where it came from," but it was his tune.

Fig. 60. "Love divine, all love excelling" (Charles Wesley, Goble no. 290) with Elder Evans's tune as sung by the congregation of Cross Roads Primitive Baptist Church, 23 June 1982, Baywood, Virginia (WI-039).

heav'n to earth come down; Fix in us thy hum - ble
dwell - ing, And thy faith - ful mer - cies crown. Je - sus,
thou art all com - pass - ion, Pure, un -
bound - ed love thou art; Vis - it us with thy sal -
va - tion; En - ter ev - 'ry trem - bling heart.

1. Love divine, all love excelling,
   Joy of heav'n to earth come down;
   Fix us in thy humble dwelling,
   And thy faithful mercies crown.
   Jesus, thou art all compassion,
   Pure, unbounded love thou art;
   Visit us with thy salvation;
   Enter every trembling heart.

2. Breathe, O breathe thy loving Spirit
   Into every troubled breast!
   Let us all in thee inherit,
   Let us find that second rest.
   Take away our bent to sinning,
   Alpha and Omega be,
   End of faith, as its beginning,
   Set our hearts at liberty.

3. Come, almighty to deliver,
   Let us all thy life receive,
   Suddenly return, and never,
   Never more thy temples leave:
   Thee we would be always blessing,
   Serve thee as thy hosts above,

Pray, and praise thee without ceasing,
  Glory in thy perfect love.

4. Finish, then, thy new creation,
     Pure and spotless let us be;
   Let us see thy great salvation,
     Perfectly restored in thee:
   Changed from glory into glory,
     Till in heav'n we take our place,
   Till we cast our crowns before thee,
     Lost in wonder, love, and praise!

The next examples show that other tunes sung in the community employ melodic phrases similar to those that Elder Evans used. The congregation of an independent Primitive Baptist church nearby sang a shorter tune that began like Elder Evans's tune but ended differently (fig. 61). A third tune sung in these churches also has similar phrases (fig. 62). This latter tune had one phrase in common with Elder Evans's tune (the second line), and it had three phrases in common with the tune in figure 61.[13]

Fig. 61. "Jesus, while our hearts are bleeding" (Thomas Hastings, Goble no. 282) with a tune similar to that of figure 60, as sung by the congregation of Woodruff Primitive Baptist Church, 11 July 1982, Glade Valley, North Carolina (WI-071).

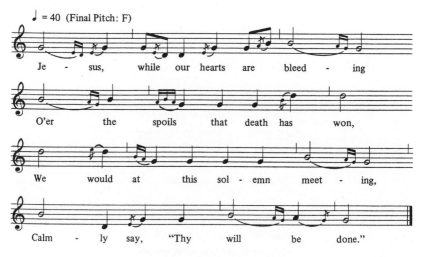

1. Jesus, while our hearts are bleeding
     O'er the spoils that death has won,

We would at this solemn meeting,
Calmly say, "Thy will be done."

2. Though cast down, we're not forsaken,
Though afflicted, not alone;
Thou didst give, and thou hast taken,
Blessed Lord, "thy will be done."

3. Fill us now with deep contrition,
Take away these hearts of stone,
And make all with true submission,
Meekly say, "Thy will be done."

4. Though today we're filled with mourning,
Mercy still is on the throne;
With thy smiles of love returning,
We can sing, "Thy will be done."

5. By thy hands the boon was given,
Thou hast taken but thine own;
Lord of earth and God of heaven,
Evermore "thy will be done."

Fig. 62. "When the day of life is brightest" (Maria [Mrs. S. W.] Straub, Goble no. 307) with a tune similar to those of figures 60 and 61, as sung by the congregation of Little River Primitive Baptist Church, 28 July 1983, Sparta, North Carolina (WI-162).

lead thou me.   And   the   steps of time beat

light - est,   O   my   Fa - ther, lead thou me.

1. When the day of life is brightest,
   Love the fondest, hope most free,
   And the steps of time beat lightest,
   O my Father, lead thou me.

CHORUS:

   O my Father, lead thou me;
   O my Father, lead thou me.
   [repeat last two lines of preceding stanza]

2. When the night of life is darkest,
   And my soul shall tempted be;
   When to sorrow's voice I listen,
   O my Father, lead thou me.

CHORUS

3. Be life's pathway smooth or stony,
   Let my faith still cling to thee;
   Be life's future bright or stormy,
   O my Father, lead thou me.

CHORUS

The full range of choices available to a song leader is not clear, but it is apparent that congregations can respond to a variety of subtle changes in singing. On one occasion, for example, a congregation sang "There is a land of pure delight" in harmony, with a definite tendency to render the tune in measured groups of three beats. A month later at the same church, the same song leader led the congregation in singing that same hymn and tune, but the harmony was absent, the tempo was slower, and the rhythm shifted toward duple meter with singers giving each syllable approximately the same amount of time and emphasis. Most likely, they were unconsciously—but quite musically—responding to cues in the song leader's voice (figs. 63, 64).

Fig. 63. "There is a land of pure delight" (Isaac Watts, Goble no. 148) as sung by the congregation of Little River Primitive Baptist Church, 20 June 1982, Sparta, North Carolina (WI-031).

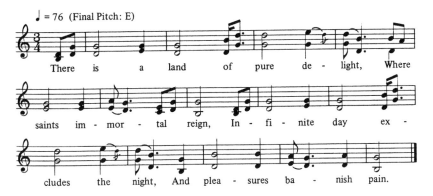

1. There is a land of pure delight,
       Where saints immortal reign,
   Infinite day excludes the night,
       And pleasures banish pain.

2. There everlasting spring abides,
       And never-with'ring flow'rs;
   Death, like a narrow sea, divides
       This heav'nly land from ours.

3. Sweet fields, beyond the swelling flood,
       Stand dressed in living green;
   So to the Jews old Canaan stood,
       While Jordan rolled between.

4. But tim'rous mortals start and shrink
       To cross this narrow sea;
   And linger, shiv'ring, on the brink,
       And fear to launch away.

5. O! could we make our doubts remove,
       Those gloomy doubts that rise,
   And see the Canaan that we love,
       With unbeclouded eyes;

6. Could we but climb where Moses stood,
       And view the landscape o'er;
   Not Jordan's stream, nor death's cold flood
       Should fright us from the shore.

Fig. 64. "There is a land of pure delight" (Isaac Watts, Goble no. 148) as sung by the congregation of Little River Primitive Baptist Church, 18 July 1982, Sparta, North Carolina (WI-089).

In addition to making choices about pairing different hymns and tunes, about making changes within those tunes, and even about constructing new tunes, congregations make aesthetic choices about what kinds of tunes they like to sing. One preference that distinguishes Primitive Baptists from mainline denominations is their acceptance and apparent enjoyment of hymn tunes many churches would reject as too short and repetitive. Even though these tunes consist entirely of one or two phrases in patterns of AA'AA' or ABAB repeated for each stanza, singers never communicated any sense of boredom as they sang. Occasionally, their singing even took on additional intensity from the frequent repetition.

Some of these short tunes are composed of phrases that appear in longer tunes. "Tarry with me, O, my Savior," for example, has only one melodic phrase that repeats in the form AA'AA' for each hymn stanza. This melody is embedded in the first half of a tune known as "The Babe of Bethlehem."[14]

Fig. 65. "Tarry with me, O, my Savior" (Caroline Louisa Sprague Smith, Goble no. 219) with tune related to "The Babe of Bethlehem" as sung by Elder Eddie Lyle, 24 July 1982, West Jefferson, North Carolina (WI-100).

| For | the | day | is | pass | - | ing | by; |
| And | the | night | is | draw | - | ing | nigh. |

1. Tarry with me, O, my Savior,
   For the day is passing by;
   See the shades of ev'ning gather,
   And the night is drawing nigh.

2. Many friends were gathered round me
   In the bright days of the past;
   But the grave has closed above them,
   And I linger here at last.

3. Deeper, deeper grow the shadows;
   Paler now the glowing west;
   Swift the night of death advances—
   Shall it be the night of rest?

4. Feeble, trembling, fainting, dying,
   Lord, I cast myself on thee;
   Tarry with me through the darkness
   While I sleep, still watch by me.

5. Tarry with me, O, my Savior!
   Lay my head upon thy breast
   Till the morning; then awake me—
   Morning of eternal rest!

Another short tune, used to sing "There is a stream whose current flows," corresponds with a phrase in "Preservation" by Elder John R. Daily. In 1918, Elder Daily published his tune with an AABA melodic form. However, in the singing we recorded, congregations invariably repeated only one tune phrase as the setting for an entire hymn (fig. 66).[15]

Fig. 66. "There is a stream whose current flows" (Vanmeter[?], Goble no. 296) with tune related to "Preservation" (Elder John R. Daily) as sung by the congregation of Antioch Primitive Baptist Church, 24 July 1982, Stratford, North Carolina (WI-222).

♩ = 42 (Final Pitch: E)

| There | is | a | stream | whose | cur | - | rent | flows |
| On | - | ward, | with | sor | - | rows, | pains, | and | woes, |

| As | cease - less | as | the | sun; |
| Its | trou - bled | wa - ters | run. |

1. There is a stream whose current flows
   As ceaseless as the sun;
   Onward, with sorrows, pains, and woes,
   Its troubled waters run.

2. Still onward, pressing to its source—
   The ocean, whence it came;
   Nor stayed by circumstance nor force,
   Is this resistless stream.

3. On its broad bosom as it glides,
   Are heedless mortals borne;
   And in the boundless ocean hides
   The friends for whom we mourn.

4. The high, the low, are swept away,
   The youth, in all his prime;
   The meek, the mournful, and the gay,
   By the great *Stream of Time!*

5. Eternity! unfathomed sea!
   Where all our hearts are drowned!
   As boundless as infinity!
   Thither the stream is bound.

6. Soon shall its current land us there,
   Soon shall our days be o'er;
   And the archangel shall declare,
   That *"Time shall be no more!"*

Several singers indicated that their current tune for the hymn "Guide me, O thou great Jehovah" has been distilled from a longer tune.[16] A Primitive Baptist elder remembered his grandfather singing the longer version and added that the churches in his area do not sing the long version any more (fig. 67).

Fig. 67. "Guide me, O thou great Jehovah" (William Williams, Goble no. 179) as sung by the congregation of Cross Roads Primitive Baptist Church, 18 July 1982, Baywood, Virginia (WI-087).

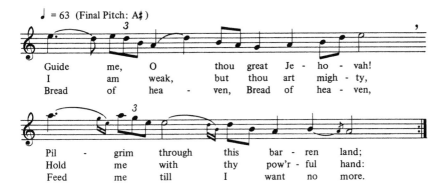

1. Guide me, O thou great Jehovah!
   Pilgrim through this barren land;
   I am weak, but thou art mighty,
   Hold me with thy pow'rful hand:
   Bread of heaven, [bread of heaven]
   Feed me till I want no more.

2. Open now the crystal fountain,
   Whence the healing streams do flow;
   Let the fiery, cloudy pillar,
   Lead me all my journey through:
   Strong Deliv'rer, [strong deliv'rer]
   Be thou still my strength and shield.

3. Feed me with the heav'nly manna,
   In this barren wilderness;
   Be my sword, and shield, and banner,
   Be my robe of righteousness;
   Fight and conquer, [fight and conquer]
   All my foes by sov'reign grace.

4. When I pass through death's dark shadow,
   Bid my anxious fears subside;
   Death of deaths, and hell's destruction,
   Land me safe on heaven's side:
   Songs of praises, [songs of praises]
   I will ever give to thee.

Scholars have been inclined to view such repetitive tunes as fragmentary and incomplete, but Primitive Baptists' deliberate use of these short tunes calls that interpretation into question. Two tunes of this type have been in publication since the mid-nineteenth century, and Primitive Baptists still sing both. William Bobo's tune "Long Sought Home" appeared with the text "Jerusalem, my long sought home" around 1835. Primitive Baptists now sing at least two hymns with that tune: "Jerusalem, my happy home" and "Before the day-star knew its place" (fig. 68). They sing at least three different hymns in the *Primitive Baptist Hymn Book* with the tune "To Die No More" (fig. 69).

Fig. 68. "Before the day-star knew its place" (Goble no. 241) with the tune "Long Sought Home" (William Bobo) as sung by the congregation of Little River Primitive Baptist Church, ca. 1960, Sparta, North Carolina. Recorded by Elder Lasserre Bradley. *Old Hymns Lined and Led by Elder Walter Evans,* Sovereign Grace 6444.

1. Before the day-star knew its place,
       Or planets went their round,
   The church in bonds of sov'reign grace,
       Was one with Jesus found.

2. In all that Jesus did on earth,
       His church an int'rest have;
   Go, trace him from his humble birth
       Down to the silent grave.

3. 'Twas for his saints he tasted death;
       All glory to his name!
   And when he yielded up his breath,
       With him his saints o'ercame.

4. With him his members on the tree
       Fulfilled the law's demands;
   'Tis "I in them, and they in me,"
       For thus the union stands.

5. Since Jesus slept among the dead,
       His saints have naught to fear;
   For with their gracious, suff'ring Head,
       His members sojourned there.

6. When from the tomb we see him rise,
       Triumphant o'er his foes.
   He bore his members to the skies,
       And with him they arose.

7. Ye saints, this union can't dissolve,
       By which all things are yours,
   Long as eternal years revolve,
       Or Deity endures.

Fig. 69. "Jesus, my all, to heav'n is gone" (John Cennick, Goble no. 41) with the tune "To Die No More" (Elder E. Dumas) as sung by the congregation of Union Primitive Baptist Church, 3 July 1983, Whitehead, North Carolina (WI-135).

He   whom I   fix   my   hopes up - on:
The   nar - row   way   till   him   I   view;

1. Jesus, my all, to heav'n is gone,
   He whom I fix my hopes upon:
   His track I see, and I'll pursue
   The narrow way till him I view;

2. The way the holy prophets went;
   The road that leads from banishment;
   The King's highway of holiness;
   I'll go; for all his paths are peace.

3. This is the way I long have sought,
   And mourned because I found it not;
   My grief and burden long have been,
   Because I could not cease from sin.

4. The more I strove against its power,
   I sinned and stumbled but the more;
   Till late I heard my Savior say,
   "Come hither, soul, I am the way."

5. Lo! glad I come, and thou blest Lamb
   Shalt take me to thee as I am;
   My sinful self to thee I give:
   Nothing but love shall I receive.

6. Then will I tell to sinners round
   What a dear Savior I have found;
   I'll point to thy redeeming blood,
   And say, "Behold the way to God."

One of the most distinctive choices singers can make with this repertory is a consciously aesthetic one. Some tunes are just more beautiful than others, according to Elder Cook. He compared three tunes his Virginia church used for "Hungry, and faint, and poor" (Goble no. 131), a text by John Newton that preachers frequently request before they take the stand to preach. The oldest tune Elder Cook remembered his home church's using for that hymn was "Idumea," a tune he sang as a child. Typical of his congregation, he sang slower and more elaborately than most other singers we recorded (fig. 70). Then he sang a second tune, "Ninety-third," the tune he said his congregation now uses for that text (fig. 71). Finally, he sang "Boylston" (fig. 72), calling that tune "the newest that it's been sung in." This tune was picked up, he explained, probably forty years ago in North Carolina. "Our people heard it, [and] some of them picked it up and brought it back home" (WI-106).

Fig. 70. "Hungry, and faint, and poor" (John Newton, Goble no. 131) with the tune "Idumea" as sung by Elder Billy Cook at his home near Chilhowie, Virginia, 29 July 1982 (WI-106).

1. Hungry, and faint, and poor,
   Behold us, Lord, again
   Assembled at thy mercy's door,
   Thy bounty to obtain.

2. Thy word invites us nigh,
   Or we must starve indeed;
   For we no money have to buy,
   No righteousness to plead.

3. The food our spirits want,
   Thy hand alone can give:
   O, hear the prayer of faith, and grant
   That we may eat and live.

As he sang the three tunes, Elder Cook was, at first, demonstrating some of the changes he had observed during his own lifetime in the tune preferences in his home church, but then he made clear that he found differences in the power of the tunes themselves to express a text and inspire the singers. The oldest tunes, "at least to me," he said, "inspire the wordings of the song, and the motive of it, more than the last that you heard" (WI-106).

Fig. 71. "Hungry, and faint, and poor" (John Newton, Goble no. 131) with the tune "Ninety-third" as sung by Elder Billy Cook at his home near Chilhowie, Virginia, 29 July 1982 (WI-106).

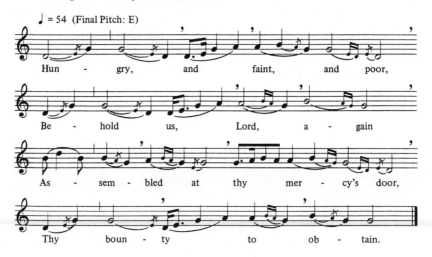

Fig. 72. "Hungry, and faint, and poor" (John Newton, Goble no. 131) with the tune "Boylston" as sung by Elder Billy Cook at his home near Chilhowie, Virginia, 29 July 1982 (WI-106).

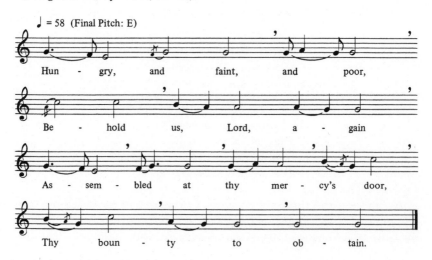

George Pullen Jackson would probably have agreed with Elder Cook's assessment of these tunes. In his own scholarly way, Jackson characterized "Ninety-third" as "an American folk-chorale of impressive native dignity" (1975 [1943]:156), and he noted that both "Idumea" and "Ninety-third" were widely copied by tunebook compilers in the South, implying that these tunes were rightfully valued and were widely and frequently sung. Of the six short-meter tunes we documented in the Primitive Baptist tune repertory, "Ninety-third" was the one we heard most often. It was used as the setting for eleven different texts on seventeen occasions consisting of interviews with two church elders and one or more meetings in seven different churches. "Idumea" was the setting for six texts in our ten recordings of it, three recordings made in interviews and the rest in meetings of four different churches. "Boylston," felt by Elder Cook to be the least inspiring, was used for only one or two texts.

Although Primitive Baptist congregations are not isolated from developments in religious song outside the denomination, as the previous discussion shows, the musical life of the church centers in its local congregations. Clearly, tunebooks and hymnals have played a role in the preservation of these older songs, but we can see also a continuing reliance on oral traditions when congregations sing all of their tunes by memory, when some of these tunes are not accessible except by memory, and when tunes are paired with hymn texts in greater variety than any of the hymnals reflect. We especially see orality at work in the countless variations that tunes exhibit.

The singing itself suggests that congregations exercise an unusual degree of control and creativity in their own singing—a musical practice all but forgotten in mainstream churches. There the printed order of worship offers a program of hymns selected in advance by the minister or choir director from hymnals that set every text to a harmonized tune. Musicians, often formally trained, use instruments to introduce, accompany, and thus control the singing. These musicians may not be members of the church or even long-time employees of the church. By contrast, in Primitive Baptist churches, song leaders—members well known to the church community—set pitches and indicate the tune with voices alone. They continue a long tradition of leading singing that requires making musical judgments about fitting tunes to a variety of texts and making aesthetic judgments about which tunes are best suited to the texts requested, and to the congregation.

The Primitive Baptists also demonstrate their musicality and independence through the tune repertory, which is marked by a cultural conservatism that parallels the church's doctrinal conservatism. El-

der Cook expressed the feeling of a number of members who preferred the most conservative elements of the tune repertory and rejected its more modern side. He is not alone in attributing to the older melodies an expressive power that exists apart from the words.
When these members lead the singing, they often choose the "old
lonesome tunes."

While their mainstream Protestant neighbors draw heavily on elitist
European and American church-tune traditions, these Primitive Baptist churches have held steadfastly to tunes that are more characteristic of traditions in American vernacular song, religious and secular. By comparison with mainstream churches, and even with other
sectarian American religions such as Pentecostals that have also em-
braced vernacularity, Primitive Baptists have always been conservative and resistant to change. They have been slow to adopt new music and even slower to adopt new singing styles. Their repertory, in
addition, shows very little ethnic diversity. It is drawn largely from
Anglo-American traditions with only traces of German and African-
American influences. But Primitive Baptists—unlike churches that
discard large parts of their repertories periodically in the scramble for
new hymnbooks and progressive ideas and practices—have retained
much of what they incorporated into their repertory over the years.

An exploration of the current tune repertory and the ways it is being used with Goble's *Primitive Baptist Hymn Book* enlarges our view
of the active conservatism and congregational control present in these
churches. How these singers match tunes and texts offers evidence
of the viability of this religious song tradition today and of the musical competence of its carriers. The absence of tunes in the *Primitive
Baptist Hymn Book* appears to have had advantages. Maintaining a
tune repertory largely by memory has encouraged creative uses of the
tunes without a simultaneous loss of stability in the repertory. It has
preserved a musical tradition that is in harmony with the doctrine
and practice of the church. Singers manipulate their tunes in ways
suggesting that, although the tune structures are firm, they are not
rigidly fixed. Whole tunes are adaptable to texts of varying lengths
and forms, and their component parts form a common stock of phrases or even smaller melodic motifs that singers can recombine in new
but familiar ways. Individual tunes may appear in different churches in various modal guises—sometimes sounding minor, sometimes
sounding major, and sometimes a mixture of the two—and not suffer a loss of recognition.

The absence of notation in the *Primitive Baptist Hymn Book* serves
some Primitive Baptists as a stimulus to the kind of heartfelt inter-

pretations they believe were characteristic of the generations before them. The satisfaction they find in singing from the *Primitive Baptist Hymn Book* has attracted singers who, in their choice and use of tunes, demonstrate that this older tradition of singing is not to be confused with singing that is static or outdated. Elder Cook expressed the feelings of one group of Primitive Baptists when he said of their old way of singing, "It takes God to bless the man to preach the gospel . . . and the same with the singing. . . . And you can tell it too, because there's a great movement in the melody, and the people that sings it. But it takes that spirit." He closed his statement with the declaration, "If we didn't get that feeling among the preaching and the singing among Old Baptists, I would be searching for the people who did sing that way" (WI-106).

6

The Influence of Notation and Gospel Songs

Now if you want to ruin a service for me, just go ahead and get the note book out and start singing by note, instead of this that you've already heard that's been passed down from generation to generation.

—Primitive Baptist elder, Virginia, 1982

ONE DEACON TOLD US he loved singing from the old-style hymnbook that had no tunes. Tunebooks, he felt, could be an obstacle to singing from the heart. But he was also practical. When he began finding it difficult to remember a tune for every hymn requested in worship services, he made preparations to turn over the role of song leader to a young man in the congregation. He could sympathize with his successor's preference for a hymnal with harmonized settings of all of the hymn tunes. When the congregation accepted the young man as its song leader, the older deacon generously helped smooth the transition from Goble's *Primitive Baptist Hymn Book* (1887) to the 1983 edition of the *Old School Hymnal*.

This change was not as difficult for the congregation as the almost one-hundred-year difference in publication dates suggests. Most members of congregations in the Mountain Association now sing from at least three different Primitive Baptist hymnbooks when they visit churches within their own fellowship network. For those who can read music, the notation is simply an "aid" to singing. Others easily ignore it. Any controversies once sparked by the introduction of music notation in the old hymn-and-tune books have faded.

A question that remains for the observer, however, is whether these changes in hymnbooks have any significant influence on the singing. A typical service in one Mountain District Association church that has long used Elder John R. Daily's *Primitive Baptist Hymn and Tune Book* (1918) offers an opportunity to explore the issue. Daily's book differs from Goble's hymnbook not only in its use of music notation, but also in its inclusion of a substantial number of gospel songs. The patterns of singing that appear in this service are typical of this congregation, and they suggest that the combination of music notation and gospel songs does represent an important departure from the older repertory—one that affects the way the congregation sings. To illustrate this, I will first describe the singing in one service in this church and then show its implications.

When we reached the church one Saturday evening in August 1983, forty or fifty people had already gathered for the usual conference meeting before their annual communion meeting the next day. Except for the few minutes given to conducting church business at the end of the meeting, the order of service was like any other—singing, praying, and preaching. The singing proceeded more or less as usual. Various men and women called out numbers from wherever they were sitting, and their requests ranged from the old hymns to some favorite gospel songs. The song leader repeated the number as he turned the pages of his hymnal. Finding the text, he began to sing and the congregation followed his lead.

The sound of the singing was quite similar to that of congregations using the old-style hymnbook, but some differences were perceptible: almost half of the songs requested had only three or four verses instead of five or more, hymns were not lined out, tempos moved a little faster, the beat was regular enough to "keep time" throughout, and the singing included harmony on all but two songs—the only two that were minor sounding. During the half hour before the preaching began, the congregation sang ten requests instead of the usual four or five common in the churches using the old-style book. They were: "Wondrous Love," "Cross and Crown" (known to many singers as "Must Jesus bear the cross alone"), "I'm Alone," "As on the cross the Saviour hung," "Suffering Saviour" ("Alas! and did my Saviour bleed"), "Sweet Name" ("How sweet the name of Jesus sounds"), "Over There," "Lead Me On," "I Want to Love Him More," and "House of the Lord." Especially noticeable was an increased number of requests for gospel songs. At the close of the meeting, two additional hymns accompanied the hand of fellowship: "Woodworth" ("Just as I am without one plea") and "Greenfield" ("How tedious and tasteless the hours"). That brought the total number of songs for that service to twelve—four gospel songs and eight hymns.

Without announcing his tune choice for the first hymn, the song leader simply started singing the second of two harmonized tunes given in the book for "Wondrous Love" (fig. 73), one of the oldest songs in the church's repertory. The congregation sang all five verses in a moderately slow unison, lightly embellishing the melody and even supplementing it with the addition of a scale tone not used in the printed version. This added tone, a minor third above the key tone, filled an important gap in the set of tones given in the printed tune. Musically, the addition confirmed the scale structure of that tune as dorian, one of the traditional minor modes. The embellishments so enlivened the slow pace of the tune that the music notation in the hymnal appeared to be just a skeletal version of the tune that singers had in mind.

Fig. 73. "What wondrous love is this" (Daily no. 383) with the tune "Wondrous Love" as sung by the congregation of Galax Primitive Baptist Church, 13 August 1983, Galax, Virginia (WI-198).

1. What wondrous love is this, O my soul, O my soul,
   What wondrous love is this, O my soul!

What wondrous love is this, that caused the Lord of bliss
To bear the dreadful curse for my soul, for my soul,
To bear the dreadful curse for my soul!

2. When I was sinking down, sinking down, sinking down,
   When I was sinking down, sinking down;
   When I was sinking down beneath God's righteous frown,
   Christ laid aside His crown for my soul, for my soul,
   Christ laid aside His crown for my soul.

3. To God and to the Lamb I will sing, I will sing,
   To God and to the Lamb I will sing;
   To God and to the Lamb, and to the great I AM,
   While millions join the theme, I will sing, I will sing,
   While millions join the theme, I will sing.

4. Ye sons of Zion's King, join the praise, join the praise,
   Ye sons of Zion's King, join the praise;
   Ye sons of Zion's King, with hearts and voices sing,
   And strike each tuneful string in His praise, in His praise,
   And strike each tuneful string in His praise.

5. And when to that bright world we arrive, we arrive,
   And when to that bright world we arrive;
   When to that world we go, free from all pain and woe,
   We'll join the happy throng, and sing on, and sing on,
   We'll join the happy throng, and sing on.

A member then called for "number 393," and the congregation sang the hymn "Must Jesus bear the cross alone" to a tune titled in the book "Cross and Crown" (fig. 74), a standard hymn tune more commonly known as "Maitland."[1] While most of the congregation sang the melody, several singers added their own harmonies. Using only the third, fourth, and fifth scale tones, a few altos and a tenor improvised a slightly plainer harmony than the alto line given in the hymnbook. One or two men added a bass line that was more melodic and narrower in range (a fifth versus an octave) than the bass line in the hymnal. Men's voices were stronger than women's and they dominated the melody. Most of the women sang the melody also, but they sang more softly and an octave higher than the men. With the addition of harmonies, the singing sounded full but it was neither cluttered nor complicated.

When they improvised harmonies, these singers only approximated the conventional chord changes presented in the book—from tonic to subdominant, tonic to dominant, and back to tonic. For example, they did not end the song with the complete chords of the standard final cadence in which the scale's important leading tone moves to its tonic to communicate a feeling of resolution in the final chord. Instead, the singers completely omitted the leading tone and sang the two tones that framed the dominant chord, an open-sounding interval of a fifth. From there, all of the voices moved together in a downward motion to end the song. All but a few voices rested on the key tone and those few harmonized that melodic note with the third scale-tone. In short, they improvised their own harmonies according to regional preferences rather than conform to the standard practice implicitly endorsed in their hymnal.

Fig. 74. "Must Jesus bear the cross alone" (Thomas Shepherd, Daily no. 393) with the tune "Cross and Crown" or "Maitland" (George N. Allen) as sung by the congregation of Galax Primitive Baptist Church, Galax, 13 August 1983, Galax, Virginia (WI-198).

1. Must Jesus bear the cross alone,
   And all the world go free?
   No, there's a cross for ev'ry one,
   And there's a cross for me.

2. How happy are the saints above;
   Who once went sorrowing here;
   But now they taste unmingled love,
   And joy without a tear.

3. The consecrated cross I'll bear,
   Till death shall set me free;
   And then go home my crown to wear,
   For there's a crown for me.

4. Upon the crystal pavement, down
   At Jesus' pierced feet,
   With joy I'll cast my golden crown,
   And His dear name repeat.

5. O precious cross! O glorious crown!
   O resurrection day!
   Ye angels, from the stars come down,
   And bear my soul away.

Another member called for "number 178." This was one of the few hymn texts published in this book without tunes. The song leader looked briefly at the text and without hesitation he began to sing the first stanza:

As on the cross the Saviour hung,
And wept, and bled, and died,
He poured salvation on a wretch
That languished at His side.[2]

The tune he sang was not printed in that or any other hymnbook used by Primitive Baptist churches in that area at the time. Nevertheless, the tune was well known to the congregation and everyone joined in singing almost immediately (fig. 75). In fact, this hymn is one that we recorded often, twenty-six times in various churches, always with the same tune.

Fig. 75. "As on the cross the Savior hung" (Samuel Stennett, Daily no. 178) as sung by the congregation of Galax Primitive Baptist Church, 13 August 1983, Galax, Virginia (WI-198).

2. His crimes with inward grief and shame
   The penitent confess'd;

Then turned his dying eyes to Christ,
And thus his prayer addressed.

3. Jesus, Thou Son and Heir of heaven,
Thou spotless Lamb of God,
I see Thee bathed in sweat and tears,
And weltering in Thy blood.

4. Yet quickly from these scenes of woe
In triumph Thou shalt rise,
Burst thro' the gloomy shades of death,
And shine above the skies.

5. Amid the glories of that world,
Dear Saviour, think of me,
And in the victories of Thy death,
Let me a sharer be.

6. His prayer the dying Jesus hears,
And instantly replies—
Today thy parting soul shall be
With Me in paradise.

Another hymn requested in the same service was number 182, which in the hymnbook was set to the tune "Suffering Saviour."[3] The song leader began singing the words in the hymnal, "Alas and did my Saviour bleed," but the tune he sang was not "Suffering Saviour." The congregation joined the singing quickly and enthusiastically. Singers followed the text in the book until they reached a chorus that began "Oh the Lamb, the Loving Lamb!" At that point, the congregation substituted another chorus from memory:

He loves me, He loves me,
He loves me this I know:
He gave himself to die for me
Because He loves me so!

In a search through additional Primitive Baptist hymnbooks, I located that particular text-and-tune combination only in the most recent editions (nos. 10 and 11) of the *Old School Hymnal*,[4] neither of which was being used in this association at the time of this service. There the tune is called "traditional." The search—which included hymnbooks older and newer than the one being used—revealed another change in the printed text. Not only has this hymn taken on a verse-and-chorus structure that it previously lacked, but it has also become progressively shorter in successive publications. Whereas Lloyd (1841) and Goble (1887) printed six stanzas without a chorus in their books, Daily (1918) printed five stanzas and added the chorus "Oh the Lamb, the Loving Lamb." The compilers of the *Old School Hymnal* (1980 and 1983 editions) published only four verses and gave the song a different chorus.

Congregations throughout the association knew this tune well and frequently used it with this hymn text and chorus (fig. 76). Like a number of other tunes in the Primitive Baptist repertory, it is major sounding and is pentatonic. Technically, this means that the tune can be reproduced from a set of five different scale tones (do, re, mi, so, la) in which "do" is the key tone. As the congregation sang, a tenor and several altos added two more scale tones ("fa" and "ti") in the harmonies they improvised. To my ear, their singing strengthened the major-sounding character of the tune. At the end of each verse, though, they again omitted the "ti"—or leading tone—and left the final cadence sounding somewhat "open." This omission, typical in Primitive Baptist singing, has implications for the larger patterns that will be discussed in the following chapter.

Fig. 76. "Alas! and did my Savior bleed" (Isaac Watts, Daily no. 182) with chorus "He loves me" and tune "He Loves Me" as sung by the congregation of Galax Primitive Baptist Church, 13 August 1983, Galax, Virginia (WI-198).

1. Alas! and did my Saviour bleed,
   And did my Jesus die?
   Would He devote that sacred head
   For such a worm as I?

CHORUS:

   He loves me, he loves me,
   He loves me this I know!
   He gave himself to die for me,
   Because he loves me so!

2. Was it for crimes that I have done,
   He groaned upon the tree?
   Amazing pity, grace unknown,
   And love beyond degree!

CHORUS

3. Well might the sun in darkness hide,
   And shut His glories in;
   When Christ, the mighty Saviour died,
   For man, the Creature's sin.

CHORUS

4. Thus might I hide my blushing face,
   While His dear cross appears;

Dissolve my heart in thankfulness,
And melt mine eyes in tears.

CHORUS

5. But drops of grief can ne'er repay
The debt of love I owe;
Here, Lord, I give myself away;
'Tis all that I can do.

CHORUS

In response to another request, the congregation sang hymn number 115, "How sweet the name of Jesus sounds" (fig. 77). Instead of singing the tune "Sweet Name" published with that text, the song leader began singing the standard hymn tune "Ortonville," by Thomas Hastings. "Ortonville" does appear in the *Primitive Baptist Hymn and Tune Book* (Daily 1918), but it is printed as the setting for another hymn, "Once more we come before our God."[5] Without hesitation, the congregation again sang by memory the tune selected by the song leader. Singers spun out the tune relatively slowly, with some of the embellishment characteristic of other Primitive Baptist singing in the association. Familiarity with the style might allow a nonparticipant to look at the hymnbook and imagine with some accuracy which notes the congregation would use in singing the melody and in harmonizing the hymn. But this congregation imprinted its singing of this hymn in a way that could not have been envisioned from the publication alone. Pausing after almost every other syllable, the whole congregation breathed as one body, sometimes in midword, and phrased its song in a pattern established by the song leader, a pattern that conformed to his phrasing of the tune rather than to that of the text.

Fig. 77. "How sweet the name of Jesus sounds" (John Newton, Daily no. 115) with the tune "Ortonville" (Thomas Hastings) as sung by the congregation of Galax Primitive Baptist Church, 13 August 1983, Galax, Virginia (WI-198).

a be - liev - er's ear! It soothes his sor - rows,

heals his wounds, And drives a - way his

fear, And drives a - way his fear.

1. How sweet the name of Jesus sounds,
   In a believer's ear!
   It soothes his sorrows, heals his wounds,
   And drives away his fear.

2. It makes the wounded Spirit whole,
   And calms the troubled breast;
   'Tis manna to the hungry soul,
   And to the weary, rest.

3. Dear name! the rock on which I build
   My shield and hiding place;
   My never-failing treasury, filled
   With boundless stores of grace.

4. By Thee my prayers acceptance gain,
   Although with sin defiled;

Satan accuses me in vain,
    And I am owned a child.

5. Jesus! my Shepherd, Husband, Friend,
    My Prophet, Priest, and King,
My Lord, my Life, my Way, my End,
    Accept the praise I bring.

6. Weak is the effort of my heart,
    And cold my warmest thought;
But when I see Thee as Thou art,
    I'll praise Thee as I ought.

7. Till then I would Thy love proclaim,
    With every fleeting breath;
And may the music of Thy name
    Refresh my soul in death.

This somewhat detailed description of how the congregation sang the hymns emphasizes what otherwise might be taken for granted because it is the most common practice in these churches—that the Primitive Baptist hymn-and-tune books prescribe tunes and harmonies but they do not necessarily dictate to the singers. In singing each of these hymns, the congregation took liberties with tunes, harmonies, rhythms, and even texts. Although their book prescribed texts, clearly the congregation did not always feel compelled to follow the printed versions. Singers took even greater liberties with tunes. Differences between the published and sung versions of hymns suggested that the whole congregation had continued to sing hymn tunes largely from an oral tradition: singers could easily follow their song leader in substituting tunes and even parts of texts for the ones printed; they sang harmonies by ear and those harmonies did not include the standard conventions reproduced in publications, such as using the leading tone in final dominant-to-tonic cadences; they chose a traditional unison interpretation for a hymn that was printed in parts; and they interpreted and embellished tunes in a style characteristic of regional traditions.

Such differences rapidly diminished, however, when this same congregation sang the four gospel songs requested. The stanzas and choruses of "I'm Alone," "Over There," "Lead Me On," and "I Want to Love Him More" corresponded much more closely to the music notation in the book. Differences from the printed score continued in harmonies that singers added "by ear," but the melodies and rhythms did not vary significantly from those printed in the hymnal. Cued by the printed music, a few singers even recreated the responsorial "echo" lines of choruses as written out in the hymnal. Their performance of these gospel songs, then, revealed an attention to the prescribed music texts that we did not find in their hymn singing.

Although tunebooks—or hymnals—have found acceptance in several churches in the Mountain Association, these congregations did not make the change from the tuneless hymnbooks easily. Music notation, including the shape-note system, represents a format that even now is not welcomed by all Primitive Baptists, but most churches have chosen to abide by congregational decisions on hymnals rather than make music notation a test of fellowship.[6] The assumption that seems to underlie their apparent acceptance of hymnals is that music notation, unlike musical instruments, has a benign influence on singing.

The general shift to music notation has been a long time coming in Primitive Baptist churches, and any changes accompanying that shift have also been gradual. Looking back over late-nineteenth-century musical developments, however, we can see a series of small shocks to congregational singing resulting from musical notation. First, notation itself appeared in hymnals. Then shape-note notation in a piano-score format became the standard for Primitive Baptists. Now, with increasing numbers of gospel songs appearing in the hymnals, the fidelity to notation is increasing.

Since 1879, when Elders M. J. Sears and Thomas B. Ausmus published their *Primitive Baptist Hymnal* with standard or "round" notes, Primitive Baptists have had music notation available in their hymnals. Sears and Ausmus apparently misjudged what type of notation would suit their readers when they decided to use standard notes instead of shape notes, for the round notes never appeared again in Primitive Baptist hymnals. Drummond found, in fact, that virtually all of the music notation in Primitive Baptist hymnals is now shape notes (1989:120). Goble's *Primitive Baptist Hymn Book*, old fashioned even in 1887 when it was new, was the last of its kind published by Primitive Baptists. Elders Silas H. Durand and P. G. Lester had already published their shape-note *Hymn and Tune Book* the year before. In their preface, they declared that their book was "in response to many requests . . . [and] to supply a need long felt in our churches." Durand and Lester's book is still used today.

The clear preference for shape notes in these hymnals commands some attention because the use of that notation carries certain cultural implications. In their strong associations with nineteenth-century southern tunebooks and singing schools, shape notes are not simply a pedagogical device. They are also a symbol of American vernacular music that has always stood apart from the standards of European mainstream or American genteel culture. Each voice part in these early shape-note tunebooks was written on a separate staff with the melody on an inner staff just above the bass. The organization of the singing was not sexually segregated, with women singing soprano and alto and men singing tenor and bass. Instead, women and men often joined in singing a part, particularly the melody and the treble. The treble harmony was on the top staff of the score, the alto (when present) on the next staff, the melody (also called lead or tenor) was on the third staff, and the bass on the lowest staff. Each of these parts offered singers some melodic interest, and when the parts were sung simultaneously they made striking and—by classical European standards—unconventional harmonies.

Except for their use of shape notes, however, the compilers of Primitive Baptist hymn-and-tune books have always adopted a conventional format when publishing songs for congregational singing. They presented the songs in a standard piano-score format of two staffs instead of the older open-score form of the earlier tunebooks in which each voice part has a separate staff. This standard keyboard-staff format, easily read by pianists and organists, divides the voices according to sex and places parts written for women (soprano and alto) on the treble staff, and those for men (tenor and bass) on the bass staff below. The melody, or lead, moves to the highest position on the staff (the soprano) instead of remaining in the tenor (with harmonies above and below), which was the practice of the early tunebook compilers.

Adopting this format presented some technical musical problems for Primitive Baptist hymnbook compilers who wanted to reprint musical settings from the older shape-note tunebooks. Occasionally, these compilers tried to preserve the independent character of the vocal parts in the early tunebook arrangements and simply transfer them from three or four staffs to two. Changes almost always accompanied this transfer. Some alterations were the practical results of reducing the parts to two staffs and trying to maintain visual clarity in the musical score by keeping the voice parts from crossing. Sometimes this adaptation required rewriting just a few notes in one or two parts to keep the alto below the soprano or the tenor above the bass. Other changes, however, seem to be related more directly to ideas about what was musically correct. Influenced by the conventions of voice-leading in music composition, compilers thought that the parallel intervals of fourths, fifths, and octaves, and the tunes based on natural minor scales (without leading tones) that often appeared in the older musical settings, reflected ignorance on the part of earlier tune writers. Accordingly, they made corrections as needed to help the tunes and harmonies conform more closely to accepted standards. Occasionally these corrections greatly reduced or even eliminated any melodic interest in the harmony parts. The harmony became increasingly predictable and began to function simply as support for the melody.

The very presence of notation in hymnals invites the singers, especially those who have music-reading skills, to abandon their traditional improvisations and conform to the tune-text combinations, the unembellished tunes, regularized rhythms, and conventional harmonies printed in the book. Primitive Baptists who compiled these books of hymns indirectly expressed some awareness of this when they acknowledged the variety that existed in the singing in their churches. For example, Durand and Lester prefaced their *Hymn and Tune Book* (1886) with an explanation about the need to make musical choices. "In the association of hymns and tunes we have in some instances had respect to long use; in others we have determined the arrangement according to our own judgment, and the character of melody preferred in different localities."

With the tuneless hymnbooks, of course, the tune choices normally would have been made locally by the song leaders of each congregation. The fact that the compilers made any statement at all about combining tunes and texts and that they identified tradition, personal taste, and local preferences as variables that affected their own choices suggests the presence at that time of musically competent and active congregations. If the hymn-and-tune book compilers had entertained questions about the potential of music notation for canonizing hymn-and-tune combinations, or about the danger of standardizing tunes and their harmonizations, they did not record them. To some degree, such concerns would have been unwarranted. The notation, by itself, has had little effect on many of these Primitive Baptists partly because of the richness and compelling nature of the oral tradition that continues to inform their singing of hymns. The singing of gospel songs, however, is another matter. As a vehicle for communicating gospel songs, music notation has played a more influential role.

For Primitive Baptists, the shift to music notation has been accompanied by an increase in the proportion of gospel songs in their hymnals and in their singing. By my estimate, less than 5 percent of the songs in Goble's *Primitive Baptist Hymn Book* (1887) are gospel songs.

Drummond (1989) estimates that 21 percent of the songs in Daily's *Primitive Baptist Hymn and Tune Book* (1918) are gospel songs, and that 46 percent of the songs in the new edition of the *Old School Hymnal* (1983) are gospel songs. Editors of this latest book emphasized their intention to include new songs as one of the purposes of the publication: "As in previous editions, we have sought to make the *Old School Hymnal* a 'living hymnal,' not one consigned to history as a closed edition. Through the years our desire has been to encourage contemporary authors and composers. Our Lord continues to bless us with 'hymns and spiritual songs' written in this day which are blended in this edition with many of the beloved hymns of yesteryear" (Preface).

Interest in newer songs (mostly gospel) is reflected in the singing that precedes worship services. Congregations request more gospel songs when they sing from hymnbooks that include more gospel songs. In contrast to their treatment of hymn tunes and texts as separate repertories, singers generally follow standard practice and treat the tunes and texts of gospel songs as inseparable. The sound of the singing, then, becomes more consistent from one church to another as the repertory of gospel songs increases.

Gospel songs are popular among Primitive Baptists even though they are more likely than hymns to present doctrinal problems for predestinarian perspectives. The certainty of salvation that is commonly expressed in gospel songs can be troublesome and "in error." That does not necessarily keep Primitive Baptists from singing some of the same songs as their evangelical neighbors, especially if the texts will yield to different interpretations. For example, when Primitive Baptists sing "Just as I am without one plea, oh Lamb of God I come," they sing the same words and the same tune that Methodists and Missionary Baptists sing, but the meaning they find in the song is radically different. While Methodists may be longing for perfection, and Missionary Baptists urging sinners to repentance and salvation, Primitive Baptists are acknowledging total human depravity. They try to avoid singing other songs that are obviously Arminian and exhortational, such as "Why Not Tonight?" and "Almost Persuaded," and they will not sing "Blessed assurance, Jesus is mine" because that seems too presumptuous for one who simply claims a hope of salvation. Drummond found (1989:293–95), as we did, that Primitive Baptists have chosen to sing "We'll Wait Till Jesus Comes" (fig. 78) instead of "We'll Work Till Jesus Comes," the text preferred by evangelical churches.

Fig. 78. "O land of rest, for thee I sigh" (Elizabeth Mills, Goble no. 264) with the chorus and tune "We'll Wait Till Jesus Comes" (William Miller) as sung by the congregation of Cross Roads Primitive Baptist Church, 4 July 1982, Baywood, Virginia (WI-083).

1. O land of rest, for thee I sigh;
   When will the moment come,
   When I shall lay my armor by,
   And dwell with Christ at home?

CHORUS:

We'll wait till Jesus comes,
We'll wait till Jesus comes;
We'll wait till Jesus comes,
And we'll be gathered home.

CHORUS

2. No tranquil joys on earth I know,
   No peaceful shelt'ring dome;

> This world's a wilderness of woe;
>   This world is not my home.

CHORUS

> 3. To Jesus Christ I sought for rest;
>   He bade me cease to roam,
>   And fly for succor to his breast,
>   And he'd conduct me home.

CHORUS

> 4. I should at once have quit the field,
>   Where foes and fury roam;
>   But, ah! my passport was not sealed;
>   I could not yet go home.

CHORUS

> 5. When by affliction sharply tried,
>   I view the gaping tomb,
>   Although I dread death's chilling tide,
>   Yet still I sigh for home.

CHORUS

> 6. Weary of wand'ring round and round
>   This vale of sin and gloom,
>   I long to leave th' unhallowed ground,
>   And dwell with Christ at home.

CHORUS

Gospel songs have widespread appeal and they are likely to remain part of the Primitive Baptist repertory. When Primitive Baptists sing these songs, however, they are doing more than simply incorporating another genre into their repertory of hymns, psalms, and spiritual songs. Gospel songs are not only a newer kind of song, they also invite a different style of performance. Now that Primitive Baptists are printing more gospel songs in their own hymnals, singers are reading the music notation more closely. Some congregations are accommodating the livelier spirit of most of these songs by setting their tempos a little faster, making the accents occur more regularly, and conforming more closely to the prescribed text. In short, instead of reinterpreting the songs in their old style of congregational singing, as their predecessors did with the camp-meeting spirituals, Primitive

Baptists today are adapting their style of singing to accommodate the newer songs. As they do this, the sound of their singing changes. Old Baptist churches sound more alike, and Primitive Baptist singing becomes more like the singing of other denominations.

7

The Sound of the Dove

It all falls back to the sound.

—Primitive Baptist elder,
Virginia, 1982

PRIMITIVE BAPTISTS FIND the singing in their own churches distinctive and compelling. When it is especially strong, they feel deeply moved. To them it is spiritually nourishing, and they have no mechanism or need to explain its beauty to outsiders. They may casually refer to their singing as "the joyful sound," but they do not generally imagine it as an expression and construction of a religious and social identity. Only an outsider, searching out some of the links between song and religion and human relationships, would be likely to exercise such an idea.

In small and often indirect ways, singers have indicated those things they notice most about their own singing. I have noted other features that seem particularly significant in their singing and its context. Here I cluster these in three groups for summarizing the practice of singing in Primitive Baptist churches and exploring some of its possible linkages to religious and social identity and even to cultural change.

The first group is a set of variables with which Primitive Baptists most often assert the song-style preferences of their local congregations: repertory, tempo, pitch, harmony, rhythm, and melody. Consistent with Primitive Baptist insistence on congregational autonomy, each congregation chooses its own song repertory and develops its preferred ways of singing. Primitive Baptists who talked with me noticed things about the singing itself that showed they were distinguishing their own association—and sometimes their own home church—from other Primitive Baptist groups. While members seemed not to give much thought to the particular discriminations they were making, they proved keenly aware of the repertories of tunes and texts preferred by a particular congregation, including the pairing of specific tunes and texts; customary pitches and tempos chosen for the singing; the presence or absence of harmony, and the particular harmonies sung; the degree of rhythmic blend of the voices in the congregation; and the particular melodic variations and embellishments sung by a congregation. A closely related feature is the role of song leader, especially the presence of one who likes to line out hymns. Choices made in all these dimensions of song subtly assert a local identity.

In recognizing these distinctions in their singing, Primitive Baptists show sensitivity as listeners; and, in consciously using these stylistic elements in ways that control and shape their congregational singing, they also show an unusual degree of commitment and competence as singers. However, the song variations that different congregations of Primitive Baptists actually produce are subtle, and an outsider is not likely to notice them or see their importance immediately. Only gradually does an observer realize that the singing of each congregation constitutes something akin to a consensus constructed in musical sound. Although members respond to general traits of Primitive Baptist singing, as when they hear them in Judy Collins's performance of "Amazing Grace," their identity as Primitive Baptists is deeply rooted in the particular sound of their own home church, normally the church where they joined and were baptized, where they must remain in good standing if they are to have fellowship with Primitive Baptists elsewhere.

A second cluster of song-related features is more stable. I have previously pointed out variations in the singing but emphasized its underlying continuities because members themselves do that. When an elder said, for instance, that Primitive Baptist singing sounds a little different from one church or association to the next, he quickly added that they still see themselves as "all the same people." His statement implies that one way Primitive Baptists can maintain their identity as a group is by keeping the congregational differences that emerge in their singing within general stylistic boundaries. These boundary-defining features with which Primitive Baptists distinguish themselves from other denominations include: the exclusion of musical instruments from the meetinghouse; the insistence that all church music be congregational song; the order of worship; the method of choosing songs; and the doctrinal criteria for evaluating hymns. These reflect beliefs about singing that most Primitive Baptists agree on, and they also provide a stable structure that helps to conserve Primitive

Baptist songs and ways of singing. It is at this more stable level that we can see relationships of this religious song to the role of women in the church and to doctrine.

On the authority they find in the King James version of the New Testament, these Primitive Baptists agree that they will not allow any musical instruments in their churches. This does not mean that they are opposed to musical instruments, to secular music, or even to dancing; and it does not mean that they do not sing with instrumental accompaniment or perform music outside the church. On the contrary, we met elders who played guitars and fiddles, and we met members who played banjos and guitars, and some who had taken piano lessons. Some of these musicians play privately for their own pleasure. Others are active as musicians in the community and perform for gatherings of family and friends, for public dances, and even for festivals and competitions.

Singing, however, is the only musical expression they permit themselves in their churches. Singing is always congregational, and it is, in fact, the only vocal expression in which the congregation as a whole may participate. No prayers are voiced simultaneously by the whole congregation, and there are no responsive readings or recitations of creeds. The basic order of worship is always the same—singing, prayer, preaching—and the congregation participates vocally only in the singing. Members request and sing the songs published in their hymnbooks, and the songs they choose are often distinctly doctrinal and are expressive of Primitive Baptist religious experience. Singing is especially significant as the only part of the formal meetings of the church in which women may normally exert influence and find a voice.

The songs of Primitive Baptists in the Mountain District Association have other, indirect links to women through the larger regional song traditions of the central Blue Ridge Mountains. These connections are especially apparent in those hymn tunes that have been adapted from the repertory of ballad tunes in the region. The transference of tunes from ballads to hymns is musically natural because the two song forms have multiple stanzas and share metrical patterns. However, the transference is also a natural and significant one socially because women have been prominent in the preservation and transmission of these tunes in both the ballad and hymn repertories. Approximately two-thirds of the informants Bertrand Bronson listed in his index of sources of Child ballad tunes were women, and a large majority of Cecil Sharp's Appalachian ballad singers were women. Even though our own sources for songs recorded outside of congregational worship were most often the men who served the church as elders, deacons, and song leaders, these individuals generally attributed their knowledge of the older tunes to their mothers or grandmothers, who sang those songs at home as well as at church.

Both men and women agreed that women's silence in church meetings is biblically authorized and is important for maintaining proper order in public worship. They also agreed, however, that this rule of silence does not apply to singing. The separate, private, and domestic nature of the woman's traditional role is contradicted in church meetings by the congregational singing. To the extent that congregational song can be considered public, it subtly reinforces the importance of women's voices.

At first glance, congregational singing seems as male dominated as the rest of the service. Men lead the singing and women take secondary roles, sometimes by providing an alto part to harmonize with a male lead, or by just singing the melody with less volume than men. Occasionally, women sing out strongly, just as men do. Twice, though, women with strong singing voices spoke to me privately and apologetically about not holding their voices down more when they sang in church. This stood in marked contrast to other occasions when I heard men who were once strong singers apologize publicly in church meetings because failing health prevented them from singing with much volume and control. It is notable, however, that the women who could sing strongly did, in fact, sing with volume and power in the meetings, and no one objected then or later. The women's apologies suggested that the convention of separate roles for men and women, with males dominant, carries over into ideas about singing, but the actual singing suggests that these roles do not operate very strongly there.

The customary practice of congregational singing, in fact, tends to balance gender relationships, enlarging the role of women while reducing that of men. During the singing, women freely request hymns they want to sing and song leaders carry out their requests. Although the song leader repeats the hymn numbers and gives the congregation its starting pitch, he typically remains seated when doing this, and he sometimes becomes indistinguishable from the rest of the congregation once the singing begins. Even the song leaders who line out a hymn for their congregations or the one or two men who sing out a high harmony above the melody often remain seated with the congregation, an indication that they are placing their voices in the service of the group.

The confinements and opportunities of congregational singing become clear when viewed in the context of a regional culture that has clearly supported male dominance and has encouraged competitiveness and individualism in males. Within the culture, for example, researchers have documented virtuoso musical performances of men who are fiddlers, banjoists, singers, and dancers. In such a culture, the unaccompanied, communal, and cooperative hymn singing of Primitive Baptist churches takes on significance for women, for it gives men no opportunity to exercise musical gifts in solo performances comparable to roles they have in secular music-making and in other churches.

Women get reinforcement not only from the public and participatory nature of singing, but also from the importance that this period of singing together has for the church. Although preaching is the ostensible focus and primary substance of a meeting for public worship and consumes the most time, church meetings always include a full half hour or more of singing before the meeting formally begins. That members voluntarily arrive in time—or even early—to sing together reveals an unusual level of commitment to singing, and it highlights the importance of this practice to the church. At the same time, the fact that most of the singing takes place "before the service" underlines its subordinate position. Peacock and Tyson allude to both the secondary formal status of singing and the informal importance of this period of singing when they write, "If you ask 'What time is the service?' an hour will be stated, but you will be later than anyone else if you wait until that hour to arrive" (1989:15).

Women not only sing, but they also request hymns during this time. Calling out numbers of their favorite texts, women often take the opportunity to direct the course of a meeting that is otherwise led by men. This is a significant opportunity, because the singing can affect participants as much or more than the preaching does. Like men, women make little attempt to vary song requests for the sake of adding variation to the singing, and no one attempts to match song selection to events in a church calendar. Christmas and Easter, for example, pass without receiving any special notice in the song choices. Instead, women request the songs they like or ones they feel a need to sing, or they choose those they know to be favorites of others. Congregations sing these songs repeatedly at different times, in different places, and for different occasions over many years.

Singing, then, becomes a powerful provoker of memories, and women become participants in the process of activating memory when they request songs. Certain hymns, they know, will evoke particular images and emotions. One woman said "they were singing 'O how happy are they' when I joined the church, and I always associate that song—when I hear it—with the day that I joined the church" (WI-029). Others remember certain friends or family members when they sing particular songs. Memories may be personal or collective or some combination of both, but insofar as they are associated with the church, they serve the whole group as a bond and they may actually be more powerful in eliciting fellowship than listening together to the sermon.

Particularly significant for women is the egalitarian nature of the predestinarian doctrine of election that appears in the sermons and in the hymns they sing. These texts not only refer to the feminine nature of the church, but they also conform to a theology in which men and women are equally powerless to effect their own salvation. Husbands do not try to persuade their wives to join the church, nor do wives try to influence their husbands. Both are alike in being equally responsible for seeking signs of grace in their own lives. Men, like women, must wait, totally dependent on God to reveal these signs of grace to them.

In all of these Primitive Baptist churches, the elders and lay members share a pervasive attitude that the songs sung in public worship need to be consistent with the doctrines of grace and predestinated election. In actual practice, this appears to be a matter that is left to the interpretation of individual churches. Even among congregations that are in agreement on doctrine, some will sing songs in their meetings that others reject as doctrinally unsound. In general, however, these Primitive Baptists choose songs that they find consistent with the concept of an unworthy sinner saved only by grace and chosen by God before the foundation of the world, songs that speak of pilgrims and strangers suffering hardships and doubt in the natural world but hoping for the full joys of an eternal, spiritual world to come. They choose texts that parallel the religious experiences reported by both men and women in the church. Uncertainty remains a strong and persistent feature of their doctrine of predestinated election, and uncertainty about this world, not to mention the next, is expressed in the texts of the older hymns these congregations sing.

The two clusters of song-related factors I have explored suggest a relationship to congregational and denominational identity. Primitive Baptists in and near the Mountain District Association show no signs of changing their musical practice in any way that would threaten the fellowship within their churches or alter their identity as "Old" Baptists. Nevertheless, their singing is marked by change as well as continuity. Especially in those churches using hymn-and-tune books, singing is undergoing subtle changes only partially explainable as natural variations in singing, or as expressions of religious identity.

A third cluster of song features that seems linked to changes includes: the acceptance of gospel songs; a tradition of absorbing tunes from various musical sources; latitude for congregational choice of hymnbooks; and the nature of music notation in these books and of a congregation's use of it. Given the strength of the doctrine of predestinated election in Primitive Baptist churches, it is somewhat puzzling that the song repertory is marked by an increasing number of gospel songs. On the surface, these songs seem unlikely candidates for the favor of a religious group that does not believe the church and its preachers are in any way instrumental in the conversion of sinners. Primitive Baptists believe, instead, that the church is a home and a resting place for those God has chosen, not those who have chosen him. Many of the old psalms and hymns are compatible with these beliefs. Gospel songs, on the other hand, have developed from Arminian ideas and practices.

Widely used in late-nineteenth-century revivals, gospel songs remain much more closely associated with popular evangelical contexts than with those groups defending predestinarian doctrines. They have evolved from a view of the church as an agent of change with a mission to save lost sinners. Gospel songs have most characteristically functioned not simply to engage participants but, more important, to encourage them to some public action: to prayer, testimony, repentance, and especially conversion. It seems paradoxical then that Primitive Baptists, who remain firmly committed to a predestinarian doctrine, are singing an increasing number of songs that do not serve their doctrinal interests. There are several possible explanations for this.

First, the survey of sources of texts and tunes in the song repertory makes clear that incorporating new songs from outside Primitive Baptist doctrinal circles is well within the tradition of Primitive Baptist singing. This song repertory has never been as static as might appear from the continuing use and repetition of eighteenth-century hymn texts, seventeenth-century lining-out practices, and even older secular ballad tunes. The tunes that Primitive Baptists are now singing have entered the repertory at different times and from different sources, and some congregations are open to further additions even now. Traces of songs from evangelical early-nineteenth-century camp meetings and revivals have found their way into predestinarian Primitive Baptist worship services, along with songs composed later in the century for Sunday schools. That these songs and tunes lost many of the associations with their earlier contexts is a comment on the interpretive power of the old style of Primitive Baptist singing. By remaining within the boundaries of their own style and practice of singing, in other words, Primitive Baptists have customarily absorbed new songs from other musical traditions into their own repertories without making significant changes in the sound of their singing. Previous experience, then, gives them little reason to think that gospel songs might not also yield to a similar transformation.

In addition, this musical shift to new hymnals and more gospel songs springs partly from a desire to appeal to younger church members and keep them interested in the church. When one deacon and song leader explained his rationale for changing from the 1887 tuneless *Primitive Baptist Hymn Book* to the 1983 edition of the *Old School Hymnal,* he indicated as much. He knew that the young people in the church enjoyed singing from the new hymnbook, he knew that they liked to sing harmony parts and could not do so without reading them from the book, and he knew that they were the singers who would have to lead the singing when he could no longer do so. The young man who eventually became the song leader reads music. He will lead singing from the new hymnal but not from the old book of hymns without tunes because he has a hard time remembering the older tunes, especially the minor tunes.

Finally, the musical shift may be associated with a more general trend on the part of some congregations to improve their social standing by moving closer to the practice and appearance of mainline Protestant churches. The purchase of comfortable new pews with engraved brass plaques memorializing family members and donors, the installation of carpet in church aisles, and the construction of a ramp entrance for handicapped members and shelters for the outdoor dinners on the church grounds are part of this trend. A wedding at the same church that adopted the new hymnbook offered a particular and striking example. The preacher's wife and daughter wanted to rent a piano for the church for the occasion of the daughter's wedding. The congregation refused permission for this but did permit the bridal party to set up a portable record player and speakers in a small foyer between the restrooms just outside the meeting room. Before the ceremony several songs, including "Love Me Tender" as a male/female duet, were sung unaccompanied. Then, as the bride began her processional, the imported sound system broadcast Mendelssohn's wedding march from the foyer, a compromise between the Primitive Baptist prohibition of musical instruments and mainline Protestant wedding customs (Peacock and Tyson 1989:160–61).

A more general example, however, is the appearance of the hymn-books themselves. Virtually all Primitive Baptist hymnbooks published since 1900 use shape-note notation and the standard keyboard-style format of two staffs, with treble and alto voices on the top staff, and tenor and bass voices on the lower staff. More and more, Primitive Baptist hymnbook editors and music arrangers are publishing new harmonizations of the old tunes and musical settings that reflect mainstream ideas about what is musically desirable and correct. Increasingly, these books dictate to the singers, as younger singers move away from their oral tune traditions and try harder to read and more literally interpret the musical scores.

At the most direct level, then, the obvious explanations for musical changes are: first, a natural continuation of a two-hundred-year tradition of absorbing new songs into the repertory; second, a desire to retain the interest and participation of younger church members; and third, an effort to meet social norms of the outside communities by moving closer to the musical practice of mainline denominations.

However, I believe the changes have implications at deeper levels also. These are more hypothetical and more indirect, but they may also be more important. For one thing, the old hymn tunes have structural parallels with the older social world from which the tunes have come. At the social level, older church members still have vivid memories of agrarian life because they were among the first in their families to turn to something other than farming to make a living. They were reared in families who, for generations, had to focus their concerns on coping with the unpredictable elements of nature, the uncertain outcomes of childbirth or sickness, and forces that were generally beyond human control. The religious and secular songs that were part of that older world for predestinarian Baptists were characterized by gapped and modal scales, and by the older style of singing with improvised embellishments and unison melodies, and occasional open-sounding harmonies in intervals of fourths, fifths, and octaves. The older tunes and the older song style in contemporary Primitive Baptist repertories link singers directly to that world and worldview because the songs connect them to their memories. In cleaving both to the old doctrinal texts and to slow and irregular rhythms in their singing, Primitive Baptists express their acceptance of a certain lack of control, and they reveal their sense of the world as a realm in which uncertainty plays a fundamental role.

The old minor tunes and the pentatonic structures that pervade most of these melodies subtly reinforce the uncertainty embodied in that worldview. For example, Primitive Baptist tunes based on these pentatonic scales have no half steps or "leading tones." The name of this tone, which is only a half step below the tonic, refers to its tendency to lead to the tonic, and to its function of setting up tensions that lead to standard musical resolutions. Pentatonic tunes, by comparison with tunes based on diatonic (seven-tone) scales, can omit such patterns of tension and resolution. These tunes often do not lend themselves to predictable harmonic progressions of major and minor chords. Instead, they are more apt to promote a sense of ambiguity.

These old "lonesome" tunes are the tunes of the older generations of Primitive Baptist men and women, of preachers and song leaders who were stonemasons, carpenters, and farmers, and of the mothers and grandmothers who taught them the tunes. In singing these songs, congregations take the same tone of stoic self-effacement used by solo ballad singers in the region. That tone, straightforward and matter-of-fact throughout, with minimal dynamic shading and vibrato, signals that singers are trying to communicate without relying on a romanticized emotional effect. They may shorten or lengthen songs at cadences or introduce other irregularities in the rhythm that suggest they are keeping their focus on the text. Unlike instrumental musicians who may be governed by outside constraints such as having to maintain a steady beat while accompanying dancers, singers will pause or move on to their next phrase according to the momentum established within the group as it sings, preferences that they seem to feel intuitively.

With vocal quality, tonal structure, and performance style, then, singers express a stoic attitude consistent with their acceptance of the tensions and uncertainties inherent in their belief in a doctrine of predestinated election. The pentatonic tunes have a capacity for expressing tensions, but they lack a musical mechanism for fully resolving that tension. These old "lonesome" tunes and irregular rhythms seem to express some of the ambiguity in the status of the believer who has a hope of salvation but cannot claim any assurance. In the sound it creates, the whole community of singers embraces the ambiguities of its world.

Gospel songs, on the other hand, are compatible with the newly industrialized world of this community. Most of those Primitive Baptist men and women who still live on farms no longer make their living from farming. Their lives are increasingly interwoven into the social and political hierarchies of textile mills and manufacturing, businesses and government, hospitals and doctors' offices. This world demands that they develop social skills and learn to cope with the problems that are constantly present when large groups of people have to live and work cooperatively. In this kind of environment, the pressures to master new technologies and new situations are constant, and the appearance of being knowledgeable and in control is important for communicating confidence and gaining cooperation.

Gospel songs offer some interesting parallels with that world. Musically they are characterized by major tonalities that express confidence and even cheerfulness. Their harmonies conform to popular and predictable conventions, and these songs generally end with perfect cadences that leave no room for doubt about the firmness and finality of their resolutions. The harmonic structures are basically hierarchical ones. Each voice part has its place on the staff with a clear relationship to those parts above and below. Their harmonies have little melodic interest in themselves. Instead, they are fully subordinated to the melodies.

Primitive Baptists have been able to absorb and transform diverse musical influences in the past. The present reliance on music notation and acceptance of increasing numbers of gospel songs in the repertory, however, may be introducing formal changes that are not compatible with the older song style and cannot be readily absorbed by it. There is, for example, an important shift in who controls the tunes, harmonies, and tune-and-text combinations. Once these were the prerogative of local congregations and song leaders. Now these powers devolve upon the more distant composers and compilers of Primitive Baptist hymnals. There is also a shift in the approach to harmony. In the earlier shape-note tunebooks used in singing schools, all of the parts were relatively melodic and somewhat independent; in the later shape-note hymnals used by Primitive Baptists, the top line is the melody and all other parts are subordinate to it, functioning only as support. Related to this is an increasing use of tunes in the major diatonic mode and a decreasing use of tunes in pentatonic and other modal systems, especially the minor-sounding ones. Acceptance of standardized versions of hymns produces gradual changes in congregational singing, as members try to conform more closely to the written versions. This modernized notation and repertory not only signal the possibility of larger change, but they also outline the direction that change is most likely to take. It is a direction that can be described in social terms as a shift from an egalitarian expressive mode to one more hierarchical in its structure, a shift from song in which uncertainty and ambiguity play crucial roles to one that communicates assurance and certainty. These are the songs of the younger Primitive Baptists—the insurance salesman, the carpet installer, the secretary, nurse, merchant, and textile worker.

Together, the new hymnals, music notation, and gospel songs represent a convergence of musical elements that have affected the whole repertory: hymns have fewer verses, they rarely get lined out, tempos for hymn singing move a little faster, rhythms are a little more regular, and harmonies are more conventional. These musical elements are at the heart of a newer sound in Primitive Baptist singing. They may resist being transformed into the old way of singing, much as newer life styles resist a return to the past. At present, however, the singing retains a sound that, for Primitive Baptists, is still distinctive. Elder Cook illustrated the power of that sound with the following story:

> A man out of the state of North Carolina was either in Japan or Korea, I don't recall which, but he'd gone over there and was in a foxhole looking for the enemy. And he started singing "Jesus, lover of my soul." And as he sang it the enemy came upon him. And the one verse, I believe it's the second verse, speaks of protecting even his head. And when he sang that, the enemy approached him. And they embraced each other, and they separated, and went on their way, both ways. I find it a very moving story, and reaction of even enemies, that they can detect the sound, which is what it's all about. (WI-106)

Their practice of singing not only reflects beliefs about singing that most Primitive Baptists agree on, but it also provides a structure that conserves the songs and ways of singing that Primitive Baptists gradually adopted to give expression to their beliefs. The structure does not necessarily prevent changes in singing, but it provides a framework within which variation can develop and change can more or less be safely contained. It is possible, of course, for congregations to change the sound of their singing more dramatically, but they cannot do this without raising some questions and perhaps creating some problems. Elder Cook mentioned one case in which a church had gone beyond acceptable limits in its singing:

> Now we were told not too long ago [that] Old Baptists, . . . [who] I don't care to speak of by name, they were singing different. They had started singing, you know, sounds of the world from the notes. And a man passed by, and he knew where he was going, to the memorial meeting that was being held. And he told the minister there, he said, "had I been looking for the Old Baptist people and not known where I was going, I would have passed you on up," he said, "because you [have] deviated and

left that sound back somewhere else and turned to a new one."
... I don't believe that they should or we should—or anybody
else should for that matter, that sings the songs of Zion—don't
believe they should ever deviate from the old tunes that's been
handed down, because it's a tradition of the fathers. (WI-106)

To Elder Cook, it did not seem at all farfetched to think that a church
could throw its identity as Primitive Baptist into question by changing the sound of its singing. Singing that violated structural boundaries would presumably result in a disruption of fellowship. This did,
in fact, occur in some Primitive Baptist churches in Georgia when they
introduced the organ as an aid to singing around 1897. The change
proved to be an unacceptable departure from the customary practice.
Drummond (1989:141–42) reports that Elder J. H. Oliphant estimated
in his 1923 autobiography that approximately two thousand members
had to leave the Old Baptists for participating in this movement. Now
called Progressive Primitive Baptists, those who use organs in their
churches have separated themselves further from the main body of
Primitive Baptists by adopting most of the institutions of traditional
Protestant evangelical denominations. They support homes for the
aged, Sunday schools, ladies aid societies, youth fellowship groups, and
a denominational college in Thomasville, Georgia.

The sound, then, is a powerful construction of identity that can
both create and destroy social and religious bonds. In these Primitive Baptist churches, song both literally and symbolically expresses
predestinarian doctrine. Although songs, like women, are assigned a
subordinate role in public worship, in effect, they often operate pow-
erfully and independently alongside doctrine. As women are the em-
bodiments and carriers of the metaphors of church, home, and family, the sound of unaccompanied congregational singing is a symbolic
but highly complex statement of who Primitive Baptists are and what
they most deeply believe and feel.

Notes

Chapter 1: Singing in Primitive Baptist Worship

1. In this book, I follow Primitive Baptist practice in using the terms Primitive Baptists, Old School Baptists, and Old Baptists interchangeably. These groups have also been called Old Line Baptists and Anti-Mission Baptists. Readers should note, however, that the Old Regular Baptists also refer to themselves as Old Baptists. Congregations in both Primitive Baptist and Old Regular Baptist churches show similarities in their practice of unaccompanied hymn singing and they share some of the same religious song repertory. One Primitive Baptist elder in eastern Kentucky reported that he had preached occasionally for the Old Regular Baptists when their own preacher could not be there. Nevertheless, Primitives and Old Regulars do not think of themselves as the "same people." Generally speaking, the Primitive Baptists are more Calvinistic than the Old Regular Baptists in their doctrines about salvation. For a detailed discussion of doctrinal differences between the Primitive Baptists and the Old Regular Baptists, see Dorgan (1987; 1989:34–40).

2. This hypothesis has an important predecessor in Jeff Todd Titon's *Powerhouse for God*. In his comprehensive study of an evangelical Independent Baptist church in Virginia, Titon looks at singing, preaching, teaching, prayer, and testimony in the church and argues that all of this religious language defines and establishes identity and community (1988:4).

3. This arrangement is reversed in some churches outside the Mountain District Association with women seated on the left and men on the right. The traditional practice of congregational seating that separates men and women is no longer strictly observed; however, members still speak of interior spaces of the meetinghouse as "the men's side" and "the women's side," and many continue to sit accordingly.

4. The churches in the Mountain District Primitive Baptist Association were not the only ones we visited, but they were the primary focus of our joint field research and they are the main point of reference for the present study. Unless otherwise noted, I draw on this group of churches when making general statements about Primitive Baptists. Some of the most insightful comments about singing, however, came from members of neighboring associations.

5. One Kentucky congregation we visited substituted an above-ground swimming pool at a member's home when its usual creek location was unusable because of damage from spring floods.

6. The undecorated walls in the North Carolina and Virginia churches contrasted with walls that held collections of objects in several eastern Kentucky Primitive Baptist churches. Here again, the displayed objects reflected the metaphors of home and family—photographs of church elders, a picture of Leonardo's *Last Supper,* clocks, calendars, hatracks, and a framed copy of a sentimental poem, "Footprints in the Sand."

7. Although this appears to be the pattern among Primitive Baptists, one notable exception is Elder Guy Hunt, who was elected governor of Alabama in 1986.

Chapter 2: Roots of Old Baptist Song Practices

1. The scriptural basis cited for this claim includes Acts 15, Heb. 9:10 and 10:1–9, and Rom. 10:4 (Pittman 1909:382).

2. Primitive Baptists do not think of themselves as either Calvinists or Protestants. Instead, they claim spiritual kinship to a succession of sectarian groups that existed outside of, and in opposition to, the Roman church long before the Reformation. In telling the history of their individual congregations, a church spokesman typically presents a line of succession that extends unbroken from the early church to the present. For one example, see West (1973:54).

In their historical view, Primitive Baptists recognize in Calvin one of the great defenders of their doctrines of grace and election, but they take strong exception to his acceptance of infant baptism and his lack of separation of church and state (Hassell and Hassell 1886:499; see also Peacock and Tyson 1989:33–35).

3. For ideas that help place Primitive Baptist singing in a theological context, I am indebted to Charles Garside's research, especially his exploration of Calvin's theology of music (1979). Garside relates Calvin's position on singing to a pastoral concern that the worship experience of each member of his congregation be edifying and intense, and to Calvin's experience with the vernacular congregational psalmody already established by Martin Bucer in the Strasbourg congregation that Calvin served from 1538 to 1541. To suggest the power of this singing, Garside quotes from a letter written "by a young man from Antwerp who had sought refuge in Strasbourg during Easter Week of 1545": "On Sundays . . . we sing a psalm of David or some other prayer taken from the New Testament. The psalm or prayer is sung by everyone together, men as well as women with a beautiful unanimity, which is something beautiful to behold. For you must understand that each one has a music book in his hand; that is why they cannot lose touch with one another. Never did I think that it could be as pleasing and delightful as it is. For five or six days at first, as I looked upon this little company, exiled from coun-

tries everywhere for having upheld the honor of God and His Gospel, I would begin to weep, not at all from sadness, but from joy at hearing them sing so heartily, and, as they sang, giving thanks to the Lord that He had led them to a place where His name is honored and glorified. No one could believe the joy which one experiences when one is singing the praises and wonders of the Lord in the mother tongue as one sings them here" (1979:18).

4. The Baptist controversies about singing in late-seventeenth-century England are documented in numerous tracts, most of which were published in the last quarter of the century. Although my accounts are limited to Baptist arguments, other sectarian views are also represented in these publications. For additional summary accounts of this period see Young (1959).

5. Thomas Crosby writes of the growth of Keach's church that "they had frequently occasion to enlarge the place of their assembling, so that at length it became a place large enough for the accommodation of near a thousand people" (1738–40, 4:273).

6. This is still a common pattern. We met a number of Primitive Baptist elders who reported joining the Primitive Baptists after becoming convinced that the Arminian doctrines of churches they had originally joined were in error.

7. See also Goadby (1871:317–49).

8. Lumpkin 1969:281. This statement is from chapter 22, "Of Religious Worship, and the Sabbath Day," of the Second London Confession adopted and approved 1677, and adopted in 1689 by the first English Particular Baptist General Assembly, a gathering of representatives of 107 churches throughout England and Wales meeting in London. See Peacock and Tyson (1989:243–55, Appendix B) for minutes of this meeting.

9. Pennepack (later called Lower Dublin), Middletown, Piscataway, Cohansey, and Welsh Tract formed the Philadelphia Association in 1707.

10. For additional information about Morgan Edwards (b. 1722 in Wales; d. 1795), see McKibbens and Smith (1980).

11. Older members of churches in the Mountain District Association said that, in the past, some women would shout regularly in Primitive Baptist services. However, shouting is rarely heard in these churches now. Women do speak in some business meetings, but this practice is not yet commonly accepted by men or women in the Mountain Association.

Chapter 3: Religious Identity and the Sound of Singing

1. According to Jeff Titon (personal correspondence), the use of solos in Old Regular Baptist services seems to be a relatively recent development, perhaps only a generation old.

2. The song leader did not forget these requests. Instead, he refreshed his memory on the tunes and honored the requests by calling for them himself in the next meeting.

3. A comparison of texts attributed to Isaac Watts in Primitive Baptist

hymnbooks with the earliest publication of some of those texts reveals numerous differences. Such changes are common practice with hymnbook compilers in other denominations also.

4. See chapter 4 for a discussion of the feminine references in these texts.

5. A few Primitive Baptists (along with a number of Old Regular Baptists) continue to line out hymns. Churches have been under pressure to abandon this practice since the early eighteenth century when it was labeled old-fashioned in England. John Rippon, pastor of a late-eighteenth-century Particular Baptist church in London, published a hymnbook that was used by Elder Wilson Thompson, one of the early predestinarian Baptist preachers in the southern mountains. Rippon's preface provides a glimpse of English efforts to rid churches of this practice: "The several ministers who preached a course of sermons in East Cheap dated 1708, 1711, 1713, and 1717, say under the duty of singing, there remains one thing we are concerned to plead for, namely, a practice which has lately obtained in some of our congregations, and that is singing of Psalms without reading. This had been [a] matter of scruple to some people, and to remove an old custom, though a bad one, is like removing ancient land marks, &c. The arguments which are given in these sermons for singing without parcelling out the lines are very convincing; and I have the pleasure to remark that this practice is gaining ground in some congregations of the first note in London, at Bristol, and elsewhere—and it is hoped that it will soon become pretty general where it can be conveniently introduced" (1801:viii).

6. For a musical example, see hymn 119 in the *Primitive Baptist Hymn and Tune Book* (Daily 1918).

7. An early publication of "Bourbon" appears in *Supplement to the Kentucky Harmony* (Davisson 1820:61).

8. The three texts are: "When I survey the wondrous cross"; "Awake, my soul, in joyful lays"; and, "I am a stranger here below."

9. This statement appears as the third article of the "Constitution" published in the annual *Minutes of the Mountain District Primitive Baptist Association* (1988). In addition to the constitution, this booklet includes the proceedings of the meeting, a list of all visiting ministers, a directory of churches, meeting schedules and statistical tables for all churches in the association, and obituaries with photographs of all members deceased since the last association meeting.

Chapter 4: Woman as Singer and Symbol

1. Women so readily defer to men when questions arise about church practice and doctrine that they might be overlooked in a study of Primitive Baptists. However, women are extraordinarily influential in their congregations. This chapter explores the complexities of their attitudes and participation in a male-dominated church.

2. As noted earlier, Primitive Baptists are not all alike in this practice. The wife of a church elder in Virginia reported that the practice of women's si-

lence was not strictly observed in an independent church where her husband preached. In the business meeting of a Kentucky church, I observed several women taking part in a discussion about whether to hold the annual association meeting at a local school or at the church. The presiding elder appeared to be soliciting their opinions in an effort to reach a consensus. Afterward, another woman said that she thought women should not participate in business meeting discussions. She reasoned that women "would take over if you let them."

3. Congregations permit and encourage only their male members to exercise their spiritual gifts publicly. A trial period in which a church "liberates" a man to introduce services and preach precedes his ordination as an elder. Members believe that, although the church may grant men permission to speak, the speaker will have little to offer unless God gives him "spiritual liberty."

4. Women have obligations to provide food only for the annual meeting of their own home church and for the annual three-day association meeting when their home church is hosting it. However, many attend the annual meetings of their sister churches, and some take food to these meetings also.

5. It is worth noting that in these texts, Primitive Baptists retain vestiges of thinking that assign feminine characteristics to strong traits such as reason and wisdom. Notably lacking in this group of traits are generosity, modesty, gentleness, and sympathy, which, feminist scholars argue, are traditional concepts of womanhood and femininity, and which are virtues that can easily be turned into negatives of exploitation, self-effacement, and servility (DuBois et al. 1985:104–6).

6. The following hymn texts also refer to the soul as feminine. It is possible that some congregations still sing these hymns, but we did not record them in any of the services we attended.

My soul stands trembling while she sings
The honors of her God. (Goble, no. 5)

My favored soul shall meekly learn
To lay her reason at thy throne. (Goble, no. 5)

My willing soul would stay . . .
And sit and sing herself away. (Goble, no. 49)

My soul looks back to see . . .
And hopes her guilt was there. (Goble, no. 64)

O, if my Lord would come and meet,
My soul should stretch her wings in haste,
Fly fearless through death's iron gate,
Nor feel the terrors as she passed. (Goble, no. 144)

7. See figure 51 for an alternate tune ("In the Pines").

8. Elder Roten was one of two Primitive Baptist preachers to refer to this hymn text as expressive of his religious experience.

9. For the full text of this hymn (Goble, no. 199) see chapter 3.

10. See figures 70 ("Idumea") and 71 ("Ninety-third") for representative tunes.

11. Quoted, with permission, from an unpublished manuscript.

Chapter 5: Creativity in the Old Way of Singing

1. This is the familiar tune for "Nearer My God to Thee." One Primitive Baptist elder claimed this as his favorite tune.

2. "Windham" was first published in Daniel Read's *American Singing Book* in 1785. It appears in many shape-note tune books, including *The Southern Harmony, Original Sacred Harp,* and in most Primitive Baptist hymn and tune books.

3. This particular fuging-tune adaptation as a unison melody appears with a different text in a hymnal used by one of the Mountain District Association churches, Monsees's *Old School Hymnal* No. 9, hymn 112. Green's editions (nos. 10 and 11) of that hymnal, Daily's *Primitive Baptist Hymn and Tune Book* (hymn 317), and Cayce's *The Good Old Songs* (hymn 10) use the text "When I can read my title clear" with other arrangements of "Ninety-fifth" that include imitative sections.

4. Jackson (1981 [1952]:20) also published his transcription of L. L. McDowell, Smithville, Tennessee, singing "Detroit" as it was sung by Old Baptists at the Old Philadelphia church near Smithville in the late 1800s.

5. See Daily's *Primitive Baptist Hymn and Tune Book,* hymn 328; Cayce's *The Good Old Songs,* hymn 282; and Green's *Old School Hymnal,* hymn 298.

6. See Daily's *Primitive Baptist Hymn and Tune Book,* hymns 305 and 365; Cayce's *The Good Old Songs,* hymn 127; and Durand and Lester's *Hymn and Tune Book,* hymn 222.

7. This tune (fig. 43) is very similar to "This Land for Me," which William Hauser arranged for the *Olive Leaf* (1878), and also to "Adieu," which Elder John Daily arranged for his *Primitive Baptist Hymn and Tune Book.*

8. For a musical example, see "Balm in Gilead" in Jackson (1953 [1937]: 147).

9. "In the Pines" exists in many variants and has been the subject of intensive research by Judith McCulloh (1970) and Norm Cohen (1981:491–502). For Cecil Sharp's minor-sounding tune transcription, see "Black Girl," in his *English Folk Songs from the Southern Appalachians* (1932, 2:278). Leonard Roberts (1980:156) transcribed a major-sounding version of "In the Pines" with a melodic form of AB that corresponds to the couplet form of the verse.

10. G. P. Jackson found the text of this chorus, an anonymous verse, in the 1859 edition of *The Sacred Harp,* and a version of the tune in William E. Barton's *Old Plantation Hymns* (1899); Jackson characterized the tune as "made of melodic scraps" (1975 [1944]:172–73).

11. For musical examples of this type of adaptation by ballad singers, see two of Cecil Sharp's transcriptions of "The Mermaid" in *English Folk Songs from the Southern Appalachians* (1932, 1:291, 293).

12. For Bronson's discussion and his musical examples, see *The Tradition-al Tunes of the Child Ballads,* vol. 2, especially Cecil Sharp's transcription of "Wife of Usher's Well," collected in Kentucky.

13. Two other related tunes, each credited to a different Primitive Baptist elder, have recently appeared in Primitive Baptist hymnals. Both tunes em-ploy phrase stock similar to that of the tunes in figures 60, 61, and 62, yet neither contains a phrase that is exactly like those being sung in the moun-tain churches. See "Lead Thou Me" (hymn 317) and "Meditations" (hymn 198) in the *Old School Hymnal,* No. 11 (Green 1983).

14. For a mid-nineteenth-century shape-note example of the "Babe of Beth-lehem" tune, see Walker (1966 [1854]: 78).

15. For a musical example, see the tune "Preservation" (hymn 53) by John R. Daily in his *Primitive Baptist Hymn and Tune Book.* The first phrase of this tune is similar to the first phrase of a shape-note tune, "Sweet Rivers," that appears in nineteenth-century shape-note tunebooks. Examples are accessi-ble in the *Original Sacred Harp* (White 1971 [1844]: 61), and *The Southern Har-mony* (Walker 1966 [1854]: 166).

16. See Patterson (1979:89) for a similar but longer tune reportedly sung at the Shaker funeral of Mother Ann Lee in 1784. The Old Baptist tune has been recorded since then in longer versions from singers in Kentucky and North Carolina.

Chapter 6: The Influence of Notation and Gospel Songs

1. For a musical example, see "Cross and Crown" (no. 393), in the *Primi-tive Baptist Hymn and Tune Book* (Daily 1918).

2. Hymn text published without tune (no. 178) in the *Primitive Baptist Hymn and Tune Book* (Daily 1918).

3. For a musical example, see "Suffering Savior" (no. 182) from the *Prim-itive Baptist Hymn and Tune Book* (Daily 1918).

4. For a musical example, see "He Loves Me" (no. 138) in the *Old School Hymnal,* no. 11 (Green 1983)

5. For musical examples, see "Sweet Name" (no. 115) and "Ortonville" (no. 272) in the *Primitive Baptist Hymn and Tune Book* (Daily 1918).

6. Use of music notation has been reported as a source of controversy in a few churches, but the controversy has been hard to document. Tallmadge (1984) quotes briefly from an interview with Primitive Baptist elders who said that a disagreement over using note books caused a split in Primitive Bap-tist churches in the mountain region. Drummond (1989) reports being unable to document the controversy in any publications within the denomination.

Selected Field Recordings

These field recordings were made by one or more of the following persons, unless indicated otherwise: Daniel Patterson, James Peacock, Ruel Tyson, Beverly Bush (Boggs) Patterson, and Debra Warner. These and other recordings and materials from the World and Identity in Ritual Action project are on deposit in the Southern Folklife Collection at the University of North Carolina, Chapel Hill, North Carolina.

WI-004. Interview. 25 May 1982. At home near West Jefferson, North Carolina.

WI-007. Interview. 3 June 1982. At home near Sparta, North Carolina.

WI-008. Worship service (Saturday). 5 June 1982. Union Primitive Baptist Church, Whitehead, North Carolina. Elder Walter Evans, pastor.

WI-009. Worship service (Sunday). 6 June 1982. Union Primitive Baptist Church, Whitehead, North Carolina. Elder Walter Evans, pastor.

WI-019. Interview. 11 June 1982. At home near West Jefferson, North Carolina.

WI-020. Interview. 11 June 1982. At home in Fleetwood, North Carolina.

WI-026. Elder Walter Evans, interview and songs. 18 November 1980. At home in Sparta, North Carolina. Recorded by Tom Davenport.

WI-027. Worship service (Saturday). 18 July 1970. Little River Primitive Baptist Church, Sparta, North Carolina. Elder Walter Evans, pastor; Cliff Holloway, song leader. Recorded by Daniel Patterson and Blanton Owen.

WI-029. Interview. 18 June 1982. At home in Baywood, Virginia.

WI-030. Worship service (Saturday). 19 June 1982. Little River Primitive Baptist Church, Sparta, North Carolina. Elder Walter Evans, pastor.

WI-031. Worship service (Sunday, communion). 20 June 1982. Little River Primitive Baptist Church, Sparta, North Carolina. Elder Walter Evans, pastor

WI-033. Worship service (Sunday evening). 20 June 1982. Cross Roads Primitive Baptist Church, Baywood, Virginia. Elder Curtis Hash, pastor.

WI-038. Hymn sing. 24 June 1982. At home in Baywood, Virginia.

WI-039. Worship service (Wednesday). 23 June , 1982. Cross Roads Primitive Baptist Church, Baywood, Virginia.

WI-042. Worship service (Saturday). 26 June 1982. Antioch Primitive Baptist Church, Stratford, North Carolina. Elder Walter Evans, pastor.

WI-045. Worship service (Saturday). 3 July 1982. Union Primitive Baptist Church, Whitehead, North Carolina.

WI-048. Worship service (Sunday, communion). 27 June 1982. Antioch Primitive Baptist Church, Stratford, North Carolina. Elder Walter Evans, pastor.

WI-059. Interview and songs. 6 July 1982. At home near West Jefferson, North Carolina.

WI-062. Interview. 7 July 1982. At home near Independence, Virginia.

WI-070. Worship service (Sunday, communion). 11 July 1982. Peach Bottom Primitive Baptist Church, near Independence, Virginia.

WI-071. Worship service (Sunday). 11 July 1982. Woodruff Primitive Baptist Church, Glade Valley, North Carolina.

WI-082. Worship service (Sunday). 16 May 1982. Little River Primitive Baptist Church, Sparta, North Carolina. Elder Walter Evans, pastor.

WI-083. Worship service (Sunday). 4 July 1982. Cross Roads Primitive Baptist Church, Baywood, Virginia. Elder Curtis Hash, pastor.

WI-087. Worship service (Sunday). 18 July 1982. Cross Roads Primitive Baptist Church, Baywood, Virginia. Elder Curtis Hash, pastor.

WI-088. Interview. 15 July 1982. At home in Galax, Virginia.

WI-089. Worship service (Sunday). 18 July 1982. Little River Primitive Baptist Church, Sparta, North Carolina. Elder Walter Evans, pastor.

WI-094. Interview, 21 July 1982. At home in Galax, Virginia.

WI-097. Worship service (Sunday). 25 July 1982. Antioch Primitive Baptist Church, Stratford, North Carolina. Elder Walter Evans, pastor.

WI-100. Elder Eddie Lyle, interview and songs. 24 July 1982. At home in West Jefferson, North Carolina.

WI-103. Mountain District Primitive Baptist Association meeting (Sunday). 5 September 1982. Sparta Elementary School, Sparta, North Carolina.

WI-105. Worship service (Sunday). 1 August 1982. Indian Creek Primitive Baptist Church on its 190th anniversary, Union, West Virginia. Elder Norvel Mann, pastor.

WI-106. Elder Billy Cook, interview. 29 July 1982. At home near Chilhowie, Virginia.

WI-109. Interview. 26 July 1982. At home in Galax, Virginia.

WI-110. Interview. 28 July 1982. At home in Sparta, North Carolina.

WI-112. Interview. 27 July 1982. At home near Sparta, North Carolina.

WI-122. Worship service (Saturday). 4 June 1983. Union Primitive Baptist Church, Whitehead, North Carolina. Elder Walter Evans, pastor.

WI-127. Interview and songs. 28 July 1982. At home near West Jefferson, North Carolina.

WI-128. Worship service (Sunday, communion). 19 June 1983. Little River Primitive Baptist Church, Sparta, North Carolina. Elder Walter Evans, pastor.

WI-131. Worship service (Monday, ordination of deacon). 20 June 1983. Cross Roads Primitive Baptist Church, Baywood, Virginia. Elder Curtis Hash, pastor.

WI-135. Worship service (Sunday, communion). 3 July 1983. Union Primitive Baptist Church, Whitehead, North Carolina. Elder Walter Evans, pastor.

WI-137. Worship service (Thursday evening). 23 June 1983. Cross Roads Primitive Baptist Church, Baywood, Virginia. Elder Curtis Hash, pastor.

WI-138. Worship service (Friday evening). 24 June 1983. Cross Roads Primitive Baptist Church, Baywood, Virginia. Elder Curtis Hash, pastor.

WI-139. Interview. 24 June 1983. At home in Baywood, Virginia.

WI-143. Worship service (Saturday). 9 July 1983. Peach Bottom Primitive Baptist Church, near Independence, Virginia.

WI-144/145. Worship service (Sunday, communion). 10 July 1983. Woodruff Primitive Baptist Church, Glade Valley, North Carolina.

WI-147. Interview. 27 June 1983. At home near Baywood, Virginia.

WI-155. Elder Walter Evans, interview. 22 July 1983. At home in Sparta, North Carolina.

WI-156. Worship service (Saturday). 23 July 1983. Antioch Primitive Baptist Church, Stratford, North Carolina. Elder Walter Evans, pastor.

WI-159. Interview. 23 July 1983. At home in Sparta, North Carolina.

WI-162. Worship service (Thursday night). 28 July 1983. Little River Primitive Baptist Church, Sparta, North Carolina. Elder Walter Evans, pastor.

WI-165. Elder Walter Evans, interview. 30 July 1983. At home in Sparta, North Carolina.

WI-168. Recorded notes. 3 August 1983. Near Sparta, North Carolina.

WI-174. Interview. 29 July 1983. At home in Sparta, North Carolina.

WI-185. Interview. 14 July 1983. At home in Winston-Salem, North Carolina.

WI-189. Association meeting (Saturday). 3 September 1983. Mountain District Primitive Baptists at Independence High School, Independence, Virginia.

WI-198. Worship service (Saturday). 13 August 1983. Galax Primitive Baptist Church, Galax, Virginia. Elder Jess Higgins, pastor.

WI-204. Association meeting (Saturday). 5 September 1981. Mountain District Primitive Baptists at Cross Roads Primitive Baptist Church, Baywood, Virginia.

WI-207. Association meeting (Sunday). 25 September 1983. Original Little River Primitive Baptists' 154th Annual Meeting at Little Flock Primitive Baptist Church, Coats, North Carolina.

WI-222. Worship service (Saturday). 24 July 1982. Antioch Primitive Baptist Church, Stratford, North Carolina. Elder Walter Evans, pastor.

Bibliographic Essay

Readers who want to acquaint themselves further with Primitive Baptists—with the sound of their singing and with related issues in religious folksong, folk religion, women's studies, and Appalachian culture—will find useful information in sources ranging from documentary sound recordings to scholarly books and articles, and denominational publications. I have already referred to some of these in the text. Here I will briefly review a few other materials to indicate directions that additional explorations might take. The list of Selected References gives full bibliographical data for these and works previously cited.

Readers who are unfamiliar with the sound of Primitive Baptist singing may want to hear recordings in addition to the one that accompanies this book. *Old Hymns Lined and Led by Elder Walter Evans* (ca. 1960) documents the oldest style of Primitive Baptist singing, still practiced in one of the churches we visited during our study. One performance from this recording has been reissued in an album available from the Library of Congress, *Religious Music: Congregational and Ceremonial* (1976). Another album, *Primitive Baptist Hymns of the Blue Ridge* (1982), recorded by Joel Brett Sutton and Peter D. Hartman, offers a rich and complex view of Primitive Baptist hymnody as performed in churches near where we worked, but in the absolutist branch of Primitive Baptists. Recordings in this album document the singing of both African-American and Anglo-American descendants of Virginians who once worshipped together as slaves and masters. In his accompanying booklet, Sutton traces patterns of change in the religious song repertories of these now-separate Primitive Baptist churches. He compares the singing styles of neighboring congregations and demonstrates the diversity of Primitive Baptist singing in a regional and multicultural context.

Another sound recording juxtaposes Primitive Baptist hymnody with other American religious folksong in the Blue Ridge Mountains. *Children of the Heavenly King* (1981), edited by Charles Wolfe from 1978 field recordings, samples a range of religious folksong in a single region. In this album, listeners can hear the contrasting song styles and repertories sung in Blue Ridge churches, ranging from the solemn, unaccompanied voices of Primitive Baptist singers in some of the very churches we visited to the amplified guitars and exuberant voices of their Pentecostal neighbors.

The older secular instrumental traditions familiar to Primitive Baptists of the Blue Ridge region can be heard in *Old Originals,* volumes 1 and 2 (1976), field recordings made and edited by Tom Carter and Blanton Owen. The musicians, many of them Primitive Baptists, perform fiddle and banjo tunes from a repertory of social music that once coexisted in the community along with the old style of hymnody. Like the song repertory of old ballads and "love songs," instrumental music remained outside the church. It preceded the string-band and bluegrass music popular today among Primitive Baptist musicians.

Of the scholarly work that preceded this documentation, George Pullen Jackson's studies in folk hymnody (1933–52) were important in identifying Primitive Baptists as conservators of an old tradition of American religious folksong. His *White and Negro Spirituals* (1975 [1944]), although flawed, still is the most comprehensive overview of the historical development of this major branch of American folksong. Numerous scholars have published studies of shape-note tunebooks that drew on and fed into religious folksongs, and some articles and dissertations bearing on Primitive Baptist song have appeared since then (Young 1959; Miller 1975; Tallmadge 1975; Temperley 1981). Only recently, however, has any extensive scholarly writing focused entirely on Primitive Baptists, notably the comprehensive booklet for Brett Sutton and Peter Hartman's album (1982) and R. Paul Drummond's *A Portion for the Singers* (1989), a study of Primitive Baptist hymnody by a Primitive Baptist. Drummond introduces the historical and theological framework within which folk hymnody survives among Primitive Baptists and traces the flow of this religious folksong into the more formal choral music of mainstream religion. Not all Primitive Baptist singing is the old style of folk hymnody, however. Drummond reviews hymnbooks used by Primitive Baptists since the mid-eighteenth century, stressing the variety of song types in their repertory, gospel songs especially.

My study of Primitive Baptist song also has numerous precedents in studies of American religious folksong that focused on the repertories of particular communities or churches. Important among these are Don Yoder's *Pennsylvania Spirituals* (1961) and Daniel W. Patterson's *The Shaker Spiritual* (1979). The most fully documented study of religious expression in a single congregation is undoubtedly Jeff Todd Titon's *Powerhouse for God: Speech, Chant, and Song in an Appalachian Baptist Church,* which has appeared in book (1988), sound recording (1982), and film (1988) formats. In these works, Titon incorporates musical expression into a broad and comprehensive study of religious language and identity among Baptists very different from those that are the subject of my study. He is currently at work on a study of the singing of Old Regular Baptists in Kentucky.

Two interdisciplinary studies of American religious song attempt to synthesize analytical approaches of anthropologists with historical research in nineteenth-century American religious song. In one of these, *And They All Sang Hallelujah* (1974), the historian Dickson Bruce chose the camp-meeting spiritual as the key to his interpretation of why southern camp meetings from

1800 to 1845 were such a powerful religious experience for participants. Those song texts, he felt, were the most valid expressions of the participants' own views, and singing them played a crucial role in achieving the religious conversion that was the purpose of the camp meeting. In the second study, *Gospel Hymns and Social Religion* (1978), another historian, Sandra Sizer, used the texts of a later religious song repertory—gospel hymns from the Moody-Sankey revivals of the mid-1870s—to interpret the religious worldview of middle-class Republicans of the urban North during that period. She saw the gospel hymn as a rhetorical strategy articulating feelings that contributed to the idea of a social religion. This social religion, she thought, united people through bonds of emotion, but the rhetoric also contributed to the isolation of home and women in ways that are complex and not yet fully understood. In part, however, the rhetoric isolates the domestic, or women's, sphere by sacralizing it. As home and family became increasingly powerful metaphors for church, they became further removed from the secular world. Bruce and Sizer provide precedent for using the religious song text as a vehicle for interpreting a worldview, but since they work from historical documents alone, they necessarily omit data essential to an anthropological interpretation: an ethnography of the singing itself.

How to interpret ethnographic data about music and singing remains problematic. In *Worlds of Music* (1984), Jeff Titon summarizes general models and categories that ethnomusicologists have developed for cultural studies of music, but there are no clear guidelines yet for how best to analyze this musical information and its accompanying contextual information or how to relate it to social and cultural patterns. Nevertheless, there has been general agreement for some time that such a relationship exists (Merriam 1964; Lomax 1968, 1976; Herndon and McLeod 1979, 1980; Frisbie 1986). Alan Lomax asserts, rightly I think, that the "song style" or performance, apart from the ideas contained in the text, is itself a communication about what is important in the culture, and in his Cantometrics project (1968, 1976) he identified elements of the song performance that may communicate cultural values. He was the first to suggest that such things as the singer's volume and vocal production, the degree of repetitiveness in the song text, and the musical organization of the singers carried messages of importance to a culture. These, of course, must be heard to be evaluated, and Lomax did listen and analyze song style from sound recordings rather than from printed texts. However, he chose his recordings and developed his analytical methods for purposes of cross-cultural comparisons. This level of comparison identifies a number of variables in song performance, but Lomax's suggested correlations with social values remain questionable for present purposes. About half of the features that I felt were significant elements of song style for Primitive Baptists—melodic variations and pitch levels, for example—are not in Lomax's list. Other elements—melodic form, metrical structure, and harmonic style—that I found important to local congregations do not appear to have orderly relationships with social structure at the larger comparative level of cross-cultural analysis.

Readers who are looking for overviews of feminist scholarship may wish to consult the collection of essays in *Feminism and Methodology* (1987), edited by Sandra Harding, or *Feminist Scholarship: Kindling in the Groves of Academe* (1985) by Ellen Carol DuBois, Gail Paradise Kelly, Elizabeth Lapovsky Kennedy, Carolyn W. Korsmeyer, and Lillian S. Robinson. For more particular studies addressing women's issues that my research touches on, such as women's silence, knowledge competence, inequality, and subordination, readers may want to consult *In a Different Voice* (1982) by Carol Gilligan, *Women's Ways of Knowing* (1986) by Mary Field Belenky and others, *Feminism and Anthropology* (1988) by Henrietta L. Moore, and *What Can She Know* (1991) by Lorraine Code, which address these issues from psychological, anthropological, and philosophical perspectives. The folklorist Elaine Lawless has done extensive field research with Pentecostals (*God's Peculiar People* [1988]) and with women who preach in these and other churches (*Handmaidens of the Lord* [1988]; *Holy Women, Wholly Women* [1993]). Her research, in a useful and dramatic contrast to my study, explores the experiences of women who are highly visible and vocal as leaders in their churches.

Readers who are particularly interested in the relationship of gender issues to musical expression will want to explore a group of essays edited by Ellen Koskoff, *Women and Music in Cross-Cultural Perspective* (1989). Although Koskoff acknowledges that theoretical statements are still premature, these essays reveal a growing interest in exploring this important relationship in a wide range of cultural settings. In her own essay, "The Sound of a Woman's Voice: Gender and Music in a New York Hasidic Community," Koskoff explores the role of gender in the musical practice of ultraorthodox Jews in New York City who require extreme separation of men and women in the synagogue. She finds their music performance not only interesting in itself but also an appropriate entrée into the group's fundamental value systems (1989:220–21).

My study of Primitive Baptist singing, while not focused exclusively—or even primarily—on women, nevertheless supports the conviction of these ethnomusicologists that analysis of musical performance can be usefully linked with gender studies to open yet another window on patterns and values that govern women's lives.

Selected References

Allen, Richard. 1696. *An Essay to Prove Singing of Psalms With Conjoin'd Voices, A Christian Duty.* London: J. D. for John Harris.

Belenky, Mary Field, et al. 1986. *Women's Ways of Knowing.* New York: Basic Books; New York: Harper Collins.

Benson, Louis F. 1962. *The English Hymn: Its Development and Use in Worship.* 1915. Richmond, Va.: John Knox Press.

Bliss, P. P., Ira D. Sankey, James McGranahan, and George C. Stebbins. 1886. *Gospel Hymns [Consolidated].* New York: Bigelow and Main, and Cincinnati: John Church Co.

Brackney, William H., gen. ed. 1983. *Baptist Life and Thought: 1600–1980.* Valley Forge, Pa.: Judson Press.

Bradbury, William B., and George F. Root. 1853. *The Shawm; A Library of Church Music.* New York: Mason Brothers.

Bronson, Bertrand. 1959–72. *The Traditional Tunes of the Child Ballads.* Vols. 1–4. Princeton: Princeton University Press.

Bruce, Dickson D., Jr. 1974. *And They All Sang Hallelujah: Plain-Folk Camp-Meeting Religion, 1800–1845.* Knoxville: University of Tennessee Press.

Calvin, John. 1541. *Calvin: Institutes of the Christian Religion.* 1960. Translated by Ford Lewis Battles; edited by John T. McNeill. 2 vols. Philadelphia: Westminster Press.

Cayce, Elder C. H. 1980. *The Good Old Songs.* 1913. 35th ed. Thornton, Ark.: Cayce Publishing Co.

Children of the Heavenly King. 1981. Recordings from the 1978 Blue Ridge Parkway Folklife Project. Edited with booklet by Charles K. Wolfe. Library of Congress AFC L69–L70.

Claridge, R[ichard]. 1697. *An Answer to Richard Allen's Essay, Vindication and Appendix.* With an Epistle by William Russel. London: N.p.

Code, Lorraine. 1991. *What Can She Know.* Ithaca, N.Y.: Cornell University Press.

Cohen, Norm. 1981. *Long Steel Rail: The Railroad in American Folksong.* Urbana: University of Illinois Press.

Collins, Hercules. 1680. *Orthodox Catechism.* An Appendix Concerning the Ordinance of Singing. London: N.p.

Crosby, Tho[mas]. 1738–40. *The History of the English Baptists from the Reformation to the Beginning of the Reign of King George I.* 4 vols. in 2. London: By the author. Reprint. 1978. Lafayette, Tenn.: Church History, Research and Archives.

Daily, Elder John R. 1918. *Primitive Baptist Hymn and Tune Book.* Reprint. Cincinnati: Lasserre Bradley.

Dalton, Elder Len, and Helen Denman Beauchamp. 1961. *Primitive Baptist Hymnal.* 3d ed. Midwest City, Okla.: Baptist Trumpet.

Davisson, Ananias. 1820. *A Supplement to the Kentucky Harmony.* Harrisonburg, Va.: By the author.

Diehl, Katherine Smith. 1966. *Hymns and Tunes—An Index.* New York: Scarecrow Press.

Dorgan, Howard. 1987. *Giving Glory to God in Appalachia: Worship Practices of Six Baptist Subdenominations.* Knoxville: University of Tennessee Press.

———. 1989. *The Old Regular Baptists of Central Appalachia: Brothers and Sisters in Hope.* Knoxville: University of Tennessee Press.

Drummond, Robert Paul. 1986. "A History of Music Among Primitive Baptists Since 1800." Ph.D. diss., University of Northern Colorado.

———. 1989. *A Portion for the Singers.* Atwood, Tenn: Christian Baptist Library and Publishing Co.

DuBois, Ellen Carol, et al. 1985. *Feminist Scholarship: Kindling in the Groves of Academe.* Urbana: University of Illinois Press.

Durand, Silas H., and P. G. Lester. 1886. *Hymn and Tune Book.* Greenfield, Ind.: D. H. Goble Printing Co.

Frisbie, Charlotte, ed. 1986. *Explorations in Ethnomusicology: Essays in Honor of David McAllester.* Detroit: Information Coordinators.

Garside, Charles, Jr. 1966. *Zwingli and the Arts.* New Haven: Yale University Press.

———. 1967. "Some Attitudes of the Major Reformers Toward the Role of Music in the Liturgy." *McCormick Quarterly* 21(1): 151–68.

———. 1979. "The Origins of Calvin's Theology of Music: 1536–1543." *Transactions of the American Philosophical Society* 69(4): 5–35.

Gillette, A. D., ed. 1851. *Minutes of the Philadelphia Baptist Association, 1743.* Philadelphia: American Baptist Publication Society.

Gilligan, Carol. 1982. *In a Different Voice: Psychological Theory and Women's Development.* Cambridge, Mass.: Harvard University Press.

Goadby, Rev. J. Jackson. 1871. *Bye-Paths in Baptist History.* London: Elliot Stock.

Goble, D. H. 1887. *Primitive Baptist Hymn Book for All Lovers of Sacred Song.* Greenfield, Ind.: D. H. Goble Printing Co.

Goins, June Hawks. 1968. *Children of Comfort.* Cincinnati: Baptist Bible Hour.

Grantham, Thomas. 1678. *Christianismus Primitivus: Or, The Ancient Christian Religion, . . . Vindicated, from . . . Many Abuses.* London: For Francis Smith.

Green, Roland U., ed. 1980. *Old School Hymnal.* No. 10. 1964. Ellenwood, Ga.: Old School Hymnal Co.

———. 1983. *Old School Hymnal.* 11th ed. Ellenwood, Ga.: Old School Hymnal Co.

Grumman, Eleanor. 1951. "Kentucky Mountain Hymn Tunes." M.A. thesis, Union Theological Seminary.

Hassell, Sylvester, and Elder Cushing Biggs Hassell. 1886. *A History of the Church of God from the Creation to A. D. 1885, Including especially the History of the Kehukee Primitive Baptist Association*. Middletown, N.Y.: Gilbert Beebe's Sons.

Hastings, Thomas. 1855. *The Presbyterian Psalmodist*. Philadelphia: Presbyterian Board of Publication.

Hayden, Roger, ed. 1974. *The Records of a Church of Christ in Bristol 1640–1687*. Bristol, Eng.: For the Bristol Record Society.

Haynes, Julietta. 1959. "A History of the Primitive Baptists." Ph.D. diss., University of Texas, Austin.

Herndon, Marcia, and Norma McLeod. 1979. *Music as Culture*. Norwood, Pa.: Norwood Editions.

———. 1980. *The Ethnography of Musical Performance*. Norwood, Pa.: Norwood Editions.

Horn, Dorothy. 1970. *Sing to Me of Heaven*. Gainesville: University of Florida Press.

Ivimey, Joseph. 1811–30. *A History of the English Baptists*. 4 vols. London: For the author.

Jackson, George Pullen. 1964. *White Spirituals in the Southern Uplands*. 1933. Introduction by Don Yoder. Hatboro, Pa.: Folklore Associates.

———. 1953. *Spiritual Folk-Songs of Early America*. 1937. New York: J. J. Augustin.

———. 1975. *Down East Spirituals and Others*. 1943. New York: Da Capo Press.

———. 1975. *White and Negro Spirituals*. 1944. New York: Da Capo Press.

———. 1981. *Another Sheaf of White Spirituals*. 1952. Preface by Don Yoder. New York: Folklorica.

Julian, John J. 1957. *Dictionary of Hymnology*. 1891. New York: Dover Publications.

Keach, Benjamin. 1682. *Tropes and Figures; or, a Treatise of the Metaphors, Allegories, and express Similitudes, &c. contained in the Bible of the Old and New Testament*. London: John Darby.

———. 1691a. *The Breach Repaired in God's Worship: or, Singing of Psalms, Hymns, and Spiritual Songs, proved to be an Holy Ordinance of Jesus Christ*. London: For the author.

———. 1691b. *Spiritual Melody, Containing near Three Hundred Sacred Hymns*. London: John Hancock.

Koskoff, Ellen, ed. 1989. *Women and Music in Cross-Cultural Perspective*. Urbana: University of Illinois Press.

Lawless, Elaine J. 1988a. *God's Peculiar People: Women's Voices and Folk Tradition in a Pentecostal Church*. Lexington: University Press of Kentucky.

———. 1988b. *Handmaidens of the Lord: Pentecostal Women Preachers and Traditional Religion*. Philadelphia: University of Pennsylvania Press.

———. 1993. *Holy Women, Wholly Women*. Philadelphia: University of Pennsylvania Press.

Lloyd, Benjamin. 1978. *The Primitive Hymns*. 1841. Stereotype ed. Rocky Mount, N.C.: Primitive Hymns Corp.

Lomax, Alan. 1968. *Folk Song Style and Culture*. New Brunswick, N.J.: Transaction Books.

———. 1976. *Cantometrics: An Approach to the Anthropology of Music*. Berkeley, Calif.: University of California Extension Media Center.

Lorenz, Ellen Jane. 1978. "A Treasury of Campmeeting Spirituals." Ph.D. diss., Union Graduate School, Ohio.

———. 1978. *Glory, Hallelujah! The Story of the Campmeeting Spiritual*. Nashville, Tenn.: Abingdon.

Lumpkin, William L. 1969. *Baptist Confessions of Faith*. Valley Forge: Judson Press.

McCulloh, Judith. 1970. "'In the Pines': The Melodic-Textual Identity of an American Lyric Folksong Cluster." Ph.D. diss., Indiana University.

McKibbens, Thomas R., Jr., and Kenneth L. Smith. 1980. *The Life and Works of Morgan Edwards*. New York: Arno Press.

Marlow, Isaac. 1690. *A Brief Discourse Concerning Singing in the Public Worship of God in The Gospel-Church*. London: For the author.

———. 1692. *Truth Soberly defended in a Serious Reply to Mr. Benjamin Keach's Book, intituled [sic], The Breach Repaired in God's Worship. . . .* London: For the author.

———. 1696. *The Controversie of Singing Brought to an End*. London: For the author.

Merriam, Alan P. 1964. *The Anthropology of Music*. Evanston: Northwestern University Press.

Miller, Terry. 1975. "Voices from the Past: The Singing and Preaching at Otter Creek Church." *Journal of American Folklore* 88:266–82.

Minutes of the Mountain District Primitive Baptist Association. 1988. Galax, Va.: Gazette Press.

Monsees, J. A. 1963. *Old School Hymnal*. No. 9. Atlanta, Ga.: Old School Hymnal Co.

Moore, Henrietta L. 1988. *Feminism and Anthropology*. Minneapolis: University of Minnesota Press.

Old Hymns Lined and Led by Elder Walter Evans. [Ca. 1960.] Recorded and produced by Elder Lasserre Bradley. Sovereign Grace 6444 and 6057–6058.

Old Originals, Vols. I and II. 1976. Recorded and edited with booklet by Tom Carter and Blanton Owen. Rounder Records 0057 and 0058.

Oliphant, J. H. 1923. *The Autobiography of Elder J. H. Oliphant of Crawfordsville, Ind.* St. Joseph, Mo.: Messenger of Peace.

Palmer, Robert. 1982. Record review in the *New York Times*, 15 Sept., C19.

Patterson, Daniel W. 1979. *The Shaker Spiritual*. Princeton: Princeton University Press.

———. 1985. "A Puzzle in Primitive Baptist Song: Two Papers in Search of an Answer." Unpublished paper.

Peacock, James L., and Ruel W. Tyson, Jr. 1989. *Pilgrims of Paradox: Calvinism and Experience among the Primitive Baptists of the Blue Ridge*. Washington, D.C.: Smithsonian Institution Press.

Phillips, R. Anna. 1875. *The Experience of R. Anna Phillips of Rome, Georgia; And Her Reasons for Uniting with the Primitive Baptists &c*. Wilson, N.C.: P. D. Gold.

Pittman, R. H. 1909. *Biographical History of Primitive or Old School Baptist Ministers of the United States including . . . Brief Sketches of a Few of Our Talented and Spiritually-Minded Sisters and "Mothers in Israel."* Anderson, Ind.: Herald Publishing.

Powerhouse for God. 1982. Recorded by Jeff Todd Titon and Kenneth Martin George. Edited with booklet by Jeff Todd Titon. University of North Carolina Press.

Primitive Baptist Hymns of the Blue Ridge. 1982. Recorded by Brett Sutton and Peter Hartman. Edited with booklet by Brett Sutton. University of North Carolina Press.

Religious Music: Congregational and Ceremonial. 1976. Folk Music in America Series, vol. 1. Edited with notes by Richard K. Spottswood. Washington, D.C.: Library of Congress.

Reyburn, Hugh Y. 1914. *John Calvin*. London: Hodder and Stoughton.

Rippon, John. 1801. *A Selection of Hymns*. 1787. Burlington, N.J.: S. C. Ustick.

Roberts, Leonard. 1980. *Sang Branch Settlers*. Pikeville, Ky.: College Press of the Appalachin Studies Center.

Scholes, Percy A. 1934. *The Puritans and Music in England and New England*. London: Oxford University Press.

Sears, M. J., and Thomas B. Ausmus. 1879. *The Primitive Baptist Hymnal*. St. Louis, Mo.: Wm. and E. Stephens.

Sharp, Cecil. 1932. *English Folk Songs from the Southern Appalachians*. Vols. 1–2. Edited by Maud Karpeles. London: Oxford University Press.

Sizer, Sandra S. 1978. *Gospel Hymns and Social Religion*. Philadelphia: Temple University Press.

Sovine, Melanie. 1979. "On the Study of Religion in Appalachia: A Review Essay." *Appalachian Journal* (Spring): 239–44.

———. 1982. "Been a Long Time Travelin': Three Primitive Baptist Women." An edited and annotated radio program transcript. Lexington: The Appalachian Center, University of Kentucky.

———. 1986. "Traditionalism, Antimissionism, and the Primitive Baptist Religion: A Preliminary Analysis." In *Reshaping the Image of Appalachia*, edited by Loyal Jones. Berea, Ky.: Berea College Appalachian Center.

Spencer, David. 1877. *The Early Baptists of Philadelphia*. Philadelphia: William Syckelmoore.

Stevenson, Arthur L. 1931. *The Story of Southern Hymnology*. Salem, Va.: By the author.

Stevenson, Robert M. 1953. *Patterns of Protestant Church Music*. Durham, N.C.: Duke University Press.

———. 1966. *Protestant Church Music in America*. New York: Norton.

Sutton, Joel Brett. 1976. "The Gospel Hymn, Shaped Notes, and the Black Tradition: Continuity and Change in American Traditional Music." Master's thesis, University of North Carolina at Chapel Hill.

———. 1977. "In the Good Old Way: Primitive Baptist Traditions." *Southern Exposure* 5 (Summer and Fall): 97–104.

———. 1982. See *Primitive Baptist Hymns of the Blue Ridge.*

———. 1983. "Spirit and Polity in a Black Primitive Baptist Church." Ph.D. diss., University of North Carolina at Chapel Hill.

Tallmadge, William. 1975. "Baptist Monophonic and Heterophonic Hymnody in Southern Appalachia." *Yearbook for Inter-American Musical Research* 11:106–36.

———. 1984. "Folk Organum: A Study of Origins." *American Music* 2(3): 47–65.

Temperley, Nicholas. 1981. "The Old Way of Singing: Its Origins and Development." *Journal of the American Musicological Society* 34 (Fall): 511–47.

Thompson, Elder Wilson. 1962. *The Autobiography of Elder Wilson Thompson.* 1867. Cincinnati: Lasserre Bradley.

Titon, Jeff Todd. 1982. See *Powerhouse for God.*

———. 1984. *Worlds of Music.* New York: Schirmer Books.

———. 1988. *Powerhouse for God: Speech, Chant, and Song in an Appalachian Baptist Church.* Austin: University of Texas Press.

Torbet, Robert G. 1950. *A History of the Baptists.* Philadelphia: Judson Press.

Tyson, Ruel W. 1986. "Voices in Primitive Baptist Calvinism." *Notebooks in Cultural Analysis.* Vol. 3. Durham, N.C.: Duke University Press.

Walker, William. 1958. *The Christian Harmony.* 1867. Revised by John Deason and O. A. Parris. N.p.: Christian Harmony Publishing Co.

———. 1966. *The Southern Harmony.* 1854. Edited by Glenn C. Wilcox. Los Angeles: Pro Musicamericana Reprint.

West, Emma Mahulda. 1973. *Primitive Baptist Ministers.* New Cambria, Mo.: West Museum.

White, Benjamin Franklin. 1971. *Original Sacred Harp.* 1844. Denson revison. Cullman, Ala.: Sacred Harp Publishing.

Whitten, A. N. 1977. *Harp of Ages.* 1925. With additional hymns. Muleshoe, Tex.: Harp of Ages.

Wicks, Sammie Ann. 1983. "Life and Meaning: Singing, Praying, and the Word among the Old Regular Baptists of Eastern Kentucky." Ph.D. diss., University of Texas at Austin.

Wyeth, John. 1964. *Repository of Sacred Music, Part Second.* 1820. New York: Da Capo Press.

Yoder, Don. 1961. *Pennsylvania Spirituals.* Lancaster, Pa.: Pennsylvania Folklore Society.

Young, Robert H. 1959. "The History of Baptist Hymnody in England from 1612 to 1800." D.M.A. diss., University of Southern California.

Note on the Recording

The sound recording that accompanies *The Sound of the Dove* represents the general practice of Old Baptist singing: unaccompanied song, often unison, that uses traditional melodies and texts voicing the doctrine of predestination as written in eighteenth- and nineteenth-century hymn texts. It also illustrates subtle differences from congregation to congregation, though not the full range of song style in Primitive Baptist churches across the country. It is limited to churches and church members we visited in the mountains of North Carolina, Virginia, and Kentucky, and a few congregations nearby pastored by elders who exchanged visits. These churches represent the conservative practice of calvinistic Baptists who split from the Arminian Baptists in the 1830s.

Most of the selections date from 1982 or 1983, when field research for this project was underway. Five others predate the project by more than a decade. One of these, recorded by Daniel Patterson and Blanton Owen, dates from their 1970 visit to the Little River Church in Sparta, North Carolina, prompted by hearing Elder Lasserre Bradley's 1960 recordings of that congregation. Four more, by William Talmadge, who recorded Primitive Baptists in North Carolina and Kentucky in 1970, supplement the repertory recorded in our field tapes. One additional selection comes from recordings made by filmmaker Tom Davenport during an exploratory field trip in 1980.

This recording, then, is a composite of recordings made across more than a decade by various individuals, using different equipment. It is intended to complement the book but does not a offer a precise correspondence with examples transcribed in the book. Where possible, however, I refer listeners to relevant transcriptions in the book. Some performances are the same ones as transcribed; others are different performances of the same tune. The following notes contain texts for the few songs that do not have references to figures in the book.

Side One: The Common Practice of Singing in Two Mountain Churches

Little River Primitive Baptist Church

The Little River Primitive Baptist Church, pastored by Elder Walter Evans, sang from D. H. Goble's *Primitive Baptist Hymn Book* (1887), which contains no musical scores. Like members of virtually all branches of the Primitive Baptists, they sing without instrumental accompaniment. Elder Evans sometimes lined out the hymns, but more often the Little River congregation simply followed the printed text. As illustrated here, members sang tunes completely by memory and rather slowly. Occasionally, Elder Evans and others harmonized the melody by ear in a style traditional in the region.

1. "There is a land of pure delight" (fig. 63) sung by the congregation of Little River Primitive Baptist Church, Sparta, North Carolina, 20 June 1982, at the church's annual communion meeting (WI-031, FT2155*).

2. "Amazing Grace" (fig. 52) sung by the congregation of Little River Primitive Baptist Church at the same meeting. Like all annual meetings in churches of the Mountain District Association, this one included a communion service followed by footwashing and dinner on the ground. Foot washing, in particular, is a deeply moving ritual that often elicits tears from participants. Led by Elder Evans, the congregation quietly and reflectively sang this unusual setting of "Amazing Grace" as deacons cleared away the pans and utensils that had been used for foot washing. The chorus after each verse, "I want to live a Christian here," implies that this version of the song originated in the camp-meeting era of the early nineteenth century (WI-031, FT2155).

3. Comment by Elder Walter Evans to the congregation at Little River Primitive Baptist Church as he announced the hymn before the church recessed for dinner on the ground. Recorded during the annual meeting described above (WI-031, FT2155):

"Turn to 214 ['O tell me no more of this world's vain store'], [it] just fell on my mind. 'They sang a hymn and went out' [quoting Scripture].

"And [we want] everybody to stay and have lunch when we get through. They've already got the tables up—Baptist recess, of course—and there'll be lunch served out here below the church. Don't go home. Everybody come and eat with us. . . . Never have run out yet, and I'll just say we won't today . . . something to eat. So stay with us and eat dinner with us.

"And we'll sing this hymn, [and] take the parting hand. The Scripture's silent [on] whether or not they had a handshake in that meeting. But the hand of fellowship is taught in the Scripture."

4. "O happy time, long waited for" (not transcribed in *The Sound of the Dove*) sung by the congregation of Little River Primitive Baptist Church, Sparta, North Carolina, 18 July 1970. Recorded by Daniel W. Patterson and Blanton Owen. This is a congregational adaptation of the tune "Liverpool," harmonized by ear and sung a decade earlier than the previous recordings (WI-027, FT2128).

> O happy time, long waited for,
> The comfort of my heart,
> Since I have met the saints once more
> May we in union part.

Temptations cease to break my peace,
And all my sorrows die;
When I with you my love renew,
O what a heav'n have I.

My sorrows past, and I at last
Have heav'nly comforts found,
My heart and treasure is above,
And I for heaven bound.

If fellowship with saints below
Is to our souls so sweet,
What heav'nly raptures shall we know
When round the throne we meet?

While here we sit and sing his love
With raptures so divine,
Our joys are more like theirs above,
While in their songs we join.

Our hearts are filled with holy zeal,
We long to see the King,
We long to see those heav'nly hills,
Where saints and angels sing (Goble no. 195)

Note: The second stanza is omitted because of technical problems on the original recording.

Cross Roads Primitive Baptist Church

Situated fifteen miles north of the Little River church, between Galax and Independence in rural Virginia, the Cross Roads church stands at the center of the Baywood community. This Mountain District Association congregation also sang from the Goble book, often led by Deacon Raymond Nichols. Evidence of the subtle differences between the singing of two affiliated nearby Primitive Baptist congregations shows up in these recordings—in the slightly faster tempos, in several hymn choices reflective of congregational favorites, and in an acceptance of more standardized hymn tunes—while retaining the repertory of traditional tunes.

5. "Glorious things of thee are spoken" (compare with fig. 12) sung by the congregation of Cross Roads Primitive Baptist Church in Baywood, Virginia, Sunday evening, 20 June 1982. The congregation had gathered for a service at the church after a baptizing at a nearby river. This text by John Newton, number 163 in the Goble hymnbook, was a particular favorite at Cross Roads. Women's participation in the singing of this hymn is especially strong, as is their role in maintaining the fellowship of this congregation. We recorded this hymn fourteen times, always with an adaptation of the tune,

"Ripley," attributed to Lowell Mason. Here, a woman requests the hymn during the period of singing before the service begins (WI-033, FT2156).

6. "A home in heaven! what a joyful thought!" (compare with fig. 57) sung by the congregation of Cross Roads Primitive Baptist Church in the same Sunday evening service in 1982. Members knew that this hymn was a favorite of one elderly member whose health was failing. Whenever he attended church, someone requested "number 277." We recorded it five times at Cross Roads, only once or twice at two other churches, but always with the same tune, one related to "Wayfaring Stranger." The tune did not appear in any of the hymnbooks used in the association but all of the singers knew it well (WI-033, FT2156).

7. Comments by the song leader, Deacon Raymond Nichols [RN], during an informal hymn sing at a home in Baywood, Virginia, Thursday afternoon, 24 June 1982. This includes a brief remark by Elder Worth Stephenson [WS] from Wendell, North Carolina.

RN: "You know, that's the secret in not having the notes to these [hymns in the Goble hymnbook]. A fellow can just sing it to suit hisself—however his heart feels. You see, Brother Worth, he's from down below Raleigh, and they turn them [the tunes] just a little different from [the way] we do."

WS: "Yeah, we use note books in two churches, and they kinda get you off, you know, a little bit."

RN: "And you kinda divide up between that and the old timey tunes. And any vicinity you go in, they'll be just a little bit different. You take that one we sung, 307 ['When the day of life is brightest']. I went down, one time, close to Mt. Airy, on a Thanksgiving day. And they had a jig tune for that thing—you could just about dance to!" (WI-038, FT2160)

8. "I am a stranger here below" (compare with fig. 15) sung by the congregation of Cross Roads Primitive Baptist Church, Baywood, Virginia, at a church service on Thursday evening, 24 June 1982. This service, held in the evening after the hymn sing mentioned above, was part of a weeklong series of meetings with a visiting preacher, Elder Worth Stephenson of Wendell (near Raleigh), North Carolina, moderator of the association in his home region. Regularly sung at Cross Roads, this tune ("French Broad") was also well known to Elder Evans and the churches he pastored. He called the tune "hard to sing." Men's voices dominate on this recording, and the tempo is slightly faster than Elder Evans would have taken it (WI-097, FT2162).

Side Two: Other Primitive Baptist
Song Traditions

Lined-Out Hymn Singing

The tradition of lining out hymns, in which the song leader chants one or two lines of text and the congregation then sings the same text to the hymn tune (see fig. 68), began in England in the 1640s and has lingered in some "Old

Baptist" churches in the mountains of North Carolina, Virginia, and eastern Kentucky, and in a scattering of churches whose members emigrated from this region. It is no longer the usual practice in any of these churches, however. The next three examples illustrate different styles of lined-out hymn singing still practiced among some Primitive Baptists in the mountain region.

1. "When I survey the wondrous cross," lined and led by Elder Billy Cook from Glade Springs, Virginia, one of several visiting preachers at Woodruff Primitive Baptist Church, Glade Valley, North Carolina, on Sunday morning, 11 July 1982. Recorded by James L. Peacock. As Elder Cook took the stand, he requested two verses of a hymn (Goble no. 94) before he began to deliver the second of five sermons preached that day at the annual meeting of this independent Primitive Baptist church. Ten men and fourteen women attended the service. Elder Cook's singing illustrates a beautiful, meditative style of lining out. The tune he used is a variant of "To Die No More" (see fig. 69), which was claimed by Elder E. Dumas, a Primitive Baptist minister from Georgia, in 1856 (WI-071).

> When I survey the wondrous cross
>> On which the Prince of glory died,
> My richest gain I count but loss,
>> And pour contempt on all my pride.

> See, from his head, his hands, his feet,
>> Sorrow and love flow mingling down!
> Did e'er such love and sorrows meet,
>> Or thorns compose so rich a crown? (Goble no. 94)

2. "How happy's every child of grace" (compare with fig. 53b) sung by Elder Walter Evans, pastor, and Clifford Holloway, song leader of Little River Primitive Baptist Church, at the home of Elder Evans in Sparta, North Carolina, 26 June 1970. Recorded by William H. Tallmadge. When a song leader lines out a hymn, he usually does it one line at a time. However, it is possible to line out two lines of text, and the singers illustrate that technique in this example (WTC #103).

3. "The day is past and gone" (Goble no. 109, compare with the tune "Idumea" in fig. 70) lined and led by Elder Teddy Ball at the Raccoon Creek Primitive Baptist Church in eastern Kentucky, 8 July 1970. Recorded by William H. Tallmadge. Lined-out hymn singing is practiced by both Old Regular Baptists and Primitive Baptists in eastern Kentucky. Elder Ball told us that he had occasionally preached for the Old Regular Baptists. Elder Ball, a retired coal miner, and Elder Evans, a retired stonemason, knew each other well and had sung and preached in some of the same churches in Kentucky and North Carolina. In the Kentucky churches, this old style of hymn singing is typically slower, more intense, and more ornamented than any of the singing in the Mountain District Association churches in North Carolina and Virginia (WTC #115).

The day is past and gone,
    The ev'ning shades appear;
O may we all remember well
    The night of death draws near.

We lay our garments by,
    And on our beds we rest;
So death will soon disrobe us all
    Of what we here possess.

Lord keep us safe this night,
    Secure from all our fears;
May angels guard us while we sleep,
    Till morning light appears.

And when we early rise,
    And view th' unwearied sun,
May we press on to reach the prize,
    And after glory run.

And when our days are past,
    And we from time remove,
O may we in thy bosom rest,
    The bosom of thy love.

4. Comments by Elder Walter Evans on the Primitive Baptist doctrine of salvation and on the church's practice of singing. Recorded and interviewed at his home in Sparta, North Carolina, 18 November 1980, by Tom Davenport:

"We believe that we're the successors of the original church as established by the Lord himself. We go back and pick up the doctrines—I'll just say in summation, not go into the different channels perhaps, and avenues of grace—but the doctrine of salvation, by the grace of God, unmerited on the part of any man or group of men. And the practice of the church, just the plain simple form of practice in the church, that is from the apostolic church, without—well, we sing, and we pray, and preaching—without instrumental music of any sort. We just feel the Bible teaches that we're to sing and make melody in our hearts. And that word is 'sing,' it's not 'play.' And we practice that" (WI-026, FT2129).

Songs Sung at Home

These songs represent a large repository of hymns that Elder Evans (and perhaps others) knew and sang at home, but seldom, if ever, sang in church.

5. "Beset with snares on every hand" (compare with fig. 14) sung by Elder Walter Evans at his home in Sparta, North Carolina, 18 November 1980. Recorded by Tom Davenport. Elder Evans reported learning this traditional tune ["Frozen Heart"] from his mother when he was a "kid boy." He did not

know where she learned it, but knew that she attended singing schools. He suggested that she could have learned it from shape-note books she used there. Elder Evans did not use this hymn in church services, but Elder Lasserre Bradley recorded him singing this song around 1960 and once used it to introduce the "Baptist Bible Hour," his radio broadcast that originates in Cincinnati, Ohio (WI-026, FT 2129).

6. "From whence doth this union arise" (compare with fig. 48) sung by Elder Walter Evans at his home in Sparta, North Carolina, 25 June 1970. Recorded by William H. Tallmadge. We recorded this tune at the Little River Primitive Baptist Church with a different text, "My gracious Redeemer I love," a hymn that shares the same metrical pattern (8s, or 8 syllables per line) with this song that Elder Evans sang (WTC #102).

> From whence doth this union arise
>   That hatred is conquered by love?
> It fastens our souls in such ties
>   That nature and time can't remove.
>
> It can not in Eden be found,
>   Nor yet in a Paradise lost;
> It grows on Immanuel's ground,
>   And Jesus' rich blood it did cost.
>
> My friends are so dear unto me,
>   Our hearts all united in love;
> Where Jesus has gone we shall be,
>   In yonder blest mansions above.
>
> Oh! why then, so loath for to part,
>   Since we shall ere long meet again,
> Engraved on Immanuel's heart,
>   At distance we can not remain.
>
> And when we shall see that bright day,
>   And join with the angels above;
> And when these vile bodies of clay,
>   Are fashioned like Jesus above;
>
> With Jesus we ever shall reign,
>   And all his bright glories shall see,
> Singing, Hallelujah, Amen;
>   Amen, even so let it be. (Goble no. 206)

7. "It is a glorious mystery" sung by Elder Walter Evans at his home in Sparta, North Carolina, 25 June 1970, during the same recording session as above. Recorded by William H. Tallmadge. A version of this song (tune and text) in early nineteenth-century shape-note tunebooks contains repetitions of "'tis a wonder" that do not appear in Goble's text (no. 207). Elder Evans's

tune fits Goble's text. His use of irregular meter, which enlivens the refrain—
and is not present in the tunebooks—suggests the creative potential of an oral
tune tradition in the mind of a gifted singer (WTC #102).

> It is a glorious mystery—'tis a wonder,
> That ever I should saved be—'tis a wonder,
> No heart can think, no tongue can tell,
>   'tis a wonder, wonder, wonder,
> The love of God unspeakable—'tis a wonder.
>
> Great mystery, that God should place ['tis a wonder]
> His love on one of Adam's race, ['tis a wonder]
> That I should also share a part,
>   ['tis a wonder, wonder, wonder]
> And find a mansion in his heart. ['tis a wonder]
>
> Great mystery, I can't tell why ['tis a wonder]
> That Christ for sinful worms should die; ['tis a wonder]
> Should leave the boundless realms of bliss,
>   ['tis a wonder, wonder, wonder]
> And die for sinners on the cross. ['tis a wonder]
>
> Oh! why was I not left behind, ['tis a wonder]
> Among the thousands of mankind, ['tis a wonder]
> Who run the dang'rous, sinful race,
>   ['tis a wonder, wonder, wonder]
> And die, and never taste his grace? ['tis a wonder]
>
> 'Twas love that spread the gracious feast; ['tis a wonder]
> 'Twas love that made my soul a guest; ['tis a wonder]
> 'Twas love that brought him from above;
>   ['tis a wonder, wonder, wonder]
> 'Twas love, Oh! matchless, boundless love. ['tis a wonder]
>
> Not all the heav'nly hosts can scan ['tis a wonder]
>   The glories of this noble plan; ['tis a wonder]
>   Oh! 'tis a glorious mystery,
>   ['tis a wonder, wonder, wonder]
>   And will be to eternity. ['tis a wonder]

Singing Influenced by Music Notation and Gospel Traditions

8. "O land of rest, for thee I sigh" (compare with fig. 78) sung by an annual association meeting in eastern North Carolina held at Little Flock Primitive Baptist Church in Coats, pastored by Elder Worth Stephenson, on Saturday afternoon, 24 September 1983. This early nineteenth-century hymn has
acquired a chorus (not published by Goble) and a gospel-style tune. The chorus, "We'll wait 'till Jesus comes," is a Primitive Baptist adaptation of a similar text common in evangelical churches, "We'll work 'till Jesus comes." As

sung here—with a steady and slightly faster tempo, conventional harmonies, and a chorus that features responsorial "echo" effects—the hymn shows the influence of later hymnbook harmonizations (WI-206, FT2257).

Credits

Recordings by Tom Davenport, Daniel Patterson and Blanton Owen, James Peacock, and others from the World and Identity project (identified by WI-xxx project numbers and FTxxx archive reference numbers) are deposited in the Southern Folklife Collection of the Manuscripts Department, University of North Carolina at Chapel Hill.

Recordings by William H. Tallmadge are part of the William H. Talmadge Collection (WTC) of Baptist Folk Hymnody, Southern Appalachian Archives, Berea College, Berea, Kentucky.

My sincere thanks to William Tallmadge for use of his field recordings; to Shannon Wilson, Gerald Roberts, Harry Rice, and the Special Collections staff at Berea's Hutchins Library and to David Camp, Amy Davis, and Steve Green at UNC's Southern Folklife Collection for their expert and enthusiastic professional assistance.

Special thanks to Ellen Evans Miles and other members of Elder Walter Evans's family; to Elder Billy Cook, Elder Worth Stephenson, and Raymond Nichols; and to members of the Little River, Cross Roads, Woodruff, Little Flock, and Raccoon Creek Primitive Baptist churches for permission to use these selections.

Index

Boldface page numbers indicate musical examples.

BEVERLY BUSH PATTERSON is a folklife specialist in the North Carolina Arts Council, Raleigh, North Carolina. She is the coauthor of the fifty-four-microfiche *Index to Selected Folk Recordings* (Curriculum in Folklore, University of North Carolina), a contributor to *Diversities of Gifts: Field Studies in Southern Religion,* and former film and video tape review editor for the *Journal of American Folklore.*

Books in the Series Music in American Life

Only a Miner: Studies in Recorded Coal-Mining Songs
Archie Green

Great Day Coming: Folk Music and the American Left
R. Serge Denisoff

John Philip Sousa: A Descriptive Catalog of His Works
Paul E. Bierley

The Hell-Bound Train: A Cowboy Songbook
Glenn Ohrlin

Oh, Didn't He Ramble: The Life Story of Lee Collins, as Told to
Mary Collins
Edited by Frank J. Gillis and John W. Miner

American Labor Songs of the Nineteenth Century
Philip S. Foner

Stars of Country Music: Uncle Dave Macon to Johnny Rodriguez
Edited by Bill C. Malone and Judith McCulloh

Git Along, Little Dogies: Songs and Songmakers of the American West
John I. White

A Texas-Mexican *Cancionero*: Folksongs of the Lower Border
Américo Paredes

San Antonio Rose: The Life and Music of Bob Wills
Charles R. Townsend

Early Downhome Blues: A Musical and Cultural Analysis
Jeff Todd Titon

An Ives Celebration: Papers and Panels of the Charles Ives Centennial
Festival-Conference
Edited by H. Wiley Hitchcock and Vivian Perlis

Sinful Tunes and Spirituals: Black Folk Music to the Civil War
Dena J. Epstein

Joe Scott, the Woodsman-Songmaker
Edward D. Ives

Jimmie Rodgers: The Life and Times of America's Blue Yodeler
Nolan Porterfield

Early American Music Engraving and Printing: A History of Music
Publishing in America from 1787 to 1825, with Commentary on Earlier
and Later Practices
Richard J. Wolfe

Sing a Sad Song: The Life of Hank Williams
Roger M. Williams

Long Steel Rail: The Railroad in American Folksong
Norm Cohen

Resources of American Music History: A Directory of Source Materials
from Colonial Times to World War II
D. W. Krummel, Jean Geil, Doris J. Dyen, and Deane L. Root

Tenement Songs: The Popular Music of the Jewish Immigrants
Mark Slobin

Ozark Folksongs
Vance Randolph; edited and abridged by Norm Cohen

Oscar Sonneck and American Music
Edited by William Lichtenwanger

Bluegrass Breakdown: The Making of the Old Southern Sound
Robert Cantwell

Bluegrass: A History
Neil V. Rosenberg

Music at the White House: A History of the American Spirit
Elise K. Kirk

Red River Blues: The Blues Tradition in the Southeast
Bruce Bastin

Good Friends and Bad Enemies: Robert Winslow Gordon and the Study
of American Folksong
Debora Kodish

Fiddlin' Georgia Crazy: Fiddlin' John Carson, His Real World, and
the World of His Songs
Gene Wiggins

America's Music: From the Pilgrims to the Present
Revised Third Edition
Gilbert Chase

Secular Music in Colonial Annapolis: The Tuesday Club, 1745–56
John Barry Talley

Bibliographical Handbook of American Music
D. W. Krummel

Goin' to Kansas City
Nathan W. Pearson, Jr.

Pistol Packin' Mama: Aunt Molly Jackson and the Politics of Folksong
Shelly Romalis

Sixties Rock: Garage, Psychedelic, and Other Satisfactions
Michael Hicks

The Late Great Johnny Ace and the Transition from R&B to Rock 'n' Roll
James M. Salem

Tito Puente and the Making of Latin Music
Steven Loza

Juilliard: A History
Andrea Olmstead

Understanding Charles Seeger, Pioneer in American Musicology
Edited by Bell Yung and Helen Rees

Mountains of Music: West Virginia Traditional Music from *Goldenseal*
Edited by John Lilly

Alice Tully: An Intimate Portrait
Albert Fuller

A Blues Life
Henry Townsend, as told to Bill Greensmith

Long Steel Rail: The Railroad in American Folksong (2d ed.)
Norm Cohen

The Golden Age of Gospel
Text by Horace Clarence Boyer; photography by Lloyd Yearwood

Aaron Copland: The Life and Work of an Uncommon Man
Howard Pollack

Louis Moreau Gottschalk
S. Frederick Starr

Race, Rock, and Elvis
Michael T. Bertrand

Theremin: Ether Music and Espionage
Albert Glinsky

Poetry and Violence: The Ballad Tradition of Mexico's Costa Chica
John H. McDowell

The Bill Monroe Reader
Edited by Tom Ewing

Music in Lubavitcher Life
Ellen Koskoff

Zarzuela: Spanish Operetta, American Stage
Janet L. Sturman

Bluegrass Odyssey: A Documentary in Pictures and Words, 1967–86
Carl Fleischhauer and Neil V. Rosenberg

That Old-Time Rock & Roll: A Chronicle of an Era, 1954–63
Richard Aquila

Labor's Troubadour
Joe Glazer

American Opera
Elise K. Kirk

Don't Get above Your Raisin': Country Music and the Southern
Working Class
Bill C. Malone

University of Illinois Press
1325 South Oak Street
Champaign, IL 61820-6903
www.press.uillinois.edu